The Writer in the Room

THE WRITER IN THE ROOM

Selected Essays

By
RAY B. WEST JR.

MICHIGAN STATE UNIVERSITY
PRESS
1968

15,021

810.9
W519

Contents

Acknowledgments

"Ralph Waldo Emerson: American Man of Letters" appeared in *Timber: A North Coast Journal*, Spring, 1963; "Primitivism in Melville" appeared in *Prairie Schooner*, Winter, 1956; "The Unity of Billy Budd" appeared in *The Hudson Review*, Spring, 1952; "Mark Twain's Idyl of the Frontier" appeared in *University of Kansas City Review*, Spring, 1948; "Stephen Crane: Author in Transition" appeared in *American Literature*, May, 1962; "Ezra Pound and Contemporary Criticism" appeared in *Quarterly Review of Literature*, No. 5, 1949; "Personal History and the Four Quartets" appeared in *New Mexico Quarterly Review*, Autumn, 1953; "Ernest Hemingway: The Failure of Sensibility" appeared in *The Sewanee Review*, Spring, 1945; "A Farewell to Arms" is reprinted from *The Art of Modern Fiction*, Holt, Rinehart, and Winston, New York, 1949; "Faulkner's *Light in August*: A View of Tragedy" appeared in *Wisconsin Studies in Contemporary Literature*, Winter, 1960; "Atmosphere and Theme in 'A Rose for Emily'" appeared in *Perspective*, Summer, 1949; "Katherine Anne Porter and 'Historic Memory'" appeared in *The Hopkins Review*, Fall, 1942; "Symbol and Theme in 'Flowering Judas'" appeared in *Accent*, Spring, 1947; "Three Methods of Modern Fiction" appeared in *College English*, January, 1951; "The American Short Story" is reprinted from *American Short Stories*, T. Y. Crowell and Co., New York, 1959; "The Modern Writer" appeared in *College English*, January, 1954.

The writer today . . . is like a man alone in a disordered room containing a door that is slightly ajar. It is not an ordinary room, for beyond the door lies mystery—the sum of all that we do not know about ourselves and fear to discover. One writer will devote his talent to an examination of the contents of the room, including the door, including, perhaps, even speculation concerning what lies outside. Another writer, armed with a knowledge of the room and its contents, will press open the door, will step out into the dangerous abyss of self-discovery. The first writer is one whose environment is a cage. The second may see it as chaos. But in our time the door *is* slightly ajar. The writer, if he has the courage, may go beyond it. This is a dangerous possibility, but the significant writer will recognize it as the opportunity that it is.

—from a speech delivered before the National Council of Teachers of English, November, 1963.

Prefatory Note

These essays by Ray B. West, Jr., are long overdue. I had read most of them as they appeared in the literary journals in the past twenty years, but the impact of this collection is more impressive than Mr. West's quiet style in the single essay could have led us to predict. I consider this book one of the three or four most important critical works on American literature since the First World War. The range of Mr. West's interests is comprehensive: he is equally good on Melville and James; and the essays on Pound and Eliot are unrivalled in their unusual combination of original perception and common sense. His approach is a little difficult to describe, as all original critical approaches are; yet one may say that he has the sharp sense of the individual work which the so-called New Criticism developed, along with the scholar's historical information. He is, in fact, that rare critic whose mind is governed not by the "historical method" of academic scholarship, but by the historical *sense*, which is a gift and not an imitative routine.

Allen Tate

Ralph Waldo Emerson:
American Man of Letters

R ALPH WALDO EMERSON remains the most difficult of all
Americans to classify. He was a poet, but his reputation
does not depend primarily upon his poetry. He dealt in ideas,
but he was no philosopher. He did not write fiction or drama.
The term by which he is most commonly known, "essayist,"
has less meaning for us today than it had a century ago. Con-
sequently, with the term out of fashion, Emerson the man,
too, seems outmoded, his work occasionally invoked in rever-
ent tones but little read except by students who ponderously
work their way through "Self-Reliance" or puzzledly recite
the lines of "Brahma" for an overworked schoolmaster.

Yet for those who learn to read him, Emerson's work remains alive and in the main current of modern American
thought and experience. As a writer, he may be called, for
want of a better name, an American man of letters, a term
which, though it is little better understood than essayist, is
more inclusive and less misleading than a term that is now
applied mainly to writers of popular magazine articles and to
literary critics. The man of letters confines himself to no single

form, but is preoccupied with all form. Above all, he is, as Allen Tate has pointed out, the person who renders the image of a man as he exists in his own time. He is literate man speaking to literate mankind; and this Emerson predominantly was.

Emerson's life encompassed the formative years in our national history. He was born twenty years after the United States gained their independence. He died seventeen years after the end of the Civil War. During his life time, the boundaries of this country extended from the Mississippi to the Pacific Ocean. The year he was born was the year of the Louisiana Purchase. In 1836, when he published his first book, *Nature*, the Texas Revolution took place. Ten years later, in 1846, the Mexican War occurred. By the time Emerson had written and published his two volumes of *Essays*, the nation had laid the foundation for its greatest expansion. When he published *Representative Men* in 1850, the California Gold Rush was underway. Just two years before the completion of the transcontinental railway, he published his last volume of poems, *May Day and Other Poems*. Thus while Emerson lived through the uncertain and unhappy years that led to and culminated in the Civil War, he also experienced fully the optimistic years of national progress, and his own career paralleled the greatness of the society he rendered.

Yet Emerson's relationship with his country was conducted on a transcendent level. He held no important offices, performed no feats of heroism, and, except for a brief and relatively unimportant act in support of abolition, joined no public causes. Despite his regard for action (it was one of the three qualities of his "American scholar"), he avoided active involvement. Although he made three extended visits to Europe and one to the Near East, although he visited most sections of his expanding homeland, he shunned travel. When he made his first trip to Europe in 1831-33, following the death of his first wife, he was more homesick than most American travellers. After a day spent visiting Paris, he wrote in his Journal: "Pray what brought you here, grave sir? the moving Boulevard seems to say." Later he was to write: "The soul is no traveller;

2

the wise man stays home, and when his necessities, his duties, on any occasion call him from his house, or into foreign lands, he is at home still."

It was duty then that called, whether to Europe to meet Wordsworth and Carlyle or onto the prairies to earn his living as a lecturer; and if these experiences enriched him, they did not change him. They did, perhaps, confirm him in his own beliefs and thus confirm his faith in the vast, inscrutable force he named the "Over-Soul," from which his own ideas derived. He believed that each man's duty was to himself and to the moment in which he lived. He should not be too much influenced by the outward demands of society, nor should he, except in moments when the light failed, pay too much attention to the past.

In all this, however, Emerson was a true American, sharing the convictions of his countrymen. America *was* the present; there had been a break with the past. He anticipated Mark Twain's *Innocents* when he wrote about America after his first trip to Europe:

> Land without history, land lying all
> In the plain daylight of the temperate zone,
> Thy plain acts
> Without exaggeration done in day;
> Thy interests contested by their manifold
> good sense.
> In their own clothes without ornament
> Of bannered army harnessed in uniform.
> Land where—and 'tis in Europe counted a
> reproach—
> Where man asks questions for which man was
> made.
> A land without nobility, or wigs, or debt,
> No castles, no cathedrals, and no kings.

Mark Twain resolved when he visited Europe to see it through his own eyes not the eyes of the art experts, the guidebooks, or the tourists around him. Whitman wrote:

I know that the past was great and the future will
    be great,
And I know that both curiously conjoint in the
    present time,
And that where I am or you are this present day,
    there is the centre of all days, all races,
And there is the meaning to us of all that has ever
    come of races and days, or ever will come.

Whitman said that he would not treat of man as "the creature of politics, aggregates, rulers and priests," but would treat
him "as he is himself in his own rights." Hawthorne and
Melville and Henry James saw the relations of past and
present as more complex, but none of them denied the vigor of
innocence or the virtue of actions performed in the clear light
of day; and, although they all seem to regret the absence of a
certain beauty in the present, they concurred in their approval
of spontaneity and sincerity. Emerson resolved when he returned from Europe: "not to utter any speech, poem, or book
that is not entirely and peculiarly my own."

Emerson's most characteristic injunction, "Trust thyself!" is
the logical result of such a resolution. It is the "good sense" of
modern times, contrasted with the European traditions of
ornamentation and authority. Such a concept had early taken
on the force of a "tradition" in American thinking. The
American Revolution was not fought only—or even primarily
—over matters of taxation and representation. Colonization
itself represented a rebellion against the elaborate forms of
aristocratic precedence and kingly rule. On the religious level,
colonization represented an objection to the imposition of
religious forms between the worshipper and his God. In
society, manners made distinctions where the colonists could
find none. How natural then to see the aesthetic act as the
breaking through barriers of imposed formality. It is true that
European society had, by the time of the Revolution and even
more so at the time Emerson was writing, begun to look in a
similar way at its traditional forms and institutions, but the

American colonists and the early citizens of the Republic were
the revolutionaries of the moment, and they were, to an extreme degree, creating a new society, not merely altering an
established one.

Emerson came to literature through the church. He was
admitted to the ministry of the Unitarian faith in 1826, and
three years later he became pastor of the Second Church of
Boston. But even the advanced views of Unitarianism were too
confining. He resigned his ministry in 1831 because he could
not conscientiously administer the sacrament. The ritual, he
stated in his apology, mirrored a concept with which he could
not agree—the concept of the divinity of Christ, whom Emerson persisted in seeing as no God, but as a greatly inspired
man. Implied in Emerson's view is the belief that such ritual
destroyed too much of Man, by depriving him of his greatest
representative, and that it served to separate Man from his
true God. Also, ritual served to make God static, by emphasizing that which God had done in the past. Emerson was most
interested in knowing what God was doing at the moment—in
coming into an immediate relation with him. "That which
shows God in me, fortifies me," he stated in his address before
the Divinity School of Harvard in 1838. "That which shows
God out of me, makes me a wart and a wen." Three years
earlier he had written in his introduction to *Nature:* "Our age
is introspective. It builds the sepulchres of the fathers. It
writes biographies, histories, and criticism. The foregoing generations beheld God face to face; we, through their eyes. Why
should not we also enjoy an original relation to the universe?"

"God and Nature!" The first American settlers, faced by a
world of nature, had already anticipated the close relationship
that later Romantics were to see between nature and God. If
the artificial forms of traditional worship served to separate
God and man, even the roof of the simple New England meet-
inghouse represented a barrier. God was not wholly visible in
the structures erected by man, simple though they might be.
His presence was most felt in the world of his own creation—
in nature. "*Nature* in the common sense, refers to essences

unchanged by man," Emerson wrote. "Standing on the bare ground—my head bathed by the blithe air, and uplifted into infinite space,—all mean egotism vanishes. I become a transparent eye-ball; I am nothing; I see all; the currents of the Universal Being circulate through me; I am part and parcel of God."

Such ideas, when applied practically to the established church in the Divinity School address, were seen as heretical and dangerous by Emerson's fellow ministers. Yet they had been stated two years earlier in *Nature* without arousing opposition; and they were to be repeated over and over again in Emerson's lectures and essays, with the only result being that he became the most respected thinker of his age. Perceptive fellow thinkers, such as Henry James, Sr., saw danger in such an attitude; and more recent critics, such as Yvor Winters, have lectured Emerson for his views; but the fact is that his ideas, in a less precise form, were the attitudes of the society of his time. Emerson was merely saying to his listeners and readers what they believed but were, for the most part, incapable of saying for themselves.

Emerson's listeners as he lectured at the Lyceum at Concord represented the first fruits of the American revolution—on an ideological level. When he ventured farther west, into the not-yet wholly settled communities of Illinois, or Iowa, or Wisconsin, he addressed audiences who were still actively engaged in winning the revolution, although the last actual battle had been fought and won. As a man of letters (and Emerson was more that than he was either a philosopher or an artist), he had simply gathered the first crop, sprung from seeds that had been dropped by the Puritans, the Quakers, the Anglican dissenters, and the deists of the first days of American self-consciousness, and which were still being carried westward by the last wave of colonists pushing towards the Pacific.

In New England and the East, the revolution was an established fact. Life in Boston and New York had become as settled and well-regulated as in any European city. After two hundred years of colonial and national life, the wilderness had not been obliterated, but it had been domesticated. The area stretching along the Atlantic coast-line was still predominantly rural, but its communities were no longer pioneer settlements. Energy that had formerly gone into the building of homes and communities, into political struggle and war, now sought another outlet. This society found it, in part, in the production of literature—the first significant literary era of our national life. F. O. Matthiessen called it "The American Renaissance." Irving, Cooper and Bryant were its forerunners; Emerson, Whitman, Hawthorne, Melville, Poe and Twain were its major products. Emerson was the first truly important voice in American letters. He was the first wholly American writer, in the sense that he summed up and expressed in his essays and poems what was the logical basis of American life and American political action from the landing at Plymouth Rock to the framing of the Constitution.

This does not mean that what he wrote always expressed the highest wisdom. His wisdom was the wisdom of American life; its limitations his limitations. The dominant tone in Emerson has been called by Matthiessen his celebration of the "positive element." This is a note that predominates in Thoreau, in Whitman, and, in part, in Twain. It is available in Hawthorne, Melville and Henry James, if only as a minor strain. It is the tone that later writers, such as Hart Crane and Thomas Wolfe, sought to strike, but which they either could not sustain or sustained at too shrill a level. It was the dominant tone in American life before Emerson's time, and society still conceives of the mythical American as positive, active, and self-reliant. Even though we have come to see the limitations of such a view in its extremes of innocence and optimism, characteristics that it took on when divorced from the older traditions, we seldom deny it, and, in times of crisis, actually rejoice in it.

But there is a sense in which Emerson was not expressing the *positive element*. It is true that he celebrated a kind of character who, in the nineteenth century represented the American ideal, and as such he was an author in tune with society and his own time. However, in a larger sense, Emerson was a revolutionary—as most artists are revolutionaries. The difference between him and later writers was that he was still a member of a revolutionary society, or of a society at least still conscious of having won revolutionary battles. Emerson, if he was not still fighting the battle against European manners and traditional European thought, was at least summing up the results. His dominant tone was suspicion of tradition, and tradition in its concrete form meant Europe. He refused to take the history of past societies as an infallible guide and model for the present. Oliver Wendell Holmes called Emerson's Phi Beta Kappa address at Harvard in 1837 "our intellectual Declaration of Independence." Emerson's writing was this and more. Perhaps it might better be called our intellectual Constitution, reflecting as it does our national aspirations, supplying as it does guides for the possible achievement of those aspirations. Not that such writing be denied the possibility of revision, as our political constitution is subject to amendment; with the need for amendment, Emerson would be the first to agree.

The story of amendment, however, belongs to a discussion of other authors, writers who recognized the limitations, perhaps even the dangers, of many of Emerson's ideas. Such a discussion would probably begin with Hawthorne and Melville, who from the beginning rebelled against Emerson's "transcendental" idealism. It would include later authors, such as Henry James and T. S. Eliot, who pointed to qualities missing or too little considered in the Emersonian concept of Man separated from a long social and ethical history. While we cannot neglect such revision, our chief concern here should be with those qualities and ideas that express Emerson's typical Yankee thinking, with those concepts that outline the hopes and beliefs of a growing nation and that have come to represent our most common understanding of what the American character assumed itself to be.

A chronological study of Emerson's writing would disclose a process of expansion of his own nature, not a process of change and development such as one most often finds in later American authors. In *Nature* and in his two addresses at Harvard, Emerson said most of what he had to say; the rest are variations—refinements—on those themes. Central is his concept of God as Universal Spirit, with nature as its most direct manifestation. "Of that ineffable essence which we call Spirit," he wrote in 1836, "he that thinks most will say least. We can foresee God in the coarse, and, as it were, distant phenomena of matter; but when we try to define and describe himself both language and thought desert us, and we are as helpless as fools and savages. . . . [Nature] is the organ through which the universal spirit speaks to the individual, and strives to lead back the individual to it." But "nature" includes Man: ". . . all other men and my own body, must be ranked under the name, Nature." As he told the Phi Beta Kappa scholars: ". . . in yourself is the law of nature." He asked them: "What would you know the meaning of? The meal in the firken; the milk in the pan; the ballad in the street; the news of the boat; the glance of the eye; the form and gait of the body;—show me the ultimate reason in these matters; show me the sublime presence of the highest spiritual cause lurking, as always it does lurk, in these suburbs and extremities of nature; let me see every trifle bristling with the polarity that ranges it instantly on an eternal law; and the shop, the plough, and the ledger referred to the cause by which light undulates and poets sing;—and the world lies no longer a dull miscellany and lumber room, but has form and order; there is no trifle, there is no puzzle, but one design unites and animates the farthest pinnacle and the lowest trench." In 1838 he told the seniors in the Divinity College at Harvard: "The intuition of the moral sentiment is an insight of the perfection of the laws of the soul."

By 1841, when Emerson published his first series of essays, he could be as explicit as he ever was to be:

Ineffable is the union of man and God in every act of the soul. The simplest person who in his integrity worships God, becomes

God; yet forever and ever the influx of this better and universal self is new and unsearchable: It inspires awe and astonishment. How dear, how soothing to man, arises the idea of God, peopling the lonely places, effacing the scars of our mistakes and disappointments. When we have broken with our god of tradition and ceased from our god of rhetoric, then may God fire the heart with his presence.

We might join with Emerson's critics here, if we wished, to point out the dangers of Emerson's position: to call attention to the similarity between his form of worship and a worship of nature itself, to suggest how Emerson's ideas tended to break down distinctions and thus to merge both the individual and God in the uncontrollable flux of nature, to decry Emerson's denial of evil, either in nature or in man ("Evil is merely private, not absolute."), to deplore his encouragement of native optimism and rational innocence. But to do so would be to become merely reactionary. These are the dangers and the limitations of Emerson's position, to be sure; just as they represent the extreme of American thought by the middle of the nineteenth century. To say as much remains only partial justification, but Emerson's ideas do not represent American thought alone, for they express the central concepts of romantic idealism wherever it flourished in the western world, whether in German and French philosophy or in the poets of England; and, for better or for worse, such ideas have permeated our thinking and will not—and need not—be wholly expelled. Too great a reaction against the extremes of nineteenth-century romanticism leads us to forget the dangers of the opposite: the veneration of tradition for the sake of tradition, ritual for the sake of ritual, social manners for manners' sake. If "utility" has become an ugly word, it is with good reason, but the implications of utilitarianism are no less attractive than the opposite view that social, aesthetic, and religious forms are absolute goods that must be maintained at all cost.

Particularly in the twentieth century, we have been made again aware of the danger of any philosophy that stresses the

value of utility as its own end, most notably when such a
philosophy serves to motivate political acts. What we tend to
forget is that the opposite extreme often masks decay. We
must remember that Emerson was writing with a memory of
social and political decadence in Europe, with a vision of a
vigorous new nation before him. When we read him today, we
are most likely to be disturbed by our recollection of the
abuses of power exercised by political dictators for utilitarian
ends. As Yvor Winters (perhaps Emerson's severest critic) has
pointed out, when Emerson wrote that we should break with
our god of tradition in order that God might fire the heart
with his presence, he himself retained enough of the traditional in his own habits of thinking to control and limit the
idea only to a more direct and personal relationship between
God and man. When Emerson wrote, as he did in 1844, concerning poetry: ". . . it is not metres, but a metre-making
argument, that makes a poem," he is not denying the value of
metre. He used metre strictly and conventionally in his own
poetry. Emerson was, however, calling for "a thought so passionate and alive, that, like the spirit of a plant or an animal,
it has an architecture of its own, and adorns nature with new
things." He maintained that, "the experience of each new age
requires a new confession, and the world seems waiting for its
poet." Emerson often used an extreme statement to make a
point, as when he wrote the following well-known injunction
in his essay, "Self-Reliance": "I would write on the lintels of
the doorpost, *Whim*." But then he went on to say, "I hope it is
somewhat better than whim at last, but we cannot spend the
day in explanation."

It is true that many of Emerson's ideas seem clearly the
product of a romantic age, original only in his manner of
stating them or in the local application that he gave them.
One way to look at America is to see it as the proving ground
of the romantic philosophies. Romanticism advised man to return to nature, to return to rural habits of mind, to a rustic
simplicity of action. American society was rooted in nature
and in rural living. European philosophies had laid out the

theoretical ground plan. In the main, and to a degree never again possible, American society of Emerson's day modeled itself after that plan.

Emerson wrote at a time when the nation was just celebrating its first cultural and political harvest. His essays represented not so much an analysis (which many of his present-day critics seem to demand), as they did a sympathetic participation in that celebration. America had produced the first of its great cities at the time Emerson was writing, but he does not reflect this. He expresses a country mind. He describes a society in which personal contact and intensely personal relationships were still possible. "Every decent and well-spoken individual effects me and sways me more than is right," he wrote. A recognition that the heroic person was not to be swayed, led him to think of the effects such a person might have, and he concluded: "An institution is the lengthened shadow of one man." If we see only the danger in such a concept, we ought to realize that Emerson was able to visualize the relationship of man to man as an adequate check against the threat of social and moral anarchy or dictatorship: "The populace thinks that your rejection of popular standards is a rejection of all standards . . . ; and the bold sensualist will use the name of philosophy to gild his crimes. But the law of consciousness abides. . . . Consider whether you have satisfied your relations to father, mother, cousin, neighbor, town, cat and dog—whether any of these can upbraid you." Even literature was the expression of common truth, as told by one man to another: "Converse with a mind that is grandly simple, and literature looks like word-catching. . . . Nothing can pass there, or make you one of the circle, but the casting aside your trappings and dealing man to man in naked truth, plain confession and omniscient affirmation."

Contrasting the world of the past, where every man stood fixed in a relationship to the universe and to the society of other men, where each value had been catalogued and pigeon-holed, where both literature and life moved according to inviolable rules—contrasting this concept with the world of

Emerson's present, where each man stood in an attitude of perceptive reverence toward nature and God and toward his fellowmen, trusting his native abilities as a guide for action and in art, we can probably understand the kind of appeal Emerson had in an age that appeared full of hope and promise. We see dangers in such a view today because we live in a world that is in flux, because our society has become depersonalized in a manner Emerson could not possibly have foreseen, but these are not reasons for denying value to Emerson's writings themselves. We can, and should, above all make use of the terms in which Emerson's contrast between the old world and the new were presented.

It has become commonplace to think of Emerson's ideas as stemming from neo-Platonism, German idealism, English romanticism, and Swedenborgian protestantism, but his actual knowledge of these movements came late, and they served him more as symbols and evidence than they did as sources. The core of his thinking came from the life around him, which he breathed as naturally as he breathed the New England air of Concord; and his principal ideas were set by the tone and atmosphere of the time and place in which he lived, which was less New England than it was America. Impressed as he was by the English poets of the nineteenth century and by Hindu mysticism, as a man of letters in a significant period of American history, he was singularly unaffected by the methods or subject matter of either. He believed he recognized in their attitudes the roots of American idealism, and it is, even now, more than a century later, too soon to say he was not right.

I have said that Emerson's ideas changed little from the publication of his first book, *Nature,* in 1836, to his last prose work *The Conduct of Life,* in 1860. However, there is another matter to consider, because of its relative neglect, and that is the writing of his poetry. Strangely enough, it is in Emerson's verse, that in many ways seems to dominate the second half of his career, that we can see, if not an idealogical development, at least the invigorating charge of a new medium. The first volume appeared in 1847, the last in 1867, and the poems serve in many ways to revivify the ideas of the essays. One way to look at them is as small sermons in verse, but to say this does not do them justice. Their didacticism is generally inoffensive because of the abundance of striking imagery and the originality of the language. They owe more to the seventeenth century than they do the nineteenth, thus showing how Emerson was in advance of the taste of his time. The value that Emerson put upon images may be suggested by the following passage from *Nature:*

The moment our disclosure rises above the ground line of familiar facts and is inflamed with the passion or exalted by thought, it clothes itself in images. . . . This imagery is spontaneous. It is the blending of experience with the present action of the mind. It is proper creation. It is the working of the Original Cause through the instruments he has already made.

This is perhaps as satisfactory an explanation as any to account for the manner in which the image works in the language of poetry—its use in the creation of an imaginative experience. It owes something, no doubt, to Wordsworth, but it stresses imagery where Wordsworth stresses metre. It may owe something to Coleridge in its joining of passion and thought. It reminds us of Bergson's concept of poetic sensibility. In its total statement, however, it seems to reflect future concepts more than it appears to derive from the past. We recall Hart Crane's attempt to define the effect of an image as "the logic of metaphor." We are reminded of T. S. Eliot's view of the poetic imagination, which reacts to the multitudinous impressions of life and seeks a fusing element in the poem itself. It reflects, in short, our present-day belief in the poetic sensibility as a means of ordering the variety of experience, except that few of us today would go so far as Emerson goes in attributing such "working" to "the Original Cause."

It was in carrying his views to this extreme that Emerson became more a "thinker" than a poet. His contrasts—his polarities, his ambiguities—are all resolved in this all-enclosing spirit of reconciliation, the Over-Soul. It is the basis of his belief in "compensation," in which the heaven of orthodox Christianity is transported to the present world, and the poetic image becomes an instrument whereby all mystery is expressed and resolved.

With such a belief, Emerson could speak of "a crack in everything God has made," he could refer to "an inevitable dualism" that bisects nature, without really meaning it. The crack is mended, the dualism unified, not in some indefinite paradise, but here and now. Emerson could thus speak of true art as "never fixed, but always flowing," and he could see a great man as "a new statue," a beautiful woman as "a picture which drives all beholders nobly mad." Manners he could see as in constant flux, where "the laws of behavior yield to the energy of the individual," and where the city and court of today are no more than the country that came to town day before yesterday.

There is important truth in such concepts. The force of them could recover vitality for art and living, a life that no longer existed in the abstract theorizing and the static traditionalism of much living and most literature of Emerson's day. In his time, such truth needed emphasis, and since it was a reflection, and a justification, of what many Americans of the mid-nineteenth century believed, it was responded to by Emerson's readers and lecture audiences. His ideas justified America's vigor in its expansion, its newness, and its necessary rejection of much of what had been believed in the past. They added prestige and honor to the pursuits of ordinary Americans, in the cities, the villages, and on the frontier, and they prepared the way for such authors as Whitman, Melville, and Twain.

But there are dangers, too, in such ideas. Remove the belief in an all-unifying spirit, and the energy may become individual power, the flux become irresponsible change. In their unrestricted excesses, such powers might become a means of enslavement rather than liberation. To the man with an axe or a gun in the forests of Oregon, nature must have had her aspects of sublimity, but she was also a terrifying presence and a practical hindrance. To many of the writers who followed Emerson, nature's contrary qualities were not to be so easily reconciled. For Herman Melville, Emerson's "inevitable dualism" became a sign of the very real ambiguity in human experience; for Henry James, the "crack in everything God has made" became a symbol of the incompleteness of man; for Hawthorne, nature did not so much reflect God as it represented the abode of evil, where witchcraft plied its devil's trade and where savagery lurked.

As we read Emerson today, therefore, we read him not as one who solved the riddle, but rather as one who posed the question, stated it in terms meaningful for his time and place. If few American writers who followed him could accept his view of nature and God, none could afford to disregard it. Thoreau and Whitman were disciples of Emerson, and it is inconceivable that either could have become what he was as a writer without having absorbed Emerson's views. Mark Twain in his major works reflects an Emersonian attitude toward nature, although he seems to have derived less from Emerson than from a similar source. Having been brought up on the frontier, Twain learned early to distrust the conventions of gentility, and he resolved to take nature as his guide. Even those authors who rejected Emerson's conclusions and rebelled against them, like Hawthorne, Melville, and James, were not unaffected, for to rebel against a position is to acknowledge its importance; and their rebellion was not so much a rejection as it was a revision. For them too Emerson had performed a valuable service, for he taught them what were the essential problems in American life. He outlined in clearer terms than we have sometimes imagined, the subject matter with which American letters were to deal for at least a century beyond his time.

Another "Look" at Walt Whitman

IT IS NOT surprising that Emerson, when he finished reading the first edition of *Leaves of Grass* in 1855, should
have been impressed by the promise of Walt Whitman. The
spontaneity, the originality, and the vigor of the verses were
qualities that Emerson had called for as early as 1836. Also,
the central theme of the twelve poems that made up the first
edition was an expression of man's relationship to God
through nature—a concept which Whitman had gotten, at
least in part, from Emerson. What does surprise us, considering Emerson's personal reticence, is that he should have written an enthusiastic letter of praise to a poet of whom he had
never before heard. The letter is important for an understanding of Emerson as well as Whitman. It said:

Dear Sir, —I am not blind to the wonderful gift of Leaves of Grass.
I find it the most extraordinary piece of wit and wisdom that
America has yet contributed. I am very happy in reading it, as
great power makes us happy. It meets the demand I am always
making of what seems the sterile and stingy Nature, as if too much
handiwork, or too much lymph in the temperament were making

our Western wits fat and mean. I give you joy in it. I find incomparable things said incomparably well, as they must be. I find the courage of treatment that so delights us and which large perceptions only can inspire.

I greet you at the beginning of a great career, which yet must have had a long foreground somewhere, for such a start. I rubbed my eyes a little to see if this sunbeam were no illusion; the solid sense of the book is a sober certainty. It has the best merits, namely of fortifying and encouraging.

I did not know, until last night saw the book advertised in a newspaper, that I could trust the name as real and available for a post-office.

I wish to see my benefactor, and have felt much like striking my tasks and visiting New York to pay you my respects.

Whitman was at the time thirty-six. He had no such long foreground as a poet as Emerson imagined. He had been a successful newspaper writer and editor, but until this time the only literary pieces he had attempted had been imitative and awkward, written in the manner of the sentimental popular literature of the time. He had written a short "temperance novel," under commission of *The New World,* a New York periodical. He had written news accounts and editorials for newspapers in New York, Brooklyn, Long Island, and New Orleans. He had written a few notices and reviews of the theatre and of books. There had been little in any of these to suggest the kind of poetry that was to appear in *Leaves of Grass.*

The first edition of *Leaves of Grass* was a slender volume, composed of only a few poems and a preface. The preface stated its author's belief that poetry should be simple, not complicated; that it should be dedicated to all persons and all classes; and, most of all, that American art should be a new art, a direct imitation of the new life that America represented. The poems themselves seemed to support these views. They were original in appearance and modern in theme. They were spoken in a voice undoubtedly American. They were engaged with American concerns.

Yet to call Whitman's themes "modern" does not mean that they were entirely new with him. Some of his ideas had been expressed by the English romantic poets; many of them obviously owed a debt to Emerson. Almost all of them were available in American society of those years, whose ideals stressed the virtues of individual competency, equality, and common sense. What is significant about Whitman's ideas as they are represented in these first poems is not the ideas themselves, but the vigor with which they were held and the clarity of manner in which they were expressed. As ideas, they were essentially the ideals of America's common life, very much as they had been observed and restated in Emerson, and Whitman wished obviously to reaffirm them:

> My tongue, every atom of my blood, form'd from this soil,
>   this air,
> Born here of parents born here from parents the same, and
>   their parents the same,
> I, now thirty-seven years old in perfect health begin,
> Hoping to cease not till death . . .

If *Leaves of Grass* was not an immediate success, and indeed it aroused the resentment of most early readers, its failure was not because of its ideas, but because of the unfamiliar and unorthodox manner in which they were presented. Even such admirers as Emerson were shocked by the frank sensuality, by the apparent egotism, and by what they considered a lack of taste. Others were offended by the unfamiliar appearance of the lines, which did not resemble poetry as they knew it.

Most of these "faults" no longer trouble us. We have seen too much sensuality in literature since Whitman, and we rejoice in him as an author who opened whole areas of experience to the literature that followed. His egotism was consistent with the extreme statement of his ideas. His occasional lack of taste was the result of his great virtue of originality. Even the appearance of his lines and the lilt of his metres have taken on the aspect of familiarity.

It is only when we come to Whitman's ideas themselves that the problem of dealing with Whitman's poetry becomes difficult, for Whitman agreed with Emerson that man (or the poet) should be more concerned with the present than the past; but while Emerson denigrated the future as well as the past, Whitman's present seemed often little more than the seed out of which would spring a future more resplendent than anything before known. In Whitman's mind, as in Emerson's, the American war for independence did not end with the surrender of troops. There was a sense in which the war continued, and Emerson's American scholar was only the old soldier in his new uniform. For Whitman, the soldier-scholar had become poet in a still active, partisan conflict that would continue until the "solid and beautiful forms of the future" had been realized.

Because Whitman conceived of himself as the revolutionary, in the front line of battle, he thought it necessary to make his position unmistakably clear, and this accounts for the hortatory nature of much of his poetry, as well as for the constantly enlarged prefaces and essays that accompanied it. Because his subject was the progressively changing face of a nation, because it was energy, not form or convention, that he wished to celebrate, he took upon himself one of the most difficult of all poetic tasks and one which may have seemed to many of his contemporaries as anti-poetic. He "put creeds and schools in abeyance," he spoke for "Nature without check with original energy." He filled his poems with endless catalogues because he wanted to encompass space as well as delineate time, "the face and movement of a nation," but he made only the slightest of distinctions between one item and another. As he wrote: "All goes onward and outward, nothing collapses." The old gods, he said, we will take "for what they are worth and not a cent more / Admitting they were alive and did the work of their days."

Where is the poetry here? we might ask, as many of Whitman's early readers did ask. Where are the images? The rhymes? Even the metre seems not too different from prose.

Another "Look" at Walt Whitman

There is energy, no one can doubt, but what is there to limit and control that energy? "All goes onward and outward," as the poet says, and this is centrifugal force. How is it then that nothing collapses?

The answer is, I think, that Whitman's poetry does sometimes collapse, in its parts, so that many readers, like Randall Jarrell, are likely to feel that its importance exists mainly in isolated lines and passages that can be judged according to the traditional standards, but not in the wholeness of its major parts. If this were the whole story, however, I think Whitman would be undeserving of the place he holds in world letters—undeserving even of the respect Mr. Jarrell shows him. Certainly, he would have fulfilled little of his own, perhaps too great, demands.

But there is another way to look at Whitman's verse. *Leaves of Grass* does have something to limit its expansiveness, a center to control its energy and movement; and that center is the "I" of the poem. Too many early readers could see in this "I" only the ego of the poet, and, this being the case, saw it only as another of the poem's whirling atoms. The actual ego in the poem, however, is a *pretended* "I", the figure of the mythical American, the heroic democrat in his traditional battle against the past, a poetic Davy Crockett. With this concept at its center, *Leaves of Grass* is not a mere miscellany of interesting excerpts separated by long-winded catalogues and didactic preachments, but it becomes, rather, something like a whirling planet, whose center has been displaced but not lost, so that, while it may cast occasional small parts of itself off into space, it yet preserves a kind of erratic shape by the novel and contrary force inhabiting its center.

Yet in supplying this image, I do not mean to imply that there was nothing more than this concept of a mythological figure to restrict the expansiveness of the poem. The poet must have known that in his first edition of twelve poems, he had gone about as far as it was possible for him to go in the direction of expansion. The editions that followed did not expand the theme, although they added details in the embodiment of it. Whitman did not so much write more books as he continued writing *the* book. He added new stanzas, and he continued to polish those that had previously appeared. The very concept of such revision implies a delimiting of expansion, a compromise with the original force, or spontaneity.

Whitman himself mentions a further means by which he provided a center for his work, one which explains the close relationship between the method of the poet and his theme:

I have allowed my poems from beginning to end to bear upon American individuality and assist it—not only because it is a great lesson in Nature, and all her generalizing laws, but as counterpoise to the levelling tendencies of Democracy.

Of this passage, Wysten Auden wrote that, ". . . one is bound to admit that Whitman was the first poet clearly to recognize what the conditions were with which any future American poet would have to come to terms." European poets had their distinctions at hand in their structured class society and in their poetic conventions. The American poet rejected class distinctions and looked with suspicion upon literary traditions, yet, he might ask himself, if there were no distinctions, would not poetry become little more than an endless catalogue? Whitman's answer to this was to express faith in the individual sensibility, at first portrayed as the mythical "I", later transferred to the person of the American who most nearly resembled the myth in its most admirable form, Abraham Lincoln.

It may well be, as Randall Jarrell insists, that Whitman wrote his most vigorous and exciting lines in the early editions of *Leaves of Grass,* but his later work was of a more consistently high level, and it did reflect a balance of freedom and restraint towards which the poet had begun to aim. In speaking of poetry in *Democratic Vistas,* which appeared in the fifth (1871) edition of *Leaves of Grass,* Whitman still called for a man who could relinquish the past and look towards the future:

America demands a poetry that is bold, modern, and all-surrounding and kosmical, as she is herself. It must in no respect ignore science or the modern, but inspire itself with science and the modern. It must bend its vision towards the future, more than the past.

Yet he could write in the opening lines of "Passage to India":

> The Past—the dark unfathomed retrospect!
> The teeming gulf—the sleepers and the shadows!
> The past—the infinite greatness of the past!
> For what is the present after all but a growth out of
>   the past?
> (As a projectile form'd, impell'd, passing a certain
>   line, still keeps on,
> So the present, utterly form'd, impell'd by the past.)

Perhaps there is relinquishment in an image that sees the present as an object conditioned by the past. This is certainly a change from an earlier poem, where Whitman referred to the past as "bygones," the proper study of the historian, while the poet's proper concern is to project the history of the future. The fact is that Whitman had begun, by the end of the war, to hold certain reservations concerning the present. He began *Democratic Vistas* by saying:

For my part, I would alarm and caution even the political and business reader, and to the utmost extent, against the prevailing delusion that the establishment of free political institutions, and plentiful intellectual smartness, with general good order, physical plenty, industry, etc., (desirable and precious advantages as they all are,) do, of themselves, determine and yield to our experiment of Democracy the fruitage of success.

The post-Civil War period was not the easiest time in American history for the poet to retain his faith in the future high destiny of the democratic system. Although the expansion of the continent that Whitman had early foreseen and favored was accelerated by the war's end, the actual accomplishment of it produced conditions that he had not anticipated: political corruption and private graft. Whitman's ideal of "individualism" seemed more often realized in the person of the ambitious and greedy entrepreneur, whose goal was wealth and power, than in the common, thoughtful American citizen.

Viewing the events of these years, Whitman concluded *Democratic Vistas* with a warning that reflects the degree in which his optimism had been tempered:

I hail with joy the oceanic, variegated, intense practical energy, the demand for facts, even the business materialism of the current age, our States. But woe to the age or land in which these things, movements, stopping at themselves, do not tend to ideas. As fuel to flame, and flame to the heavens, so must wealth, science, materialism—even this democracy of which we make so much—unerringly feed the highest mind, the soul.

Just as Whitman's optimism had become qualified by the 1870's, so did his poetry undergo a certain change. If the earliest versions of *Leaves of Grass* express an extreme (almost an eccentricity) of individuality and of expansiveness, the revisions and the later poems display an increased recognition of the need for order. The difficulty of the poet in making such an adjustment is for him to do so without loss of creative energy, without frustrating the creative spirit. The highest art requires a blending of creative power with an understanding of just how far that force may go without curb or control. A poet's originality consists in his vital struggle to break the old forms, but his final excellence must be judged by his success in creating new ones.

There is no doubt that some of Whitman's original force had been curbed by mid-career, but by his revision of the early poems he had greatly improved them. His later poems present more of a problem, because they were less daring in conception, yet composed with a sure skill that he had lacked in the early days. There is no doubt that such a poem as "When Lilacs Last in the Dooryard Bloom'd" is a superior poem to the original version of "Song of Myself." Whether or not it is better than the revised and final copy is another question, but an irrelevant one, if not futile to ask. The later poem has been a great popular success, but it has been little considered by critics (Randall Jarrell does not mention it, while saying that over half of Whitman's best lines are to be found in "Song of Myself"). One has the feeling that critics do not like it, but that they are too uncertain to say so. "When Lilacs Last in the Dooryard Bloom'd" is most obviously a celebratory poem, even though an elegy, and such poetry has not been in vogue in America since Whitman's day. It is not a superior poem because it is celebratory, but because of its craftsmanship and because of the rightness of its concept. In it Whitman discovered a subject that called forth his full energy and at the same time provided him with an object for his mature emotions both more inclusive and more exact than he had found before.

The subject of this poem is the death of Abraham Lincoln; but Lincoln as a representative figure, not the actual man. Lincoln was the embodiment of those virtues Emerson had celebrated and Whitman had incorporated in the "I" of "Song of Myself." Whitman's discovery of this mythical Lincoln (the idealized concept of the Yankee character), removed the poet from the center of the stage and replaced him with the American Hero. Secondary images are the lilacs that bloomed in the spring of Lincoln's assassination, representing the emotion aroused by the death of the hero, and the bird, singing in the secluded recesses of the swamp, that is the poet himself, singing his love. Whitman calls these controlling images a "trinity," brought by "ever recurring spring":

> Lilac blooming perennial and drooping star in the west,
> And thoughts of him I love.

With the thought of death that the bird's song recalls, Whitman introduces his "Hymn to Death," which is the counterpart to the bird's song, which is also the poet's celebration of an idea. These twenty-eight lines of verse embody the emotion and the consolation the poet felt upon the death of the great man; yet it is more than the death of the hero, it is the knowledge that even heroes must die that motivates the idea (the consolation), and the idea is Emersonian: the merging of the individual with the Over-Soul.

Fortifying and enclosing this lyric passage is the image of the funeral train, carrying the dead hero's coffin home for burial. It is a movement through space, as the train passes through towns and villages, by "Ohio's shores and flashing Missouri, / And over the far-spreading prairies cover'd with grass and corn"; it is a movement through time, as the poet's thoughts revert to the past, with its memories of war, and to the future, which lies westward.

Whitman's hero was a man of the present who had engaged in a crusade for human rights and dignity. He was also, as a man from the West, a man of the future. But the West in this poem is not only, or even primarily, the geographical West; it is what Archibald Macleish called the West, "a country in the mind." It is a land of the future, a land of promise, but it is also a land that symbolizes the end, not only of the hero, but of all men: death.

Whitman's preoccupation with death is, in many respects, a puzzling characteristic of his verse; but it is puzzling mainly because it is so ambiguous. In an earlier poem, titled "Poets to Come," he had written:

> I myself but write one or two indicative words for the
> future,
> I but advance a moment only to wheel and hurry back in
> the darkness.

Here death is the future of the individual, as contrasted with a more distant moment towards which the individual contributes. In another curious little poem, titled "To Think of Time," we have the concept of death as a casual occurrence in a world where all men are equal:

Another "Look" at Walt Whitman

> He that was President was buried, and he that
> is now
>> President shall surely be buried.

Such lines express confidence in man living to continue and
supplant the labors of those who have died.

Some critics have seen in Whitman's preoccupation with
death the typical "romantic agony" of nineteenth-century English poetry. Others have viewed it as a traditional "poetic"
attitude, signifying man's common humanity. Most recently,
Yvor Winters has objected to Whitman on grounds relevant
to our discussion by attacking him through both his master,
Emerson, and his disciple, Hart Crane. "Most of Crane's
thought," Mr. Winters writes, "was . . . derived from Whitman. In turn nearly all of Whitman's thought was derived
from Emerson, or easily could have been." Winters' objection
to Emerson was the lack of any adequately formulated religious or philosophical concepts to limit his use of indefinite
terms. In commenting upon a passage from *Nature* ("Man
imprisoned, man crystallized, man vegetative, speaks to man
impersonated"), Winters says:

In the last sentence, "man imprisoned" is in apposition with "man
crystallized" and with "man vegetative," terms which may be translated respectively as "God in the form of a crystal" and as "God
in the form of a cabbage"; the expression "man impersonated" may
be translated as "God in the form of man," or more simply, as
"man." The passage, like many others in Emerson, indicates that
man in death remains immortal while losing his identity.

Winters demands a more specific referent for "man in
death"—a referent that, if I understand him correctly, may be
satisfied in several ways, among them through the concepts of
orthodox religion. His general criticism of Emerson seems to
be that though Emerson the man practices a traditional
decorum as a result of temperament and training, his expressed views did not supply such props for us who were to
follow after him. Poetry, too, Winters implies in his criticism

of Whitman, needed such props in the form of established concepts.

On the whole, this is legitimate, if narrow, criticism; but it is legitimate only if it can be shown that the references were, in fact, vague. We might quarrel with Mr. Winters' pejorative translations of Emerson's images, but it is more to the point to question his implied objection to Whitman's imagery, particularly since it appears to question the use of the death images in "When Lilacs Last in the Dooryard Bloom'd."

Insofar as Whitman's poem is an expression of conscious intent (and I believe such intent does make up part of the meaning), Winters is correct in attributing to Whitman many Emersonian concepts. Such a line as "Undulate round the world, serenely arriving, arriving" is reminiscent of passages in Emerson, and I believe it is fair to Whitman to say that he consciously intended the idea of death to symbolize whatever it was he understood by man's merging with the common spirit.

The success of the poem does not, however, depend upon such an interpretation. The ambiguity of Whitman's use of the term death makes it mean a great many other things as well. If such terms as "equality" and "the future" are too indefinite, so must be the term "love" and the relationship between love and loss; and if this were true, how many poems in the English language would become invalidated. If we can see the situation of the bird in "Out of the Cradle Endlessly Rocking" as the specification of the loss of the beloved, then certainly Whitman's reference is no less vague than most traditional poetry when dealing with so subtle a relationship. If we can see the singer of "When Lilacs Last in the Dooryard Bloom'd" as singing a similar song of love, then certainly the reference is specific enough to tell us that the poet is grieving over the sense of loss he feels at the death of Lincoln, as well as celebrating his love.

Similarly, if we wish to see the concreteness of the death image in a purely traditional sense, we can say that death in the total poem means merely "the last adventure"—an adventure under uncertainties as great as those one encounters in life. In this case, the referent is clear, concrete, and sensual. The specific adventure is the journey across the continent from East to West of the funeral train, which is a real journey and a symbolic one, both a personal adventure and a mythical experience, an adventure in life and an experience in all those mysterious realms which are of the imagination or of God (whatever name we wish to assign them, but for which Whitman chose the image of death).

By the time Whitman came to write "When Lilacs Last in the Dooryard Bloom'd," he had lost some of his Emersonian optimism. How much still remains an important question. Certainly his best work displays, if not an attempt to return to an old mythology, an effort to discover or to create a new one. Abraham Lincoln, he saw, in life, as the American hero, and certainly millions of Americans have seen him in such a light since Whitman's time. Yet the poem is more than the celebration of a single person. It is a celebration of those typical American virtues that Emerson had called for, made available in verses worthy of their subject matter, by a poet whose long and serious dedication of that subject had earned him the right and provided him the skill to be its spokesman.

The qualities that made Walt Whitman the kind of poet he was (perhaps even the qualities that made him a poet at all) were qualities that existed in the extreme form that he knew them for only a short period in American history. A war of liberation had been fought and won. Emerson outlined the ideals of an emerging society, and Walt Whitman celebrated them. As an expression of one side of American life (perhaps even the best side), they are not only real, they are a formulation of what most Americans think about themselves and what many foreigners consider America's most admirable qualities. Even as Emerson and Whitman wrote, however, conditions had begun to change. The emergent states of the East, who as colonies had banded together to protect their freedom, were no longer either a pioneering or a revolutionary society. Only in the West, where the nation struggled to achieve what it considered to be its destiny, did the revolutionary ideals still seem immediate and real. In the East they had left their mark, but by now they had become a subject for examination and reappraisal. In the West they were still a living force, demanding affirmation and justification. Mark Twain, growing up on the frontier in Missouri and later traveling in the Far West, sensed this, as had Emerson and Whitman, so that it is from him that America obtained its last important work, portraying in the form of the novel those qualities of the American character that Emerson had attempted to define in his essays and Whitman to celebrate in his verse.

Primitivism in Melville

I N A LETTER to Nathaniel Hawthorne in 1851, Herman Melville wrote: "Lord, when shall we be done growing. As long as we have anything more to do, we have done nothing." Contrary to most opinion concerning Melville's career, which saw an abrupt decline after the publication of *Moby Dick,* Melville never did stop growing. He never again achieved the greatness of *Moby Dick,* yet his most important works all came after, not before, the writing of *Moby Dick.* And there is good reason for this: Melville's life is a history of self-education and growth. When he sailed on the whaler *Acushnet* for the South Seas in January, 1841, he was a youth of twenty-one with little formal education. When he returned in 1844, he had the subject matter for most of his important works, and his account of the library aboard the man-of-war described in *White Jacket* suggests that he had begun the habit of intensive reading which was to continue throughout the remainder of his life.

Although Melville wrote in *Moby Dick,* "a whale-ship was my Yale College and my Harvard," the statement is true only insofar as whaling supplied the means by which he came into contact with the adventurous life of the sea—a life which was to supply the general background and the central images for his major works. The adventurous life did not teach him how to write or how to evaluate his experience. Earlier he had written to Hawthorne: "My development has been all within a few years past." In the same letter he exclaimed: "Think of it! To go down to posterity . . . as a 'man who lived among the cannibals!' " The career of Melville as a writer is of a man who sailed on a whaling ship, "who lived among the cannibals," but who came only gradually to see what those experiences represented, both for himself and for posterity. He saw in them finally a quality less of reality, less of actual experience, than a metaphor for the condition of Man. In his late years, in *Clarel,* he was to write:

> Historic memory goes so far
> Backward through the long defiles of doom;
> Whoso consults it honestly
> That mind grows prescient in degree;
> For man, like God, abides the same
> Always.

In his discovery of the primitive races of the South Seas, Melville was stimulated to a consultation of "historic memory" which did indeed carry him "far backward," but it is not likely that he came immediately to the conclusion that God and Man remain the same. For this he needed more than the impressionable years spent as a sailor, important though they were. He needed the knowledge which he was yet to gain of Homer, Shakespeare, Milton, and Hawthorne, who were to serve him as masters. He needed to become aware of the problem which was to become the central concern of all his important works: why was not the modern world, and particularly America, the best of all possible worlds?

The case of Melville's development as a writer, despite the mistakes which have been made about it, is one of the clearest in all literary history. He was born in 1819 into a family which was predominantly Dutch and English and into a society which combined Calvinistic seriousness with typical nineteenth-century hopefulness. He served as a sailor for three years, between 1841 and 1844, and his voyages carried him once to England, where he was most impressed by the poverty and suffering possible in an enlightened civilization, and then halfway around the world—principally into the South Seas. In the Pacific he made the acquaintance not only of an unspoiled native society, but also of a society corrupted by the intrusion of western ideas and western commerce. He returned from his voyaging to write the account of a primitive idyl in his first book, *Typee,* and an account of the corruption of that idyl in his second work, *Omoo.*

Both of these early books were in many ways typical of popular writing done at that time. Upon one level they were travel books. In part they were nature studies. The combination of these two characteristics made them immediately popular. Already, however, there were qualities in both books which puzzled the ordinary reader, and which led some reviewers to conclude that *Typee* was a hoax. Melville had not been satisfied merely to report his personal experiences. He struggled to give his material some kind of shape and design. He read voraciously in all the books on the subject of the South Seas in order to understand his subject wholly and to increase its scope. Where his own experience seemed lacking, he did not hesitate to borrow from other sources. Most important, he developed a point of view towards his material, which was a strong feeling of sympathy for the primitive society which he visited, a strong revulsion against the corruption of it by modern influences.

This was not an unusual attitude for his time. Something happened to that attitude, however, between 1847, when *Omoo* appeared, and 1849, when he completed his third book, *Mardi.* The third volume begins as if it were to be a continuation of the first two, to round out and form a trilogy of the South Seas. But Melville's subject was to have but two sides, the idyl of nature and the corruption of the idyl—what he called later in *Clarel* "the harps of heaven and the dreary gongs of hell"—and these he had discussed in his first two volumes. His sensitivity was too acute to be satisfied with doing the same thing over again, even with a new setting. As he progressed in his third book, he found it difficult to locate a theme which would not be merely repetition. Perhaps even more important, as he progressed with the writing of *Mardi,* he had begun his extensive reading in the Duyckinck library. Late in 1847 or early in 1848, he read Rabelais and Sir Thomas Browne. In 1849 he took out books by Hawthorne, Carlyle, and Thoreau. He must at this time have read Emerson and Milton. From this time onward, his personal experience became less important *as experience,* more important as objective events to reflect ideas that were stimulated by his reading.

In *Mardi,* it is possible that experience dropped too far into the background—the ideas became too prominent. *Mardi* became an allegorical criticism of modern life, more extreme in its abstraction than anything he was ever again to write; but it has been rightly said that it was in *Mardi* that Melville discovered his method—the techniques that were to come to fruition in *Moby Dick.* To say that he "discovered his method," however, does not mean that he was immediately conscious of such a discovery. He was undoubtedly disappointed by the unhappy reception of the book when it appeared. In his next two novels, *Redburn* (1849) and *White Jacket* (1850), he reverted somewhat to his earlier manner. But not altogether. In these novels his experiences as a sailor were heightened by the themes of social reform. By the time he came to write *Moby Dick,* Melville had not only the background of whaling, he had developed attitudes towards primitive life in the islands, towards commerce among those islands, towards poverty, ignorance, and injustice in modern life, towards religion as it is preached and religion as it is practiced; and he had become acquainted with enough of the great writers and thinkers of the past to be accounted one of the most completely educated Americans of his time. He had discovered his technique in *Mardi* and refined it through his intense reading of Shakespeare. It should not, therefore, surprise us that he created at this time, out of a combination of native energy and thoughtful perception, what is undoubtedly the first truly great book in American literature.

We cannot explain the production of a masterpiece. Nevertheless, two facts seem of particular importance in the writing of *Moby Dick*. First is the fact of Melville's acquaintance with, and interest in, the primitive societies which he had come to know as a sailor. Second is Melville's discovery of Hawthorne and Shakespeare during the period of composition. This interest in primitive societies was the early attitude displayed in *Typee* and *Omoo,* in which Melville is not untypical of his age. This is an attitude inherited from the extremes of French and English romanticism. Melville never held such views with the assurance of a Rousseau, a St. Pierre, a Wordsworth, or even an Emerson; but it was a concept which was to remain with him and influence his work down to, and including, his last novel, *Billy Budd.* Yet to say so demands certain strong reservations. In actual practice, he rated Hawthorne far above Emerson. Of Emerson, he said in a letter to Evert Duyckinck: "I could readily see in Emerson, notwithstanding his merit, a gaping flaw. It was the insinuation, that had he lived in those days when the world was made, he might have offered some valuable suggestions." Of Hawthorne, at least when he first read him, he had no such feelings: "The soft ravishment of the man spun me round in such a web of dreams, that when the book was closed, when the spell was over, this wizard 'dismissed me with but misty reminiscences, as if I had been dreaming of him.'" Melville announced to American readers that Hawthorne "is one of the new, and far better generation of your writers. The smell of your beeches and hemlocks is upon him; your own broad prairies are in his soul; and if you travel away inland into his deep and noble nature, you will hear the far roar of his Niagara. Give not over to future generations the glad duty of acknowledging him for what he is."

Melville had just discovered Shakespeare when he read Hawthorne, and he felt only a slight hesitation in comparing one to the other. The sense of discovery he felt in both cases was profound. In Hawthorne he was most impressed by the ability to penétrate "the deep mystery of sin." In Shakespeare it was the ability to see the truth and to reveal it clearly through the rich texture of his style. In both cases he was struck by the deeper meaning lying beneath the deceptively simple surfaces. Beneath the surface of his own story—the surface of sailors at sea engaged in the hunt for a white whale—he added deeper currents in the allegorical method of Hawthorne; his own native style he enriched and controlled by adopting the full tones and the ambitious metaphors of Shakespeare.

"Great geniuses," Melville said, "are part of the times, they themselves are the times, and possess a corresponding coloring." He was not talking about himself, but we have come to see him as an excellent example of it; for despite his borrowing from many sources, his principal interest was always in problems located particularly in his time and place. Emerson's genius led him to an exploration of the basis upon which American culture was founded—a relationship of Man to God and to Nature. Hawthorne's genius led him to the rediscovery in American history and American society of traditional limitations of Man and so curbed the excessive optimism of his time. Mark Twain's genius led him briefly, but concretely, to expose America's moral dilemma as it was represented in both the view of Emerson and the view of Hawthorne and to suggest the relative weight of each as they existed in a typical American society. Herman Melville's greatness lay, not only in his ability to see the whole problem as Twain did, but to see it in its more profound and universal aspects. His subject was particularly American, but its implications were an extension of the problems faced by all Western culture.

Melville's immediate subject, the American whale fishery, was perhaps as completely topical an American subject as any he could have selected. Its success in Melville's time was as much a source of patriotic pride as is the development of nuclear energy in our own time—more dramatic and more easily comprehended. By adding to this a parody of the scientific examination of whales and by drawing upon legends concerning a mysterious albino whale, he reflected the two common extremes of modern culture—the new science and primitive superstition—and he posed one against the other. By creating such a character as Captain Ahab of the whaler *Pequod,* he portrayed what he conceived of as possibly the last example of heroic man, whom he described with typical imagery as one who "lived in the world as the last of the Grisley Bears lived in settled Missouri." He created, in addition, a cast of characters which represents a remarkably full range of the possibilities and the limitations of modern life. In the search for the whale itself, which proceeds from the safety of the land to the dangerous unknowns of the sea, he found an almost perfect symbol for the restless rational and irrational, actual and metaphorical, struggle of Man to achieve completeness—absolute understanding—in the face of the unknown and the ubiquitous.

The story itself is simple, and it is too well known, even to those who have not read it, to demand recapitulation. In its setting, the novel achieves its necessary complexity. Life aboard the whale ship is reported in great detail, even to the inclusion of the background of whales and whale-fishing. In a sense the book is what it at times pretends to be—a detailed account of what became known as the whaling industry. In another sense, it is the epic portrayal of the first American Hero. In its most complex aspect, however, we can see it as a monumental and detailed allegory of the predicament of Man (a human comedy)—man with his immediate practical needs and the forms he has discovered partially to alleviate them and man with his undercurrent of irrational fears in the face of the uncontrolled forces of the universe.

The term "allegory" has been used often to describe Melville's method, but it is apt only when loosely used. *Moby Dick* is allegorical, but only in the sense that its events exemplify and define a concept of the human predicament held by Melville and based upon certain traditional concepts. That is, it is allegorical only in the sense that all epic and tragedy is allegorical, presenting events against a defined background and resolving them according to the view as achieved in the definition. Melville accepted Hawthorne's view of the reality of the existence of evil, and he added to it a respect similar to Mark Twain's for the terms in which the moral plight of our times may be represented. With a secular scepticism nearer the Greek view than it was to the eventual hopefulness of traditional Christianity, Melville recovered (in this one book, at least) a concept of the epic as tragedy at a time when such a view seemed on the point of becoming irrecoverably lost. Where *Moby Dick* differs most from traditional tragedy is in its necessary complexity—a complexity which I call necessary because the events of the action could not be merely presented, with the assumption that its readers would understand the underlying social and mythical concepts—those concepts must be exposed and defined at length.

It is just here, too, that the difficulty of treating so complex a work as *Moby Dick* in a short space arises. As I have suggested, almost every character and every event in the novel has a particular function to contribute towards the final definition. Most of these characters and events have been the subjects of the many separate studies made of Melville since the great revival of his reputation began in the 1920's. The Greeks had no need to ask upon what terms the tragedies of Sophocles were presented, whereas one of the pressing critical demands of our age, with its multiplicity of beliefs, is just this need. Yet the critic is overwhelmed by such a necessity in dealing with the inclusiveness of *Moby Dick*. Perhaps the most satisfactory expedient, in such a case, is to focus upon one aspect of the work, with the hope that by elucidating that, the method by which Melville has created his "tragic" background will at least come clear.

As we have seen, one of Melville's most constant subjects was the relation of primitive virtue to modern life. Yet the subject of primitivism in *Moby Dick* has seldom been treated. One of the first characters we meet in the novel is a figure whom we can conceive of as coming into the "civilized" life of modern society (as represented in the ship the *Pequod*) straight from the innocent and simple society of a community such as Melville knew in Typee Valley. He is the harpooner, Queequeg, whom Ishmael meets in the Spouter Inn in New Bedford and whose native superstition leads him to sign aboard the same ship as his newly-made friend. He is a simple and likeable person and an accomplished harpooner. His meeting with the owners of the ship allows Melville the opportunity to compare, humorously, the simple superstitions of the savage's beliefs with the solemn Calvinism of Bildad and Peleg, two of the *Pequod*'s owners. His assignment to duty as harpooner to Starbuck, the chief mate, allows him comparison with a typical Yankee of the most admirable sort, a man who was "no crusader after perils," but who looked upon courage as one of the staples of the ship, "like her beef and her bread."

But the comparisons are not to be carried out on so simple a level as this. The ship carries three mates, and each mate has his harpooner. Each of the mates characterizes a different quality of modern life, a different attitude towards the voyage of the ship. The harpooners are all products of a primitive society. The second mate, Stubb, is described as "A happy-go-luck; neither craven nor valiant; taking perils as they came with an indifferent air; and while engaged in the most imminent crisis of the chase, toiling away, calm and collected as a journeyman joiner engaged for the year." His harpooner is Tashtego, a pure American Indian, whose "long, lean sable hair, his high cheek bones, and black rounding eyes—for an Indian, Oriental in their largeness, but Antarctic in their glittering expression— . . . sufficiently proclaimed him an inheritor of the unvitiated blood of those proud warrior hunters, who in quest for the New England moose, had scoured, bow in hand, the aboriginal forests of the main." The third mate is Flask, characterized as "a short, stout, ruddy young fellow, very pugnacious concerning whales," who somehow seemed to think that the great Leviathans had personally and hereditarily affronted him; and therefore it was a sort of point of honor with him to destroy them whenever encountered. Flask's harpooner was Daggoo, "a gigantic, coalblack negro-savage, with a lion-like tread." Suspended from Daggoo's ears were two golden hoops, so large that the sailors called them ring-bolts, and would talk of securing the top-sail halyards to them. In his youth Daggoo had voluntarily shipped on board a whaler, lying in a lonely bay on his native coast. "And never having been anywhere in the world but Africa, Nantucket, and the pagan harbors most frequented by whalemen; and having now led for many years the bold life of the fishery in the ships of owners uncommonly heedful of what manner of men they shipped; Daggoo retained all his barbaric virtues, and erect as a giraffe, moved about the decks in all the pomp of six feet five in his socks."

Nor is this all the primitive complement of the *Pequod*. In the usual whale ship, the captain seldom had his own boat and crew, so that if he decided to participate in the chase himself, he had to take over the boat of one of his mates. It was thought that the captain, like the general of an army, was too valuable a person to be endangered by actual participation. Unknown to the owners of the *Pequod,* and for a long time to members of the crew, Captain Ahab had spirited aboard a harpooner and a boat crew of his own, to use in running down the white whale. Captain Ahab is a tremendous and singular figure, whose passionate temper seemed almost to match the malignancy of the white whale itself; whose arrogance in the face of fate is exemplified by the artificial limb which he has constructed to replace the leg lost to Moby Dick on a previous voyage—fashioned from the ivory of the whale-bone itself. Captain Ahab's missing leg is significant as a motive of his need and desire for revenge, as well as symbolic of the incompleteness of the man himself, who is represented as a descendant of all heroic men of the past, a man who rushes into the sublime and ubiquitous face of the unknown, under the power of a rage as eloquent as that of Achilles or of King Lear. Captain Ahab's crew is made up of ghost-like phantoms, resembling spirits more than they do men, who are captained by a giant, turbanned harpooner by the name of Fedallah. "He was," Melville says, "such a creature as civilized, domestic people in the temperate zone only see in their dreams, and that but dimly; the like of whom now and then glide among the unchanging Asiatic communities, especially the Oriental isles to the east of the continent—those insulated, immemorial, unalterable countries, which even in these modern days still preserve much of the ghostly aboriginalness of earth's primal generation, when the memory of the first man was a distinct recollection, and all men his descendants."

With the appearance of Fedallah, we begin to see that the comparison between primitives and moderns is to be developed along no such simple lines as those suggested by the South Sea islander, Queequeg; the Gay-Head Indian, Tashtego; and the African Negro, Daggoo. The very terms of the description of Fedallah suggest something deeper and more comprehensive. If Melville means to consult "historic memory" as a means of creating his fictional world, it is a history which goes beyond the brief, though mysterious, histories of the Islander, the Indian, and the Negro. It is to extend to the very source of prehistory (a kind of Jungian myth-world), into the very cradle of the race. The three harpooners come from races which have retained a close and practical relationship with nature. Even their religions, though superstitious, aim at practical ends. They are primitive societies, but their primitivism is a form of innocence—society newly introduced to the evil of western society, subject to corruption by contact with civilization. Fedallah's land, on the other hand, is described as "unchanging"—one of which "domestic, civilized people in the temperate zones" have almost no recollection or knowledge. It is described as "insulated," "immemorial," and "unalterable"—a society which, by its absolute, unchanging nature, must be close to either heaven or hell.

Melville, in his description, leaves no doubt. By its closeness to nature and by its unalterable form it is a society which suggests a close relationship with evil. The members of Fedallah's boat crew are described as spirits, any one of whom might have been mistaken for Beelzebub himself; they are called "tiger yellow," compared with the sharks in the "audacious seas." Fedallah and his crew are primitives, but primitives raised to the highest and purest form of primitivism, instinct raised to the degree that it has become a spiritual quality— pure nature; but nature in such a degree of refinement is inhuman, it is a kind of innate evil.

As I have suggested, the other side of primitivism, which Melville sometimes characterizes as "savagery," sometimes ironically as "cannibalism," is a form of innocence; it is not so much inhuman as it is a-human. But innocence blends into evil, just as it can rise to good; and in the three harpooners we have a kind of chart of the degrees of primitivism in stages from the almost saint-like innocence of Queequeg, through Tashtego and Daggoo, to the pinnacle of Fedallah. They stand as the primitive counterparts for the mates and captain of the *Pequod,* who are depicted similarly in degrees of heroic virtue, from the hereditary audacity of Flask, through Stubb and Starbuck, to the singular heroic qualities of Captain Ahab.

Yet the comparison is not a simple one of black and white (although the color has some importance), in which the qualities on one side are admirable, those on the other hateful. There is a point at which the two worlds tend to merge, to produce a balance. It is a dual world in which the qualities of the three mates are balanced by the qualities of the harpooners. On the level of Flask and Daggoo it seems almost a purely physical, purely utilitarian relationship. Flask is short; Daggoo is tall; the qualities and limitations of one are compensated by the qualities and limitations of the other. In the case of Starbuck and Queequeg, however, it becomes almost a perfect balance between one kind of development and the other. On the whole, the qualities of western man are represented as intellectual, reasonable, and courageous; the qualities of the savage as spontaneous, colorful, and active. One is the guiding intellect, the other is the intuitive act. The true center is as ambiguous as the color of the whale which it has become the crew's duty and the captain's necessity to capture. (The whale's whiteness, Melville tells us, is not due to its absence of color, but to its representing an accumulation of all colors.) If nature is, as Captain Ahab maintains, the mere mask of reality through which the seeker after true knowledge —the modern hero—must strike to disclose the true reality, it is a mask as blank as the whiteness of the whale. Ahab's heroism consisted in this necessity to strike through the mask, to penetrate beyond the uncertainties, to the absolute truth; and in the hope of achieving it, he was both willing and under the necessity to borrow, Faustlike, the power of Fedallah—the spirit of the devil.

Yet, "Cannibals?" Melville asks, "who is not a cannibal?" To be an artist is an occupation often calling for qualities of savagery. "I am myself a savage," he has Ishmael say at one point, "owing no allegiance but to the King of the Cannibals; and ready at any moment to rebel against him." Also, he says: "As with the Hawaiian savage, so with the white sailor-savage. With the same marvellous patience, and with the same single shark's tooth, of his one poor jack-knife, he will carve you a bit of bone sculpture, not quite as workmanlike, but as close packed in its maziness of design, as the Greek savage Achilles' shield; and full of barbaric spirit and suggestiveness, as the prints of that fine old Dutch savage, Albrecht Dürer."

Savagery—that is, primitivism—represents the qualities of life and nature which give man the ability to act, whether as artist, sailor, or ship's captain. It is the duty of the intellect to keep such energy in check, to direct it towards reasonable and possible ends. Captain Ahab's quest for knowledge becomes inhuman as soon as he loses sight of the reasonable ends of his voyage and concentrates upon thoughts of revenge. It is Starbuck who attempts to dissuade him: "Vengeance on a dumb brute," he cried, "that simply smote thee from blindest instinct! Madness! To be enraged with a dumb thing, Captain Ahab, seems blasphemous."

Starbuck is right, but not wholly right. It is blasphemous—it becomes madness. Ahab discards or destroys all man-made guides, including his quadrant and his compass and depends upon blind instinct; he disregards the warnings of others or appeals for human compassion; he concentrates every ounce of human energy upon his one hopeless task, to strike through the mask of ambiguous reality and discover the "higher reality" beneath its shifting and ambivalent surface. As the action progresses, it leaves in its wake the wounded feelings of the three mates, the madness of the cabin-boy, Pip, the crucifixion of Fedallah on the body of the wounded whale, and finally the splintered wreck of the *Pequod* and the destruction of the captain and his crew. What survives the disaster is the memory of the destruction of evil and the singular heroism of Ahab. The memory survives because the narrator Ishmael (the artist) is saved, allowed to float to safety on the buoyant coffin of Queequeg—the primitive islander. It is as though Melville were saying, he had been allowed to record the destruction of the modern hero through a vision he had received of an innocent society on the island of Typee years before.

The lessons of *Moby Dick* are many and many-sided. Nevertheless, it is not difficult to discover in this work the combining of an essential romanticism, such as that which formed the basis for such relatively simple works as *Typee* and *Omoo,* with the traditional values of philosophy, religion, and aesthetics—the values and the limitations of primitive man contrasted with like values and limitations of cultivated society. Such contrasts were not unusual in American literature of Melville's day, and they have continued to preoccupy our authors to the present. The two principal aspects of the view that the primitive is, at once, a regenerative force and a mysterious source of evil are available in Hawthorne's two principal works. In *The House of the Seven Gables,* the wronged family Maule maintains a physical supremacy over the descendants of Judge Pyncheon, and they are destined to revive the decayed family through the marriage of one of their members into the Pyncheon family. In *The Scarlet Letter,* the dark woods are always symbolic of a diabolic spirit which stands close to nature, but which is also the source of physical regeneration.

Primitivism in Melville

Henry James stressed the innocence and energy of the traditional American character, then contrasted it with the sophistication and the decay of the European. In William Faulkner it is the primitive energy of the Negro and the Indian which represents the only force capable of holding the crumbling structure of Southern society together. "They endured," Faulkner wrote in describing the Negro Dilsey of *The Sound and the Fury,* and it is nature that is finally to endure in his fine short story, "The Bear." For T. S. Eliot, the problem of time and change seems to signify our concern with nature and with the primitive qualities of nature. In the "Dry Salvages" section of *The Four Quartets,* he speaks of

> The backward look behind the assurance
> Of recorded history, the back-ward half-look
> Over the shoulder, towards the primitive terror.

The river, which is both nature and time, he speaks of as "a strong brown god," "Keeping his seasons and rages, destroyer, reminder/Of what men choose to forget." The rhythm of the river he remembers as being present in the nursery bedroom, where it was felt with more intensity than by the "dwellers in cities," who believed they had tamed the god with their bridges and barges and dikes.

The river and the seas are reminders of an earlier creation —a pre-history—just as they were to Melville. It is "historic memory" which takes us back through "long defiles of doom" to disclose a kind of truth for the present moment. And so it is to "historic memory" that Melville continues to appeal in his major works. His long poem *Clarel* sees modern man posed against a background of Christian history. His final work, *Billy Budd,* is based upon an incident at the beginning of the French Revolution, but which thrusts us backward in time to our remote beginnings. These two works are so related in terms of theme that one can draw upon the statements of the poem to elucidate the meanings of the allegorical terms of the novel, for *Billy Budd* is almost wholly an allegory, although it uses the terms of heroism and of tragedy to mirror its meaning.

There is perhaps little in *Clarel* or *Billy Budd* that Melville had not stated earlier in *Moby Dick*. The important thing is that there is much in all these works that had been recognized as early as *Typee*. If one went far enough back into history, one traversed "long defiles of doom"; if one dug deeply enough into human nature, noble though it might be, one encountered the far roar of a Niagara. In *Moby Dick* this concept had been embodied in epic action; in *Billy Budd* it was stated as an allegory for our times. Do we owe our allegiance to Nature or the King? Too great an allegiance to Nature leads to the excesses of the French Revolution; too great an allegiance to the King results in injustice.

Melville is most specific on this subject in *Clarel,* where the opposites later to be incorporated into *Billy Budd* were represented in a series of images followed by a warning:

> Yea, *ape* and *angel,* strife and old debate—
> The harps of *heaven* and the dreary gongs of *hell;*
> Science the feud can only aggravate—
> No umpire she betwext the *chimes* and *knell:*
> The running battle of the *star* and *clod*
> Shall run forever—if there be no God.

Science cannot solve, it can only aggravate the strife between ape and angel, the clod and the star, hell and heaven, birth and death. The nature of Melville's religious beliefs is not my concern here, but two things can be said of them: he believed in the efficacy of the concept of original sin; he believed in the necessity of a faith in some kind of god. It is necessary to state this, because somehow what he considered the qualities of primitive life entered into both his concept of evil and his concept of good. Billy Budd is as much a primitive—a barbarian—as Fedallah; but Billy's innocence is virtue, while Fedallah's immemorial knowledge of nature is evil. The strife, then, finally is between two qualities of primitive life; a solution—insofar as there is a solution—can be found only in terms of art and religion; but they must be an art and a religion quickened by primitive powers. *Moby Dick* is an epic illustration of man's greatness in his battle with all those forces doomed to defeat him. *Billy Budd* is an allegory of the triumph of innocence over modern rationalism, and finally over evil itself. But the seeds of Billy's existence were planted many years before, in Typee Valley, and they developed through all the works that preceded *Billy Budd* into a final statement of Melville's moral and aesthetic creed.

The Unity of *Billy Budd*

MELVILLE'S LAST COMPLETE work, *Billy Budd,* was not finished until 1891, the year of Melville's death, and it
did not appear in print until 1924. Even then, the first printed
version, prepared by Raymond Weaver, was not completely
authentic because of the chaotic condition of the manuscript.
A final, scholarly transcription was made by F. Barron Freeman in 1948.[1] Freeman's verified version, however, revealed
nothing startling in itself. What it did do was indicate the
tremendous seriousness with which Melville took the labor of
composing his final work, the conscious effort and energy
which he expended on it almost up to the last hours of his
life. Most important, it removed doubts concerning the final-
ity with which *Billy Budd* could be read critically, for it established a text which we can be reasonably certain represents
Melville's final and deliberate intention.

This is important because so much that has been written
about this short novel has been tentative and uncertain. In
brief, the criticism of *Billy Budd* has represented two points of
view. The first is that which sees the work as Melville's "testament of acceptance," without making it in any way clear what

[1] *Melville's Billy Budd,* ed. F. Barron Freeman. Harvard University
Press.

The Unity of Billy Budd

that acceptance represented; the second the view that *Billy Budd* is a reflection of its author's final confusion and disappointment, an unnecessarily expanded and wasteful work. Both judgments are, in my opinion, wrong, and their error arises from an original error in reading.

Billy Budd has been seen as an attempt at conventional tragedy, with Billy as tragic hero confronted by the fateful choice between two traditional extremes: order at the expense of justice or justice at the expense of order. Had Billy demanded justice, he would not have accepted Captain Vere's judgment. Not to have accepted the judgment would have represented a denial of the law (and order) upon which the judgment was based. Since order represents a means of controlling evil, the choice of anything else would have represented the triumph of evil (Claggart). Melville has set the whole sequence up cleverly to parallel the crucifixion, so that the incident mirrors Christ's agony and depicts Christ's choice of death in the service of the law. The law is God (Vere). It is absolute. Justice is for Man. Christ (and Billy) as God-Man chose the law and suffered death, for it is only in terms of the law that evil can be defeated. The very concept of justice gives reality to evil—a choosing between the ambiguities of right and wrong. Billy's choice is thus read as equivalent to Christ's agony and as an indication of Melville's final acceptance of the doctrine of Christian atonement.

Having taken such a position, however, the critic finds himself in difficulty, for what is he to do with the events of the novel which are not concerned directly with Billy's defection and punishment? Billy's career, while representing the central events of the narrative, makes up approximately one-third of the total story, and it is surrounded by events and references dealing with philosophical, political, and aesthetic matters apparently only distantly related to Billy's personal predicament. The easiest answer to this problem, and the one most frequently given, is merely to suggest that such matters are extraneous: obvious but minor defects in an interesting work, shortcomings which Melville, had he lived, would have corrected. The second, and most obvious answer, is to say that such apparent disorder was simply a mirroring of Melville's own confusion and uncertainty and that the work is a failure in consequence of it.

The fallacy of the first position is obvious since the publication of Mr. Freeman's edition of *Billy Budd,* for it shows us that Melville had worked out a short version of the tale, entitled *Baby Budd,* in which Billy occupies a dominant position and there is little "digression"; but Mr. Freeman shows also that this version was discarded by its author as unsatisfactory and evidently incomplete. Since Melville worked at the writing of *Billy Budd* for more than two and one-half years, we can consider the work nothing less than the result of his considered and mature deliberation. The fallacy of the second position can be disclosed only by showing that there is no moral equivocation, as Richard Chase calls it, in *Billy Budd* and that the apparent digressions are part and parcel of the total unity of the work.

The initial mistake is to persist in thinking of *Billy Budd* as a tragedy at all. The subject of the novel is adequately suggested in Melville's brief preface, the opening sentence of which reads as follows:

The year 1797, the year of this narrative, belongs to a period which as every thinker now feels, involved a crisis for Christendom not exceeded in its undetermined momentousness at the time by any other era whereof there is record.

This crisis, of course, represents the events surrounding the revolution in France, and it is significant that Melville apparently saw the events of the mutinies at Spithead and at the Nore as symbolic of the threat to world order posed by the revolution. Any reader of Melville knows that he was greatly concerned with the historic development of mankind and that he saw Christianity as the center of an order which seemed gradually but inevitably to be passing away. It was probably because of this view that he could think of himself only as a nominal, not an orthodox, Christian. Any reader of *Clarel* understands the approximate terms upon which this state of mind was based during the later years of Melville's life. Both *Clarel* and *Billy Budd* might have been titled, less imaginatively, "The Crisis of Christendom," with Christendom standing not only for the formal aspects of religion, but for all of the philosophical, political, and moral concerns of Man.

In these terms Billy Budd is Man—Christian man as well as historic man. Though he is presented with obvious simplicity, he contains the ambiguities of all of Melville's heroes from Ahab to The Confidence Man. In Christian terms he is Christ, but with typical Christian ambiguity, he is both the Son of Man and the Son of God. Whence came he? In philosophical and political terms, he sailed first as a common sailor on the *Rights of Man,* but was later impressed aboard his Majesty's warship the *Indomitable.* It is remarkable how little attention critics have paid to the names of these two vessels, as well as to the ship which appears at the end of the story: the French warship *Atheiste,* formerly the *St. Louis.* The contrast between life aboard the *Rights of Man* and that aboard the *Indomitable* is the contrast between the Lockean and the Hobbesian points of view. The order of the first is that imposed by Billy's primitive innocence: the common-sense example of good backed up by physical force when necessary. The *Indomitable* is ruled by a concept of absolute order imposed by authority and depending upon fealty to the source of legislated power. Historically, however, it is the distinction between primitive society (which, of course, Melville knew well and at first hand) and the era of what he called "citified man." Theologically, it is the contrast of pagan and Christian order.

Freeman presents evidence to show that at one point Melville considered naming the *Indomitable,* the *Bellipotente.* Such a title must have seemed to him finally too inclusive, too pointedly aimed at the religious level of his tale. Nevertheless, the religious level is primary during the period of Billy's difficulties aboard the second ship, and the parallel of Billy's execution for technical mutiny and the crucifixion have been clearly and commonly seen. Christ's godlike innocence is mirrored in Billy's natural innocence; Christ's humanity in Billy's natural (physical) defect of speech; Christ's agony in submitting to the Will of Heaven in Billy's submission to the authority of Captain Vere. Captain Vere's exclamation following the death of Claggart (the naturally depraved) by the hand of Billy—"Struck dead by an angel of God. Yet the Angel must hang!"—reflects the paradox of atonement by which Christ suffered the agony of death in order to release mankind from the bondage of evil.

It is clear that Melville saw the idea of the Fall and the Atonement as an accurate image of man's predicament (See *Clarel*, XV, 249, *The Works of Herman Melville*, 1924); this level of *Billy Budd* is the one with which critics have primarily concerned themselves. What is important is that Melville held it *as image*, not as orthodox religion. As such it was nearer an aesthetic than a theological concept. This is important, because it follows that the crucifixion becomes tragedy, mirroring man's incompleteness; the victory over evil is transient and incomplete. Such a view is expressed in the Christ-like aspect of Ahab in *Moby Dick*. Whereas in *Moby Dick*, however, we have the tragic view expressed directly, in *Billy Budd* it is merely reflected as parable. Melville had written in *Clarel*:

> Historic memory goes so far
> Backward through the long defiles of doom;
> Whoso consults it honestly
> That mind grows prescient in degree;
> For man, like God, abides the same
> Always. (XV, 248)

In *Billy Budd* Melville is merely consulting "historic memory," and what he discovers is that man and God are always the same. Billy is budding man, yet he is also the budding God. As primitive man Billy lives at comparative ease with his shipmates aboard the *Rights of Man*—a society similar to that pictured in *Typee.* Transferred, however, to the *Indomitable* —emerging into the era of citified man, he has left nature behind him, except as he himself represents it aboard the second vessel. As a representative of nature, he does the *natural* thing, strikes out at the evil with which he is confronted. It is Claggart's eloquence (the ability to make a fair case for an evil cause) which is the mark of his duplicity. The mark of primitive man is his completeness, his oneness with nature; but he lacks eloquence, he depends upon intuition and action. Citified man faces nature, as John Crowe Ransom has stated handsomely in a recent article, "in guilt and fear toward that Nature who no longer contained him but indifferently confronted him." Melville has Captain Vere say, after acknowledging that Billy's action was no more than "natural": "But do these buttons that we wear attest that our allegiance is to Nature? No, to the King."

The question I take it Melville is raising here is this: If the King's authority is gone, and Nature's, what then supports us? Billy dies for his impulsive act with a prayer for Captain Vere (*vir*—man) upon his lips. A little later the *Indomitable* meets up with the French warship *Atheiste* (formerly the King's ship, the *St. Louis*) and engages her. The *Indomitable* survives the engagement, sinking the *Atheiste,* but Captain Vere, who is also the old god, perhaps even the father of Billy, dies with Billy's name upon his lips, not, as Melville says, "in accents of remorse," but as though transferring his authority to his son: Billy the Son of God and the Son of Man; God become Man and Man become God.

It seems clear that this is Melville's view of the crucifixion— the old God superseded by the new; God as myth. The story of Billy Budd then represents the origin of myth, myth which mirrors man's tragic situation; but is not an attempt at tragedy itself. It is set in a period which represents, in Melville's words, "a crisis for Christendom," a period in which atheism is averted but which has only (possibly) in the story of Billy Budd brought forth a new myth to replace it. *Billy Budd* is to be seen, then, somewhat as prophecy, or as an expression of faith. Such an idea had been expressed earlier in *Clarel:*

>   . . . the gods are gone.
> Tully scarce dreamed they could be won
> Back into credence; less that earth
> Ever could know yet mightier birth
> Of Diety. He died. Christ came.
> And, in due hour, that impious Rome,
> Emerging from vast wreck and shame,
> Held the forefront of Christendom.
> The inference? The lesson?—come:
> Let fools count of faith's closing knell—
> Time, God, are inexhaustible.
>   (XIV, 128-129)

Billy Budd is an example of how the new birth will come, winning for mankind a unity such as they knew under Christianity, under the gods of antiquity, or in their primitive innocence. Is this too optimistic a view? Melville's last years have been seen as full of darkness and despair. He himself said of these years that he was neither optimist nor pessimist, nevertheless he relished the pessimism of Thomson's *City of Dreadful Night,* "if for nothing else than as a counterpoise to the exorbitant hopefulness, juvenile and shallow, that makes such a bluster in these days—at least in some quarters." If he was optimistic, then, at least it was not the kind of optimism which he recognized "in some quarters."

If the subject of *Billy Budd* is, as we suggest, the renewal of myth, is it Melville's intention to imply that we are simply awaiting the arrival of a new Messiah? In one sense, yes. We must not assume, as did Tully, that since the old gods are gone no new ones will arise to perform the unification performed by the old. On the other hand, Melville is quite specific about a certain danger—the danger of following false gods; and he is equally specific about the method whereby he believes the new will be enabled to arise. It is this which the critics of *Billy*

Budd have heretofore failed to see in those passages which they have labeled extraneous.

Let us begin first with the danger. I have said that the victim of Billy's natural wrath, Claggart, clothed his duplicity by a fairness of appearance which included his ability to speak falsehood under the appearance of truth. Undisguised truth (which is what Billy's innocence represents) is hateful because antipodal to evil. Billy is budding man—primitive man: John Locke's *tabula rasa.* Claggart is the Hobbesian man in whom cunning and intelligence have been substituted for brute force. Mythical man (or Captain Vere) stands squarely between these two opposing concepts. He is intelligent but dreamy—sometimes known as "Starry" Vere. He wears the authority of his office openly and plainly, as did Lord Nelson, who insisted upon wearing the scarlet and gold-braid even in the midst of battle. The life of Vere (and Nelson) is open to scrutiny, and upon a certain level it is reflected in the beauty of their vessels, the ornaments of their office, the attractions of ceremony, and the eloquence of their commands. Upon another level, however, such ornaments only served to mask the ugly injustices afflicting the common sailors under their command. Here is Melville's dilemma, and the dilemma which supplies the dramatic framework for his tale. If we correct the injustices in the name of humanity, do we not also commit ourselves to the giving up of all of those beauties which the old order had cherished? Yes, Melville finally concedes, we do. We exchange Nelson's ornate dress for drab, because in calling attention to himself, Nelson endangered the lives of those under him. We relinquish the ceremony of authority, because to delay weighing anchor as Nelson did was dangerous and impractical in a world where ceremony is no longer observed. We surrender the grand lines of Nelson's flagship *Victory* to the more functional and less beautiful design of the *Monitor.* Yet we do not accede to the demands of revolution—atheism. We have come full circle, but only in the sense that pagan civilization had come full circle at the time of Tully. We are faced with what Melville, in *Clarel,* had called "civil barbarism": "Man disennobled—brutalized/By popular science —atheized/Into a smatterer" (XV, 250).

We then are faced by the same danger which Captain Vere faced in his engagement with the *Atheiste:* civil barbarism. The *Atheiste* is, significantly, not a vessel in its own right, but one merely captured and renamed. The question of identity here is related to Melville's concept of truth and reality. Atheism, which was the product of popular science, was doomed simply because it did not express truth and reality. Captain Vere was doomed, but for an entirely different reason ("The gods are gone"); the *Indomitable* survived both the *St. Louis* and the *Atheiste,* but the implication is clear that the crisis is one merely of discovering a new captain. Melville's attitude toward popular science is further clarified in an ironic passage labeled "A Digression," which occurs in the narrative just after Billy's death. The Purser and the ship's Surgeon are discussing what everyone had considered the remarkable nature of Billy's dying. The Purser suggested that willpower might have been responsible for the absence of the usual physical manifestations, but the Surgeon ridicules such an idea, saying it is no more attributable to willpower than to horsepower. He admits that the event was phenomenal only "in the sense that it was an appearance the cause of which is not immediately to be assigned." The Purser then suggests euthanasia. *"Euthanasia,"* the Surgeon replies, "is something like your *will-power;* I doubt its authenticity as a scientific term. . . . It is at once imaginative and metaphysical,—in short, Greek."

It seems clear that if Melville was optimistic it was not with the arrogant optimism of nineteenth-century science. This is further indicated in the report of Billy's death supplied by a writer of popular prose, the reporter of *News from the Mediterranean;* here (as with the Surgeon) the truth is hidden beneath a false appearance of truth. If Claggart represents malicious evil (natural depravity), the Surgeon represents the evil of ignorance, while the popular reporter, pretending to serve constituted authority, tells the grossest falsehood of all.

The Unity of Billy Budd

All are forms of dissimulation—the dangers confronting modern man in his search for truth. Where then does truth lie?

The answer, of course, is inherent in the novel itself. As is so often the case, however, Melville had considered the problem explicitly in *Clarel:*

> Suppose an instituted creed
> (or truth or fable) should indeed
> To ashes fall; the spirit exhales,
> But reinfunds in active forms:
> Verse, popular verse, it charms or warms—
> Bellies philosophy's flattened sails—
> Tinctures the very book, perchance,
> Which claims arrest of its advance.
> (XV, 105)

Here is an almost exact duplication of the situation in *Billy Budd.* Christianity and all it implies has fallen into decay. The spirit exhales, but only momentarily, awaiting the propitious moment again to belly philosophy's sails. Billy's act of innocent heroism supplies the opportunity—creates the situation. Authoritarianism and a changing concept of man's individual worth had conspired to bring about the destruction of the old gods. Billy's act (and by extension, Christ's) is seen more as tragic circumstance than as actual atonement. From Billy's act then springs the new myth, sung to the tune of a simple sailors' ballad. It is "verse, popular verse" which bellies the sails, which supplies the common man with a means of confronting the facts, not only of Billy's death, but of his own. It is not orthodox Christianity. It is not popular science. It is the simple creative act which pierces the mask of falsehood and error, which sees man's existence as an heroic submission to fate, but which is in constant rebellion against those forms which result in man's injustice to man.

If it seems odd that so apparent and so integrated a theme should have been missed by so many readers, the fact of its having been missed is only additional evidence of the difficulty which the modern has with the ironic style in which *Billy*

Budd is composed. The difficulty is multiplied in this case, because Melville did not employ (indeed, could not have employed) the lyric-ironic style of *Moby Dick,* to which we have after a lapse of many years, become accustomed. Accompanying the positive theme of man's rejuvenation through myth, there is also, as we have indicated, the negative one of modern man's situation in an over-materialistic society: "atheized into a smatterer." In a satiric-ironic manner, Melville pretends to adopt the very style of the popular-prose writer against whom his book is at least partially directed. Despite the fact that his central theme betrays his principal intention —he had elsewhere written, "It is not the purpose of literature to purvey news,"—he pretended to have written a story which, as he says, "has less to do with fable than with fact." He speaks of digressions and ragged edges, as though the very essence of truth lay in its absence of form. He pretends, in other words, to have written the very book which claims arrest of the advance of truth, or fable, or of instituted creeds; but the theme itself, the form which he has created in *Billy Budd,* tinctures the very book which he pretends to have written—the book of factual information concerning a mutiny at sea.

Contrary to current critical opinion, then, *Billy Budd* as a unified work not only is not marred by digressions and irrelevancies, it is a triumph of architectonic structure. When Melville protests that as a writer of "facts" he is prevented from achieving "an architectural finial," he is merely calling attention (in a method not uncommon in literature) to his central theme, which is in fact presented as an architectural finial, since it lies imbedded in the popular ballad "Billy in the Darbies," which ends the book.

> But they'll lash me in hammock, drop me deep.
> Fathoms down, fathoms down, how I'll dream fast asleep.
> I feel it stealing now. Sentry, are you there?
> Just ease these darbies at the wrist,
> And roll me over fair.
> I am sleepy, and the oozy weeds about me twist.

The Unity of Billy Budd

This is not great poetry, but it was not intended to be. Neither is it, as one critic calls it, doggerel. It is intended merely to represent the primitive, but universal, ability of man to temper the harsh facts of death, to come to terms with nature, through art. It represents Melville's final expression of faith in mankind—faith in the ability of the common man to see beyond the misrepresentations of evil, however disguised; faith that the essential beauty and heroism of man will always be recognized and celebrated in artistic form, however crude.

Billy Budd is not in itself a tragedy, although it is an expression of belief in the tragic predicament of man. If we need distinguish it by supplying a name, I would suggest that it be called satiric-allegory. It does not pretend to the organ voice of *Moby Dick*. It combines the biting irony of Swiftian satire with the lyric hopefulness of John Bunyan. That it has been so little understood need not finally surprise us when we consider the history of Melville's literary career from *Mardi* onward. Among other things, *Billy Budd* suggests the possibility that Melville believed the rich tongue of Shakespeare (the use of which he borrowed in *Moby Dick* and *Pierre*) to be as obsolete as the scarlet and gold of Lord Nelson's office. Perhaps this is why he chose to write otherwise in his final work.

Henry James: The American[1]

THE AMERICAN CHARACTER is firmly embodied in the person of Christopher Newman, whose name ironically suggests both his qualities and his function. He is the *new* man of the Western world, contrasted with the *old* of Europe. He is ironically reversing the voyage of his namesake, Christopher Columbus—the *new* man discovering the *old* world. James calls him "the superlative American," and his chief characteristics are a physical and moral health which have come from the grounding of his virtues in a world of action. "If he was a muscular Christian it was quite without knowing it." Like Mark Twain's Innocents he had no eye for art ("he had often admired the copy much more than the original"), but he likewise lacked the barbaric cynicism which would have made dramatic action impossible and which left Twain's American figures isolated and lonely in the midst of Europe's plenty. "His attitude was simply the flower of his general good-nature, and a part of his instinctive and genuinely democratic assumption of every one's right to lead an easy life."

Christopher Newman, though his early innocence is con-

[1] Chapter references are based on the Rinehart Edition, which is a reprint of the first edition.

stantly stressed by James, is not unintelligent. He is an out-growth of the typical Yankee character, a figure in a long line of American mythical and fictional characters which would include Tyler's Jonathan, Davy Crockett, and Huckleberry Finn. Nowhere in James's work is his admiration for this side of the American character more clearly shown than in the figure of Christopher Newman. Of the other Americans in the novel, Mrs. Tristram comes the nearest to representing a unique American personality, but she was obviously intended as a portrayal of a character occupying that middle ground between American and European culture which Newman must traverse to conduct his courtship of Claire. She is the European-American in the best sense. "She told [Newman] that he was 'horribly Western,' but in this compliment the adverb was tinged with insincerity." She tells him that he flatters her patriotism (in a later edition, James revises it to her "latent patriotism" and has her say, "Deep within me the eagle shrieks"). She remains in Europe because it is more convenient and because she (like James's Mrs. Medwin in one of his short stories) had found it possible to capitalize upon the fact of her difference. She does, however, together with her husband, who is little more than an amiable simpleton, represent at a much lower level a repetition of that pattern suggested by Newman and the Bellegardes. They are the American equivalents of the French family Nioche, standing in a relationship to Newman comparable to the relation of Noémie and her father to the French aristocracy. Mr. Babcock, the young Unitarian min-ister from Dorchester, Massachusetts, is a more complicated kind of innocent than Newman, and while he enters the story briefly, his purpose is obviously to suggest the limitations of the New England character as a symbol of the American cul-ture of the nineteenth century. Babcock's unitarianism has a deep tinge of Calvinism, which, while innocent enough in its own way, is an additional contrast to Newman's Yankee nature, not an ingredient of it.

The Bellegarde family, on their side, are more European

than French. The marquise is the daughter of an English nobleman whose family dates from the sixteenth century. Her husband, the old marquis, dates from "somewhere in the ninth century, under Charlemagne." As Valentin characterizes them: "My mother is strange, my brother is strange, and I verily believe that I am stranger than either. You will even find my sister a little strange. Old trees have crooked branches, old houses have queer cracks, old races have odd secrets. Remember that we are eight hundred years old!"

The chief characteristics of the Bellegardes are (1) their survival as a symbol of European aristocracy removed from its function; (2) their moral strangeness (note that Valentin uses this adjective as well as "crooked," "queer," and "odd"), which in this case includes the harboring of the evil deed which Newman discovers from Valentin's hint upon his death-bed; (3) their formal emptiness in contrast to Newman's utility and naturalness, a relation which is conceived in an aesthetic, not a social sense. If Newman's innocence is a mark of his racial youth, the evil deed in the background of the Bellegardes is an objectification of their age and knowledge. It was an act of self-protection—absolute form defending itself against the threat of change. Form exists only in a changeless order, and the old marquis had acquiesced in the first stage of the destruction of his class. He was prepared to uphold his daughter in her objection to her early marriage for humanitarian, not formal, reasons.

What James described in the preface to the 1910 edition of *The American* as the weakness of this early novel—his making the outrage more "showy" than "sound"—consisted in his making the contrasts between Newman and the Bellegarde family so great. What he did, however, was to present dramatically the great dilemma of American society, a dilemma that received particular attention before and after the turn of the century. What is Melville's Ahab and his battle with the malignant whale but an attempt to come to grips with absolute truth? Socially, the novels of Twain, Howells, and

Hamlin Garland[2] depict the case for humanitarian values as opposed to the restrictions of an empty formalism. In our own time, such authors as Ernest Hemingway and William Faulkner have been concerned with the problem of developing a new form to clothe the particular concepts of our age. Henry James did not see the problem or the relation of the artist to it in so simple a light as most of these authors, and in such later novels as *The Ambassadors* and *The Golden Bowl* it was to become very complicated indeed; but that he recognized it in similar terms is clear from *The American*. It is clear, too, that James was wholly upon the side of Newman, his expatriation and his personal regard for traditional modes of living notwithstanding; but in speaking of Newman we mean the Newman of the last chapter, not the first, for it is Newman's triumph that he did not push action beyond its proper bounds —he did not, finally, make use of the letter written by the old Marquis de Bellegarde. He observed proprieties that few characters in American literature would have observed. Though he did not, certainly, condone the empty ritual of Valentin's duel over a Parisian coquette, it is undoubtedly true that he and Valentin come nearer to representing James's ideal, within the limits of human possibility, than any other characters in the novel. It is likewise true that Valentin could no more have broken the bonds of his own existence in the world of the Bellegardes and become a bank clerk in the new world than Newman could, once Claire de Cintré was lost to him irretrievably, continue his prosecution of revenge against the old marquise and her son. He could not use his own weapon (the letter) to fulfill the merely formal purpose of upholding

[2] Garland wrote, for instance, as follows: "Obscurely forming in my mind were two great literary concepts—that truth was a higher quality than beauty, and that to spread the reign of justice should everywhere be the design and intent of the artist. The merely beautiful in art seemed petty, and success at the cost of the happiness of others a monstrous egotism." But Garland was here mistaking the function of the artist with the function of the sociologist and politician, a mistake which James never made.

THE WRITER IN THE ROOM

his honor; although Valentin felt obliged to use his (pistols) in an affair involving a woman for whom he no longer cared and whom he would never see again. The irony here indicates not only the relationship of the two characters, but also indicates James's attitude toward them. Newman, the man of action, is put in the position of revenging himself in an abstract and judicial way by the disclosure of the Bellegardes' guilt, while the representative of the Bellegarde family engages in an active and physical, though empty, gesture which results in the loss of his life.

Perhaps the most misleading feature of *The American* for the inexperienced reader is its similarity in dramatic structure to the popular romance, in which one is accustomed to expect virtue to triumph in the cause of love at any cost. According to this view, Newman would have been obliged to act upon his knowledge of the family crime and thus release Claire from her confinement in the Abbaye Auebert. For a great many readers, the problem is no more complicated than that, for what they wish to witness is the triumph of American individualism over the decadent traditions of Europe. On the level of action, we must admit that such a conclusion is as reasonable as the victory of Colonel Manly over the Europeanized Billy Dimple in Royall Tyler's early American play *The Contrast;* it is as reasonable as much of the laughter of Mark Twain's Innocents at the expense of European culture or of Sinclair Lewis's sympathetic portrayal of Sam Dodsworth in comparison with the silly pretensions of his wife Fran. But for Henry James the problem *was* more complicated, and it is James's reservations (because they disturbed the total affirmation which so many American readers have been taught to expect) that have been weighed against him and labeled "European"—if not, "un-American."

Our introduction to Claire de Cintré is made through the eyes of the Tristrams. For Tom Tristram she is "a great white doll of a woman, who cultivates quiet haughtiness." He says: "[She has] a kind of beauty you must be *intellectual* to understand."[3] Mrs. Tristram is more sensitive to the particular value which Claire's beauty represents. "She is perfect!" she says. "I won't say more than that. When you're praising a person to another who is to know her, it is bad policy to go into details. I won't exaggerate. I simply recommend her. Among all women I have known she stands alone; she is of a different clay."

Claire's "difference" lies not alone in that she is a member of the Bellegarde family, but in her perfection. It is a different kind of strangeness from that of her family. She is a representation of the ideal woman—the golden mean between the two extremes of aristocratic pride and democratic simplicity. It is in terms of this perfection that she is described to Newman by Valentin:

"You have seen her; you know what she is: tall, thin, light, imposing, and gentle, half a *grande dame* and half an angel; a mixture of pride and humility, of the eagle and the dove. She looks like a statue which had failed as stone, resigned itself to its grave defects, and come to life as flesh and blood, to wear white capes and long trains. All I can say is that she really possesses every merit that her face, her glance, her smile, the tone of voice, lead you to expect; it is saying a great deal. As a general thing when a woman seems very charming, I should say 'Beware!' But in proportion as Claire seems charming, you may fold your arms and let yourself float with the current; you are safe. She is so good! I have never seen a woman half so perfect or so complete. She has everything; that is all I can say about her. . . ."

(VIII)

These words are not merely compliments by an admiring brother. The intent of the author shows through: "She looks like a statue which had failed as stone, resigned itself to its grave defects, and come to life as flesh and blood. . . ." Tom Tristram detected the coldness, but called it the kind of beauty which demanded an intellectual (i.e., abstract) appre-

[3] In a later edition, James revised this sentence to read: "She's as cold herself as a porcelain stove, and has about as much expression."

65

ciation. Mrs. Tristram and Valentin agree on her perfection. Through the eyes of Newman we detect the special problem which Claire represents, stated upon all three levels, the moral, the social, and the aesthetic:

Madame de Cintré gave Newman the sense of an elaborate education, of her having passed through mysterious ceremonies and processes of culture in her youth, of her having been fashioned and made flexible to certain exalted social needs. All this, as I have affirmed, made her seem rare and precious—a very expensive article, as he would have said, and one which a man with an ambition to have everything about him of the best would find it highly agreeable to possess. But looking at the matter with an eye to private felicity, Newman wondered where, in so exquisite a compound, nature and art showed their dividing line. Where did the special intention separate from the habit of good manners? Where did urbanity end and sincerity begin? Newman asked himself these questions even while he stood ready to accept the admired object in all its complexity; he felt that he could do so in profound security, and examine its mechanism afterwards, at leisure.

(IX)

The social terms are here stated: urbanity and sincerity. Newman, at the beginning of the novel, has sincerity without urbanity; Valentin, perhaps, urbanity without sincerity. In terms of the aesthetic theme we have urbanity equated with art, sincerity with nature; urbanity with superb craftsmanship, sincerity with the special intention of the artist. Claire is compounded of the terms which represent, when taken together, the special problem of all of Henry James's works. In these abstract terms she is as unattainable as Melville's white whale, and Newman sensed this when he commented to himself: "The only trouble, indeed, was that when the instrument was so perfect it seemed to interpose too much between you and the genius that used it." That "too much" is, of course, Claire's perfection: the very fact of her combining in proper degree the elements of art and nature, of which perfection is compounded. Her name suggests a halo: Claire de Cintré—an arch of light—a lighted window, the bright window through which the reader peers toward perfection. Claire's mother and her elder brother, likewise, may be taken as figures in this metaphor. They are the wardens of her beauty (Bellegarde); but only of her superficial beauty, for they are depicted as wholly artful. To have married Claire to Newman, as they perceived, would have brought out her human qualities at the expense of the artificial culture which they represent and thus estranged her from them. To have married her to Lord Deepmere, as they finally hoped to do, would have accented the artful and bound her more firmly to them.

The only repository for such perfection as that possessed by Claire is the convent—a removal from the constant tensions of life into the timeless death in life—just as the legitimate end of Valentin is the life in death gained at the expense of the murderers of his father. There is in Claire and in Valentin an area of consciousness which might, under other conditions, have made it possible for them to come to terms with what Newman represented. When Newman is sitting with Valentin after his duel, he says:

"It's a bad case—it's a bad case—it's the worst case I ever met. I don't want to say anything unpleasant, but I can't help it. I've seen men dying before—and I've seen men shot. But it always seemed more natural; they were not so clever as you. Damnation—damnation! You might have done something better than this. It's about the meanest winding-up of a man's affairs that I can imagine!"

(XIX)

Valentin's death is unnatural because his own value was so much greater than the cause for which he elected to sacrifice himself. Somehow—perhaps as a result of Newman's speech—he recognizes this:

Valentin feebly waved his hand to and fro. "Don't insist—don't insist. It is mean—decidedly mean. For you see at the bottom—down at the bottom *in a little place as small as the end of a wine-funnel—I agree with you!*"

(Our italics, XIX)

Claire de Cintré agreed this far too, else she could not have agreed to the marriage in the first place. But her agreement was not large enough to prevent her acceding to the demands of her mother and elder brother when they saw a way out of the alliance with Newman; large enough, however (and especially after her meeting Newman), to make it impossible for her to marry her cousin. Her retirement to the abbey is a death more complete than Valentin's, for it is really *unnatural* —an abstract death only. It is a relinquishing of life while yet remaining alive, and this is the meaning Newman makes of the chant of the Carmelite nuns: "It was their dirge over their buried affections and over the vanity of earthly desires." In accepting the discipline of this order, Claire has gone even beyond the understanding of the Bellegardes: her virtue is even more abstract than their evil. Newman's last visit to the convent is like a visit to the tomb:

From without Newman could see its upper windows, its steep roof and its chimneys. But these things revealed no symptoms of human life; the place looked dumb, deaf, inanimate. The pale, dead, discolored wall stretched beneath it, far down the empty side street— a vista without a human figure. Newman stood there a long time; there were no passers; he was free to gaze his fill. This seemed the goal of his journey; it was what he had come for. It was a strange satisfaction, and yet it was a satisfaction; the barren stillness of the place seemed to be his own release from ineffectual longing. It told him that the woman within was lost beyond recall, and that the days and years of the future would pile themselves above her like the huge immovable slab of a tomb. These days and years, in this place, would always be just so gray and silent. Suddenly, from the thought of their seeing him stand there, again the charm utterly departed. He would never stand there again; it was gratuitous dreariness. He turned away with a heavy heart, but with a heart lighter than the one he had brought.

(XXVI)

Claire's sacrifice is sterile because all beauty is sterile when it is not wedded to utility. But utility is a human term. Utility (action, nature) is the crack in James's "golden bowl." It is like Hawthorne's "Birthmark" or the cracked marble fountain in Dr. Rappaccini's garden—it is death. In Claire de Cintré we have the opposite of Beatrice Rappaccini or Georgiana, for their human defects allow them to suffer physical death as a consequence; Claire, who is without blemish, can suffer only a spiritual death, because she has become all spirit—a saint.

James's allegory in *The American* is almost as complete as Hawthorne's in "Rappaccini's Daughter" or Kafka's in "The Hunger-Artist"; it subsists on three levels: (1) the social, the theme of the Americans in Europe, the active life as contrasted with the mannered life of European aristocracy; (2) the artistic, the plight of the artist, the contrast between spiritual (perfect or abstract) beauty, or form, and natural beauty; (3) the moral, in which the moral innocence of Newman is contrasted with the knowledge and evil of the Bellegardes. This third contrast we have noted in the inhuman deed which the Bellegardes performed in defense of their mannered lives—the murder of the old marquis by his wife and son. That the triple theme is repeated at a lower level in the activities of old M. Nioche and his daughter and finally incorporated in the total pattern has not, however, been pointed out; nor that they are intended to portray that physical evil which the author did not see fit to depict through the characters of the Bellegardes themselves.

Socially the Nioches represent a lower strata in the aristocratic structure, but one which observes, outwardly at least, the same strict decorum as their betters. Morally, however, their alliance with the aristocracy must be an extralegal, unpunishable one (despite M. Nioche's hope that Noémie's alliance with Lord Deepmere will eventually be announced in the newspapers). Aesthetically, the Nioches represent the flaw in the golden bowl, the objectification of that imperfection on the physical (even sexual) level. Newman in his aesthetic, moral, and social innocence imagines that by commissioning Noémie to perpetrate her bad imitations of the masters he can subsidize her marriage to a petty clerk and thus preserve her moral status. Valentin at first glance (and out of his own deeper knowledge) knows better. As he says to Newman:

"She has taken the measure of life, and she has determined to *be* something—to succeed at any cost. Her painting, of course, is a mere trick to gain time. She is waiting for her chance; she wishes to launch herself, and to do it well. She knows her Paris. She is one of fifty thousand, so far as the mere ambition goes; but I am very sure that in the way of resolution and capacity she is a rarity. And in one gift—perfect heartlessness—I will warrant she is unsurpassed. She has not as much heart as will go on the point of a needle. That is an immense virtue. Yes, she is one of the celebrities of the future."

"Heaven help us!" said Newman, "how far the artistic point of view may take a man! But in this case I must request that you don't let it take you too far. You have learned a wonderful deal about Mademoiselle Noémie in a quarter of an hour. Let that suffice; don't follow up your researches."

"My dear fellow," cried Bellegarde with warmth, "I hope I have too good manners to intrude."

"You are not intruding. The girl is nothing to me. In fact, I rather dislike her. But I like her poor old father, and for his sake I beg you to abstain from any attempt to verify your theories."

"For the sake of that seedy old gentleman who came to fetch her?" demanded Valentin, stopping short. And on Newman's assenting, "Ah no, ah no," he went on with a smile. "You are quite wrong, my dear fellow; you needn't mind him."

"I verily believe that you are accusing the poor gentleman of being capable of rejoicing in his daughter's dishonor."

"Voyons," said Valentin; "who is he? what is he?"

"He is what he looks like: as poor as a rat, but very high-toned."

"Exactly. I noticed him perfectly; be sure I do him justice. He has had losses, *des malheurs*, as we say. He is very low-spirited, and his daughter is too much for him. He is the pink of respectability, and he has sixty years of honesty on his back. All this I perfectly appreciate. But I know my fellow-men and my fellow-Parisians, and I will make a bargain with you." Newman gave ear to his bargain and he went on. "He would rather his daughter were a good girl than a bad one, but if the worst comes to the worst, the old man will not do what Virginius did. Success justifies everything. If Mademoiselle Noémie makes a figure, her papa will feel—well, we will call it relieved. And she will make a figure. The old gentleman's future is assured."

(XI)

Noémie's painting (her art) and her father's manners (his art) are both a trick to gain time. Neither is a master; both imitate the masters: Noémie, the masters in the Louvre; her father, his masters in the social structure. And Noémie does become a "success," as Valentin predicts, first as the cause of Valentin's fatal duel with the Dutch merchant, and then in her alliance with Lord Deepmere, that distant cousin of the Bellegardes whose marriage to Claire had been envisioned by the old marquise as an escape from Newman. When Newman sees her in London, "The perfume of the young lady's finery sickened him. . . ." He lacked Valentin's admiration for her artfulness, and we can assume that by now he would have been capable of judging her pictures rightly. We feel that he sees depicted in the small English bulldog, to whose attendance the "fine" M. Nioche has been degraded, a symbol of an even worse degeneration than that described in the figures of the Bellegardes: "The pug was sniffing at the fashionable world, as it passed him, with his little black muzzle, and was kept from extending his investigation by a large blue ribbon attached to his collar with an enormous rosette. . . ." The final irony occurs when Lord Deepmere suggests that the Bellegardes had explained Valentin's death by announcing that his adversary had "said something against the Pope's morals." Valentin's only physical activity before the duel had been his short service with the Pope's army—an empty cause, since the Pope's military prerogatives had long since been usurped. Lord Deepmere sees the joke without its implications: Valentin had not fought over a slight to the Pope's morals, but a slight to Noémie's morals. As the Englishman says: "*she* was the Pope!"

Love and religion—both are reduced to an empty formalism. Noémie's affair with Lord Deepmere will one day be sanctified for M. Nioche *dans les feuilles*—the newspapers, a substitute for the cathedral. Nevertheless, M. Nioche, like the Bellegardes, maintains his hold upon the world by adherence to a rigid code of manners in which he must believe. In his embarrassment at meeting Newman in London, he attempts to escape unobserved, but failing that he braves the interview and is degraded only when Newman makes a move to leave him. "I should have left you," he says, "—from consideration. But my dignity suffers at your leaving *me*—that way." Likewise, the Bellegardes retire to their country place at Fleurières, "spending the year in extreme seclusion," as Mrs. Tristram says; keeping quiet on their own scale much as M. Nioche sat quietly beside Newman on the bench in the London park, hoping to escape unobserved.

It is the knowledge of evil, suggested first in the estimate Valentin makes of Noémie, which is, of course, Newman's weapon against the Bellegardes. Specifically, that knowledge is symbolized by the letter, in which is revealed the depths of evil concealed by the elaborate façade of the degenerate aristocracy. Mrs. Tristram, in referring to the letter after it has been destroyed, speaks of it as *his secret;* she asks: "How did you come into possession of your secret?" "It's a long story," he replies. "But honestly, at any rate." (He came into possession, it must be remembered, through the English servant, Mrs. Bread, who is in many respects Newman's English counterpart.) It is Newman's honesty—no longer spoken of as his "innocence"—which has embarrassed both the Bellegardes and M. Nioche: his bravery in confronting their evil. If, in the end, he does not employ his "innocence"—which has embarrassed both the Bellegardes and M. Nioche: his bravery is shown in confronting their evil. If, in the end, he does not employ his knowledge, it is because he is too honest for mere revenge. All of his action had been directed toward a practical end: his marriage to Claire. During his last visit to the convent, he measured the wall which separated him from her. It is his final confirmation of the truth. Though he still had some thought of scaling it, he is convinced now, as he tells Mrs. Tristram, that there was nothing to do but look at the place a few minutes and then come away. (In the later edition, James revised this passage to read: "I measured the wall. I looked at it a long time. But it's too high—it's beyond me.") His honesty was not enough to match Claire's abstract perfection. The wall would always remain between them—the symbolic wall. And his charge against the Bellegardes—it was "burnt up"—"quite consumed"—"there was nothing left of it," for even the honesty of a Newman can do no more than learn the nature of evil. It cannot destroy it. Such is the tragedy of our world as seen by Henry James, and it is an *American* story (if not entirely a tragedy), because it is told in the terms of James's "superlative" American—Christopher Newman.

Henry James:
The Ambassadors

Henry James recorded the origin (the "germ") of *The Ambassadors* in his notebook on October 31, 1895. Five years later, in September, 1901, he sent a synopsis to a magazine editor. It was rejected. The novel did not get into print until 1903, when it ran serially in a magazine in twelve installments and was also published in book form. It was reprinted six years later with some revision and with James's typical explanatory preface in the famous New York edition of his works.

These facts do not, except for the fact of its early rejection (which was unusual for James) constitute an unusual publishing history. They do, however, present us with an unusually clear account of how a novel was conceived, executed, and judged by its author. The account of its initial conception is well known. James had just spoken with a young American who had met William Dean Howells in Paris. Howells, who had only been in Europe a short time, was being called home by some event in his family. He spoke feelingly of Paris, and, at some point in the conversation, put his hand on the shoulder of the young man, saying, according to James's notebook account of it, "Oh, you are young, you are young—be glad of it: be glad of it and *live*. Live all you can: it's a mistake not to. It doesn't so much matter what you do—but live. This place makes it all come over me. I see it now. I haven't done so—and now I'm old. It's too late. It has gone past me. I've lost it. You have time. You are young. Live!"

This account of the novel's origin seemed significant enough that James repeated it as an introduction to his synopsis. In the synopsis itself he outlined the action, delineated all the major characters, and hinted at the theme. The finished novel differs from it only in certain small details, such as the altering of two of the characters' names and a more complete rendering of another than had been originally planned. When James came to look back upon the finished product, in the preface to the New York edition, he pronounced it as probably his most significant work. "Never," he says, "can a composition of this sort have sprung straighter from a dropped grain of suggestion, and never can that grain, developed, overgrown and smothered, have yet lurked more in the mass as an independent particle."

Neither the notebook entry (intended originally as an aid to the author's memory) nor the synopsis (intended to present the projected work to a publisher) has yet become fiction. In the synopsis James continuously admonishes his reader to "trust me," trust me to bring it off, to make it right. He had decided on the particular point of view. It was to be "scenic," by which James meant closely rendered through the eyes of his principal character, Lambert Strether. He had recognized that the drama lay in Strether's consciousness, his blindness as well as his awareness, and that it would be necessary to discover some means of outside illumination of the character of Strether himself. There are two primary "reflectors" in the novel (James called them *ficelles*); they are Maria Gostrey and Waymarsh, both Americans, but of contrasting type. In a note on Maria Gostrey, made later in the preface, James described her function. She is to serve as a friend to the reader; "she is enrolled, a direct aid to lucidity; she is, in fact, to tear off her mask, the most unmitigated and abandoned of *ficelles*." James recognized, however, that the use of Strether as the intelligent surveyor of events was a strategy that, like all strategic fictional devices, would not always work:

I am moved to add after so much insistence on the scenic side of my labour that I have found the steps of re-perusal almost as much waylaid here by quite another style of effort in the same signal interest—or have in other words not failed to note how, even so associated and so discriminated, the finest properties and charms of the nonscenic may, under the right hand for them, still keep their intelligibility and assert their office.

What James is saying is that some scenes may suffer from being too scenic—too closely rendered. Characters that demand heightening may be reduced by too much scenic detail. The scene of the first meeting in Paris of Strether and Chad, for instance, where everything depends upon the reader seeing, not what Chad is as we come later to know him, but what it is that Strether sees in him at that particular moment, must be presented lightly. "The book," James says, ". . . is touchingly full of these disguised and repaired losses, these insidious recoveries, these intensely redemptive consistencies."

The problem, as James certainly knew, was one of authority, a problem of the author's remaining true to his own vision of what the various scenes should be made to accomplish. In the case of James's late novels like *The Ambassadors,* these intentions are not at all simple. James uses the contrasts he had used in such early novels as *The American* and *The Portrait of a Lady,* the contrast between Americans and Europeans; but the differences are now more complex and more meaningful, less black against white, evil against virtue. It is as though James were saying, there is a way to blend the characteristics of America and Europe; but first the different qualities must be selected, then scrutinized for all the least obvious implications, then rendered in fictional form.

It is, perhaps, in the very conscientiousness with which

James accomplishes this search for meaning that many readers are thrown off, including the publisher's reader who reported: "The scenario is interesting, but it does not promise a popular novel." Popularity must have been one of the author's aims, but among the least significant. First in importance was the lifelikeness of the characters and their actions; second, the relating of these people and events to the meaning they were intended to convey.

Some authors begin their works with a complex situation and end by disclosing its inherent simplicity. James begins with the simple-appearing and proceeds to uncover layer after layer of unsuspected meaning. This initial simplicity, in the case of *The Ambassadors,* may be suggested by saying that it is the story of an apparently easy mission. Lambert Strether, as emissary for a wealthy New England widow, goes to Europe to persuade the woman's son, Chad Newsome, to return home and take his rightful place in the family business. He is known to be in Paris, and it is suspected that he has become entangled with a Parisienne. It is as simple as that. The first complication is introduced when Strether begins to suspect that Chad is much improved over what he had been in America; another is added when Strether cannot determine whether it is an older woman with whom Chad is allied or whether it is with her daughter, who is too young for him; another when Strether begins to doubt whether Chad should return to America at all. The latter complication is compounded when Strether discovers the "vulgar" side of Chad's relation with his mistress and still does not take the easy way out by taking him at once back to his homeland.

The concepts upon which the characters are based begin simply too: 1. There are fundamental differences between Americans and Europeans; 2. Europe is old, weary, decadent, while American culture is young, energetic, and innocent; 3. Europe represents beauty, America materialism. There is a certain tempting truth in all these oversimplifications, and James recognized them in the first notes he made for his novel. The view of Paris as the seat of art and sophistication, he considered the city's "banal note." Yet he utilized this note in describing the first impact of Paris upon Lambert Strether; and he utilized an equally banal note, the view that America is all sincerity and commonsense, in his presentation of such a character as Waymarsh in the early scenes. At once, however, he begins to introduce complications. Maria Gostrey, whom Strether meets even before he meets Waymarsh, and Little Bilham, whom he finds occupying Chad's apartment in Paris, are also Americans, but they are Americans who have somehow been altered by residence abroad. Have *they* been improved or tainted by this contact? This is one of the early dramatic questions that the book raises, for it foreshadows the problem Strether is to face in his relations with Chad.

It is clear to Strether, even before he meets Chad in Paris, that he has been improved. He judges him by the quality of the house he occupies and by the company he keeps; but the question kept uppermost in the reader's mind is the question of Chad's Americanism. Little Bilham and Maria Gostrey are portrayed as *intense* Americans, in some ways more American for having been away a long time, yet somehow also able to blend with the intensity of Paris. Waymarsh stands out in their company as the stolid, relaxed, frank, and honest person that the typical American is supposed to be. Miss Barrace recognizes him at once as the type she had met before in American diplomatic circles—"the grand old American." He could become a sensation in Paris, she tells Strether. All this talk about Americans is really preparation for the meeting with Chad, raising the question, what kind of American will he turn out to be?

If Chad is much improved, as Strether believes him to be, the questions are, in what way and by whom? Maria Gostrey, as a result of her European residence, can see things that Strether is not yet prepared to see. For one thing, she sees that he is entangled, "not free," and the cause of it is certainly a woman, an excellent one to all appearances, but one who will not be easily cast off. Furthermore, Maria warns, Chad is not as good as he appears in Strether's eyes. Little Bilham also raises doubts when he admits that Chad is changed, and not for the worse, but that he is not sure he did not like him better in his former state.

What is Chad's former state but his quality as an American? What is the cause of his change except a supremely "European" woman? Madame de Vionnet, once James allows us to know that it is she and not her young daughter whom Chad is allied with, is as much the extremely European type as Waymarsh, or Mrs. Newsome herself, is the extreme American. What she exemplifies, on the one hand, is a studied grace and charm; on the other, discord: a broken marriage, separation, and no possibility, under French custom, of divorce.

James's view of European culture is as ambiguous as his view of America. Europe presents a surface of beauty, but there are hints of evil in its depths: the appearance of tranquility achieved by a disordered past. The de Bellegarde family of James's *The American* is a clearer but cruder rendering of the decadent aristocracy of Europe, struggling to perpetuate its forms, though now deprived of any effective power; but it is essentially the same situation as that portrayed by Madame de Vionnet and her daughter, as we come to see when that view is not obscured by Lambert Strether's too innocent vision. Madame de Vionnet's evil is more human than the melodramatic and monstrous crimes in the background of the de Bellegardes; but it is similar in its necessity for deception, and it is as sordid in its inevitable struggle to perpetuate itself. She aquiesces to the engagement of her young daughter to an older man for the sake of property and position, when this is exactly the situation that caused her own unhappy plight.

Set alongside Madame de Vionnet and her daughter to heighten both sides of their nature are the American Pocock women: Sarah, who is Chad's sister, and Mamie, who is Sarah's sister-in-law. The Pococks arrive as a second wave of ambassadors when it has seemed clear to Mrs. Newsome that Strether is not adequately fulfilling his mission. Sarah is as set in her manner as is Madame de Vionnet, but what we see of her (again through Strether's eyes) shows her as willful, direct, and blind to the finer qualities of Europe; but she is, of course, right—right in every way except her manner. Madame de Vionnet *is* guilty. To see her through Sarah's eyes, she is an adulteress and a liar. But her manner is impeccable.

These two women are extreme contrasts. Less extreme is the contrast between Mamie Pocock and Jeanne de Vionnet, but Mademoiselle de Vionnet is less a character than she is a pale representative of the marriageable aristocratic female, highly bred, but serving purposes other than her own womanhood—a pawn in the politics of social survival. Mamie, on the other hand, is all firm flesh and independence. In James's notes and in the synopsis, it appears that Mamie was originally intended as little more than bait to be tendered Chad by his sister in the foolish hope that he would thus recall his sense of duty to his family. But Mamie is the type of American young woman that James was extremely fond of, a Daisy Miller or a younger Isabel Archer, and she is given considerable stature as a character. A fledgling sensibility, she recognizes that Chad has grown away from her, but she is less judging than she is understanding.

Perhaps, James is saying, Chad's manner is inevitable, given the complexity of the European setting. As a kind of parable, Strether's belated discovery that Chad and Madame de Vionnet are, as James wrote suggestively in his synopsis, "positively and indubitably intimate with the last intimacy" represent an initiation for him, a recognition that beauty is, in one sense, merely a disguise for what is essentially ugly and vulgar, a recognition that below the surface of good lies a world of evil. In a note written earlier for *The Wings of the Dove,* James recognized the problem as one of concealment. "One can do so little with English adultery," he wrote, "—it is so much less inevitable [than the French], and so much more ugly in all its hiding and lying side. It is so undermined by our immemorial tradition of original freedom of choice, and by our practically universal acceptance of divorce." One might say that Madame de Vionnet's absence of choice in her own unhappy marriage and her belonging to a society that denied her divorce made her adultery inevitable; but such an explanation does not wholly suffice to justify it or to explain it away, especially in the mind of a Sarah Pocock. What Lambert Strether has learned, presumably, is that while evil need not be condoned it must be recognized. Madame de Vionnet shows an understanding of this in her final scene with Strether, where she tells him, "You may, no doubt, pull up when things become *too* ugly; or even, I'll say, to save you a protest, too beautiful. At any rate, even so far as it's true, we've thrust on you appearances that you've had to see and that have therefore made your obligation. Ugly or beautiful—it doesn't matter what we call them—you were getting on without them, and that's where we're detestable."

This is what James's Europe does to James's Americans. It makes them face the too ugly or the too beautiful. American innocence tends to turn away or to make too hasty judgments. The simple view, either of Europe or of America, however, is not the true one. Truth is ambiguous, but it can be tracked down and identified in all its bristling meaningfulness. What Lambert Strether meant when he clapped Little Bilham on the shoulder and exhorted him "to live" is really an oversimplification of an early recognition that "to live" in Paris is a richer experience than anything America appeared to offer. Yet it also had something to do with the relative ages of the two characters. Lambert, at his age, is too old for the full experience; Little Bilham is young and has his "life" before him. Implicit, however, is the implication that Paris is the *old* world; America, the *new*.

This seeming paradox is a typical Jamesian irony, but it is also part of the fundamental dramatic structure of the novel; and it is brought into sharper focus through the character of Lambert Strether. In the final chapters, he ponders his own situation in scenes with Madame de Vionnet, with Chad, and with Maria Gostrey. If he has not "lived," the life of Paris has certainly had its effect on him. He will return to Woolet, but not to marriage with Mrs. Newsome. "Too much has happened," he tells Maria Gostrey, "I'm different for her." He is different for himself too, he admits, because, while Mrs. New-some has not changed, he now sees her as she is for the first time. His eyes have been opened. She is all that Madame de Vionnet is not, virtuous, direct, and master of her own fate. Strether is, symbolically, caught between these two women, the wealthy and influential American widow, who had pro-posed marriage to him before he took over the mission to save her son; the charming, aristocratic, and intelligent French woman, who appears to speculate on what it would have been like if Strether had been her lover instead of Chad. Maria Gostrey stands, with the now-initiated Strether, somewhere be-tween the two—the Europeanized American; and it must have been a great temptation to James to solve all of his structural problems in one swoop by having Strether take Maria as wife at the end of the book. Maria does, in effect, propose, and Strether is tempted. Such an ending would have been tidy, but it would also have been false—an escape, not a facing up to the final problem. The great virtue of Strether's situation, with all that he had gained and lost, was, as he came to see it, that he had not gotten anything personal out of it. Maria objects: "With your wonderful impressions, you've got a great deal." Strether agrees: "A great deal, but nothing like you. It's you who would make me wrong."

What Strether would have got is exactly that "life" that he had earlier felt himself incapable of experiencing. He proves himself here as incapable, not because he is old, but because of his fine scruples, his "sharp eye," as Maria calls it, for what he considers to be his duty—to himself, to society. Like Milly Theale, the heroine of the novel written immediately after *The Ambassadors,* who struggled "to live" while doomed to die, Strether turns his face to the wall. He does so, not to die, as Milly did, but to stay true to himself as American, to reject "life" in the complex form that it appeared to him in the light of his three ladies, to renounce life in favor of both European manners and American morality. Strether thus represents what James elsewhere described as "moral sensibility," but he does so only after he has undergone his belated initiation.

Mark Twain's Idyl of
Frontier America

ALMOST ALL THE critical writings concerning Mark Twain have dealt with his life, the psychology of his twisted later years, and with his social background. They have treated his works only by implication. The challenge of Samuel Clemens' personal frustrations and his relation to his frontier background have attracted the sociologist, the historian, and the biographer, while the numerous failures and partial successes of Mark Twain, the artist, have so complicated (and in a certain sense weakened) his status that they have obscured the values of his major works.

It is certainly true that Mark Twain's personal relationship to his environment (frontier America) is more pertinent than is the case with most authors. It is also true that certain gross misunderstandings of that environment needed correction before a critical structure could be established. Bernard DeVoto has, I think we may assume, disposed of Van Wyck Brooks's mistaken view of the frontier, though he has, as a result of his argumentative nature, swept away Brooks's occasional valuable insights along with it. He has at least made it clear that

Mr. Brooks had little conception of the affirmative values in American frontier development, less even than Henry James, who at first glance would appear to represent the antithesis of everything Mark Twain stood for and who scarcely can be said to represent the high point in appreciation of Twain, but who in making his most completely representative American character a product of the western environment indicated an awareness of frontier values wholly lacking in Brooks's *The Ordeal of Mark Twain*. Even Sherwood Anderson, who as a personal friend of Brooks was extremely anxious to approve of *The Ordeal* when it first appeared, recognized at once the injustice of Brooks's position. Mr. DeVoto, up to the time that he relinquished custody of the Twain documents, seemed to be working toward a critical position, especially in the volume *Mark Twain at Work,* but the more ambitious *Mark Twain's America* is marred as criticism by a preoccupation (valuable in itself) with revaluating the influence of the frontier and by his Brooks-phobia. In justice to Mr. DeVoto it must be pointed out that he made no pretentions of writing literary criticism, and certainly the meaning of the frontier represents a valuable and necessary pre-critical occupation.

It is in America's nineteenth-century development that we recognize the essential features of our great national dilemma outlined in its boldest and perhaps most disturbing clarity. The frontier was, as Van Wyck Brooks recognized, the meeting place of traditional conservative and liberal opinion, but it was also, as he failed to note, a conflict in which traditionalism most often went down in defeat, the seed-bed of political and economic innovation, of reaction against eastern conservatism, just as the colonies had at one time represented a reaction against the conservatism of Europe. The development of this attitude toward the frontier can be traced from the social historian Frederick Jackson Turner, through the socio-literary historian V. L. Parrington, down to the socio-literary critic, the late Constance Rourke, to whom Mr. DeVoto is, as he acknowledges, enormously indebted. It is an attitude which has led increasingly toward a concern with literary values, but one which, along with the footnotes and personal details of the academic scholars and biographers, has never completely succeeded in catching hold of the works themselves, of explaining the enormous vitality which we acknowledge them to possess, the constant appeal of such works as the better short fiction, *Life on the Mississippi, Tom Sawyer,* and *Huckleberry Finn.* It would seem logical that the next job should be just such an examination, a bringing of these works into focus alongside the works of James, Hawthorne's *The Scarlet Letter,* and Melville's *Moby Dick,* a position which at least *Huckleberry Finn* would seem to occupy despite its critical neglect, despite even a great deal of obscure disparagement by critics from Henry James to Mr. Brooks.

II

The bulk of Mark Twain's early writings were personal records or humorous sketches pretending to be personal accounts. This was in the accepted tradition of American journalism of his time, especially in the rural outposts and upon the frontier. It was an era of personal journalism, and in the tradition in which Twain received his training both in Hannibal, Missouri, and in the Far West. The jump from newspaper reporting to the lecture platform and into book publication was, therefore, not great, the success of all of these activities depending as they did upon the personal manner of the reporter—not upon the personal manner of Samuel Clemens, but of Mark Twain, the humorist. Samuel Clemens had several pseudonyms before he settled upon the final one, and it is perhaps fortunate that Mark Twain was the one which he retained, for the earlier disguises were exactly in the tradition of the popular humor of the time, no less crude and no more subtle. In a sense, the name "Mark Twain" was to symbolize those two elements in Samuel Clemens' approach to his material which are the clue to his importance: (1) the humorous tradition of the frontier, which had created, as Constance Rourke has pointed out, a vast reservoir of folk material, and which had developed a technique of dealing with that material; (2) a knowledge of and a regard for life within the orbit of the Mississippi River Valley.

It is no doubt natural enough that most biographers and scholars have been impressed by the necessity of explaining the psychological changes which occurred in Mark Twain following his tremendous popular success and after his settlement in the East. These changes are significant if we are to understand the many failures in Twain's literary career. Their importance, however, would seem to be no greater than the similar tragedies of Melville, Hawthorne, Whitman, or Hart Crane, except in degree, and except to the extent that there has been more interest aroused in the personal predicament of a man who came very near to representing our national public jester—against his will; whose every quip was broadcast by most of the newspapers of America, whose every move was watched and applauded by an inquisitive and delighted public. The truth is, Mark Twain the humorist became himself almost a national mythical figure, and the fact was tinged with a romantic poignancy when it became known that he was, beneath his mask, a bitter and tortured man.

The facts of his pessimism have been sufficiently treated that they need no repetition here, except to point out that there have been others who suffered personal tragedy without the need to express their despair and bitterness in such short stories as "The Mysterious Stranger" and "The Man that Corrupted Hadleyburg." Whitman's "Democratic Vistas" is full of a similar disillusionment, as are the late letters and stanzas of Hart Crane, but neither Whitman nor Crane felt a compulsion to formulate a philosophy of despair and to build a body of works upon it. Disillusionment meant, for them, a revision of a former optimism, a recognition of a complexity in American life with which their art, finally, was unable to cope. For Mark, who had been raised in the heart of the Mississippi River country during its most exciting and colorful period, whose visit to the Far West had occurred at a time when its boisterous laissez-faire existence had seemed like nothing less than a Utopian freedom from the restraints of an artificial morality, domestic economy, and even aesthetic theory, personal frustration was to become a harness from which he could free himself only by a process of disassociation.

The fact is that Mark Twain wanted to affirm life. In the beginning his humor was directed against all of those associations which seemed to falsify his concept of reality; the romantic views of Cooper and Scott, social obligations, the traditions of culture which seemed remote to life in Hannibal or Virginia City. Mark was a hedonist because the philosophy of the frontier put great value upon even the most minor sensations: the excitement of gambling, heavy drinking, cigar-smoking, exotic dress; it looked with a skeptical eye upon intellectual life which did not provide immediate physical excitement or upon any social or aesthetic restraint which seemed to frustrate it. In the beginning of his life in the East, the family seemed to provide a similar kind of excitement, as did his early financial success, and as his popular success as an author never failed to do. Put down in the midst of a genteel society, however, it was inevitable that he should also seek affirmation there. That he found great value in his friendship with Willian Dean Howells is not as surprising as it is sometimes made to seem, because Howells himself had, as a Westerner come East, undergone much the same experience, and (as it turned out) with much the same result. Howells could understand and appreciate Twain the rebel, as could Mark's general reading public, but the genteel intellectual society of New England could not, as the Whittier birthday dinner of 1877 testifies. Nevertheless, there is evidence that Mark attempted to conform to New England standards in his family life, the conscientious revision of his works, and in the great emphasis put upon the making of money. It is this last fact, more than any other, which contributed most to the impact cf disillusionment when his family life was disrupted by illness and death and when his personal financial structure collapsed.

Mark Twain could not, however, in his writing, at least, compromise himself in the manner that Howells did—not even when he tried. There is no doubt that Howells possessed a keener intellectual insight into the social and moral problems of American life, but he lacked both the aesthetic sensibility of Twain and the aesthetic-moral sensibility of Henry James and Nathaniel Hawthorne. Mark never lost his feeling of nostalgia either for the Mississippi River country where he was raised or for the Far West, where he first experienced the kind of personal freedom for which he yearned. Life in the Far West was not, however, a suitable subject for first-rate literature, as the works of Bret Harte have amply illustrated. It was a first-rate subject for the businessmen of literature, whether of literary talent like Twain and Harte or not, but it was too new, too isolated, and too chaotic to have accreted to itself the necessary myths against which its life could be examined and made real and meaningful. That section of the Midwest where Mark had grown through boyhood was not. It was the meeting place of American mythology, creating as a result of its geographical and historical situation an amalgam of regional folk literature which transcended the areas from which it had come, the South, the North, the eastern seacoast, and the Far West. Tales of frontier violence merged with a folk literature which could trace its roots into those lands from which the American colonists had come. Tales of pre-Civil War tension over slavery and the difference between northern and southern ways of life merged in the river lore which was a part of the life in which Mark Twain grew up. Perhaps at no time in American history has so significant a background been provided for the use of any American artist, and it is natural that an author of Mark Twain's temperament should have been drawn to it. It was, however, almost pure accident that a literary technique should also be provided, a technique which made it possible for Mark to treat that material in a manner which would raise it above the level of personal sentiment and into the realm of literature, but nevertheless a technique which was not so much consciously acquired as it was devel-

oped by the time and place in which its owner was born and
raised.

III

America's most consistent mythical figure is that of the
Yankee—shrewd, good-natured, and skeptical of all sophisticated values, lacking a formal education but exercising
abundant common sense. Sometimes this character is elevated
to a sentimental celebration of dubious manly virtues; other-
times he degenerates into the burlesque figure of the country
bumpkin or the rogue. At his best, however, he represents an
objectified folk concept of democratic values more valid than
any ideological statement—a norm against which may be measured the vagaries of false sophistication or of downright dull-
ness. He achieved his greatest stature during the period of
America's expansion onto the western frontier, when his qualities of ingeniousness and self-reliance were necessary con-
comitants of successful pioneer life. He achieved his foremost
portrayal in the figure of Abraham Lincoln, whose personality
was so nearly identical with the folk concept that little literary
distortion was necessary. The historical figure and the mythical figure were, as is seldom the case, indivisible; and the
historical figure arose at precisely that moment when the myth
was at its point of greatest public availability. In popular
opinion, the triumph of republican ideas over federalism and
the aristocratic social concepts of the South seemed complete.
The excesses of personal greed and industrial rapacity were
not yet anticipated. Lincoln embodied the concepts of rustic-
ity, sagacity, and, above all, humor, which had become the
most marked characteristics of the myth, during a period when
those concepts had risen above the level of merely oral trans-
mission and overflowed onto the pages of popular periodicals,
primarily the rural newspapers and popular magazines of
prewar America.

This was the period of Mark Twain's youth in the heart
of America's frontier. He was engaged as a printer at his

brother Orion's rural newspaper, and thus educated, in a sense, by the flow of magazines and newspapers which came in as exchanges, as well as by the small stock of religious books, classics, and romantic novels which were among the literary possessions of most middle-class frontier families. We know, for instance, that he read and even contributed to B. P. Shillaber's *Carpet Bag*, and that his early contributions were little different from the bulk of crude, humorous parodies which made up the popular writings of his day. The frontier humorist was usually, like Mark, a writer for some small-town newspaper. His early contributions usually took the form of letters written to the editor, in the best of which shrewd comment was disguised beneath the mask of misspellings, wrenched syntax, typographical oddities, and other forms of rural impersonation. The comic figure took many forms, but all were derivations of the mythical Yankee, the frontiersman Davy Crockett, the river man Mike Fink, the humorous Negro slave, and the stoical Indian. The humor usually consisted in the ironic distance achieved between the manner of presentation and the pretentiousness of the subject. Accepted social, religious, and political forms were fair game for such humorists, who posed as common sense sweeping away the accumulated prejudices of an overcivilized social structure. Most of the attempts were crude, even vulgar, but when they were not they approached characterizations at least suggestive of Christopher Newman in Henry James's *The American*, who was a product of the myth, not too different from Twain himself who reported unashamedly (in *Innocents Abroad*) that he often preferred the copy of an Italian painting to the original.

As such humorous authors as Charles Farrar Browne (Artemus Ward), George Horace Derby (John Phoenix), and Henry Wheeler Shaw (Josh Billings) became well known, they transferred their activities from the columns of the press to the lecture platform, as Mark Twain also did after his trip to the Sandwich Islands in 1866. While the pseudonymous mask had been used to disguise the man in such comic papers as *The*

Brickbat, the *Jolly Joker,* and *Merryman's Monthly* (to mention only a few characteristic titles), the mask became the man on the lecture platform. In this manner, the method, though it seemed to be highly personal, was really an objectification, in that the personality of the man was submerged by the humorous characterization. Samuel Clemens *became* Mark Twain, which may have had something to do with later psychological difficulties following his conflicts (symbolic rather than actual) with the intelligentsia of the East. Most important to our purpose here, however, is the fact that such apprenticeship, both in the papers and upon the lecture platform, supplied Mark Twain with a method (humor) of objectifying his subject matter (frontier life), and it developed an attitude toward that subject matter which was not to be overcome even by Samuel Clemens' developing philosophical pessimism during the very long period when he was composing his most important works.

The attitude of the frontier humorists toward American life, even when their writing was the most crude, was one of sympathetic appreciation. When the mask failed, as it often did, the writings sank into bathos. When it succeeded it was, at its worst, no more than simple burlesque. At its best, it became a kind of social satire (as in much of *Tom Sawyer*) or even (as in *Huckleberry Finn*) national epic. Innocent as the American national character appeared before the closing of the frontier, it lacked that element of primitive innocence necessary to the production of a serious work celebrating its national life. It possessed, however, for a few years, that other ingredient: a workable mythology. It had, fortunately and at the same moment, a method which, in the hands of an expert craftsman such as Mark Twain became, was a successful instrument for an idyllic presentation. Though the method failed often enough in such humorous reporting as *Innocents Abroad* and *Roughing It,* these early works represent an important phase in the development of a career which was only briefly to attain the heights of which it was capable, and it is in an understanding of these two important factors (subject matter and technique) that the key to Mark Twain's importance lies.

In the light of these facts, it is difficult to understand the conclusions of many critics, particularly so mistaken a critic as Fred Lewis Pattee, who concluded in an article written in 1935, that: "Mark Twain has been overrated. His compelling personality blinded the earlier critics. He worked in vaudeville materials, he worked without plan and by improvisation. He dramatized himself, never for a moment escaped from the little circle of himself, had no adequate philosophy of life, and no upward look." Mr. Pattee has confused the mask with the man. Mark Twain's personality was compelling, there is no doubt of that, but it was the disguise of the humorous reporter, which Twain finally became in his public life. How he succeeded in obscuring his personality in his best works is evident to anyone who attempts to discover either Samuel Clemens or Mark Twain in the character of Tom Sawyer, despite years of scholarly attempts to prove that they were one and the same. Compare the objectivity of *Huckleberry Finn* with that achieved by another author in the idyllic tradition— Thomas Wolfe—and you will understand how much Mark Twain owed to the training he acquired in the school of frontier humor. It is true that some of his lesser writing was treating with "vaudeville materials," but we are to be concerned with the successful works, not the failures. As for "improvisation," who is to say how much of the creative process is improvisatory—how much is conscious, how much a part of all the previous experimentation, acceptance and rejection not only of ideas and of subjects, but also of methods of composition? We can admit that Mark Twain was no conscious critic of his own work without condemning the principal products of his genius. Likewise, we can acknowledge occasional lapses of taste without assuming, with Mr. Pattee, that Mark Twain did not "possess those timeless qualities that render a piece of humor forever laughable."

What Mr. Pattee and many another scholar failed to recognize was that Twain's humor consisted not alone in the occasional use of what he calls the "popular joke," but in his fundamental approach to his subject. We can agree that his personal success (before *Life on the Mississippi*) was only a degree above that of other humorists of the century, and the degree which distinguishes him from Artemus Ward and John Phoenix is represented by little more than his essential seriousness and by a quality which defies definition—aesthetic sensibility. It is the absence of conscious intent (the improvisation) which, perhaps more than any other thing, accounts for the pervading sense of folk-nearness which has been pointed out as one of *Huckleberry Finn*'s most admirable qualities. Bernard DeVoto is certainly right when he comments: "Throughout the book [*Tom Sawyer*] time curves back upon itself and boyhood is something more than realism, it is a distillation, a generalization, a myth."

If, however, we think of *Huckleberry Finn* and *Tom Sawyer* as superior even to so interesting a short story as "The Mysterious Stranger," it is not a difference of the author's technique alone which makes them superior, but a difference of attitude *plus* technique. Mark Twain belongs with those American writers who possess a high degree of personal sensitivity to their environment: Walt Whitman, Ernest Hemingway, Hart Crane, and Thomas Wolfe. Like them, he had little ability to intellectualize his feelings. Hemingway and Crane represent essentially negative natures who, at some point in their careers, felt a need for affirmation. Whitman and Wolfe, while recognizing an ultimate need for some revision of their early optimism, were essentially affirmers of American life. The pessimism from which Twain spun his whole later philosophy was, likewise, not natural to him. He could damn the whole human race in theoretical terms, but the background of the country and the life which he had known as a boy was always treated with nostalgia and sympathy. It has been pointed out that the boys of "The Mysterious Stranger" and the citizens of "The Man that Corrupted Hadleyburg" were only Tom and Huck and the townspeople whom he had known in Hannibal dressed up in a foreign setting and given foreign names. The implications of the masquerade have not, so far as I know, been deduced. Is it not because he could not bring himself to apply his rational philosophizing about man's state to a locale for which he felt more affection than bitterness? Life in the Mississippi River Valley and in the Far West represented for him an idyllic existence which could be treated humorously, but not with personal rancour. The world of politics, business, even of rational ideas was another matter. Sensitive to their rewards, he was also aware of their shortcomings; but even more important, he came to recognize finally (though only vaguely and intuitively) that they were not his world. He belonged to the world of boyhood on the Mississippi, riverboating, and carousing in the mining camps of Nevada and California. His contact with Europe, with eastern sophistication, and with the life of business deepened his insights, but did not corrupt his essential innocence nor turn him into a philosopher. They made him a more fit instrument for depicting the boyhood of Tom Sawyer and Huck Finn, adding an edge to his writing tool which was lacking in even the best of his predecessors in the humorous field. The complicated and tragic worlds of Hawthorne and Melville were not for him, nor could he like Walt Whitman take the whole of national life for his province, yet he succeeded in depicting what now seems to have been most typical of America at any time, past or present, treating it with sympathy and with humor.

IV

Mark Twain's three most lasting and impressive works were all published between 1876 and 1884—a period of only eight years out of a publishing career which must have begun around 1850 and which continued for approximately sixty years, until his death in 1910. Important as two of these works are, however, their chief value would seem to consist in their importance as additional apprenticeship toward the completion of the third, *Huckleberry Finn. Tom Sawyer* explored the boyhood of Tom and Huck in St. Petersburg, depicting the small-town fears and superstitions of the elders as well as the children, the mixture of Puritan morality, romantic imagination, and frontier reality which made up life in this crossroads of America. *Life on the Mississippi* remains an outstanding example of personal reminiscence, but was of the utmost value in refreshing Mark Twain's memory concerning details of the Mississippi Valley, which he had traversed as a young river pilot for three years before the Civil War and which was to become the setting for the more pretentious *Huckleberry Finn*.

With the exception of an occasional aside, there is little in these books to reveal Mark Twain's bitterness or his deterministic personal philosophy. Man's foolishness and natural terror in the face of superstition and danger (real or supposed) is exploited, but so are the common virtues. *Huckleberry Finn* in particular is a mosaic woven of numerous moral concerns, all of them appropriate to a deeper awareness of the problems of human living, though presented in such a manner as to disguise, but not blind us to, their essential seriousness.

Tom Sawyer is marred by a formal structure only partially necessitated by its characters and subject-matter. Such structure, even when employed by so accomplished a craftsman as Henry James, must have a logical and natural relationship to the themes which lie embedded in it, and demand an awareness of intentions and an expertness of all techniques of which Mark Twain was certainly incapable. The two principal threads of action (the enmity of Injun Joe culminating in the discovery of the treasure and the childhood love affair between Tom and Becky) are all too obviously conventional and superficial attempts to construct a "plotted" story. More successful is the consistent characterization of the two principal characters, Tom and Huck, with the subtle and ironic contrasts which they afford. Tom is the highly imaginative, romantic boy, pretending to be Huck's mentor, but forced to the limit of his ingeniousness to retain the role against Huck's innate common sense. Huck's natural inclination is to take reality as his guide until it fails, then to apply his knowledge of primitive lore picked up from the Negroes, the squatters, the woodsmen, and the rivermen. His instincts rebel against the forms of civilization as represented in frontier society (school, church, personal cleanliness, etc.), while retaining a respect for its ends. Together the somewhat sophisticated Tom and the more primitive Huck embody at their best the two principal traditions of the western frontier. Beyond this contrast, however, there is little recognizable pattern in the characterization. Sid is a minor embodiment of sophisticated conceit and cleverness. Injun Joe and Pap Finn (the latter playing no definable role here) tend toward an extreme of evil upon Huck's level, Aunt Polly and the Widow Douglas toward an extreme of moral virtue. Becky Thatcher is primarily a conventional figure, who comes alive only briefly during the scene at the schoolroom where she tears the page in the schoolmaster's book. Likewise, the minister and Judge Thatcher are ordinary examples of types common in American fiction both before and after Twain's time. The structure achieved in Tom Sawyer is not an integration of action with theme and character, but is rather that of the conventional plotted story, an artificially contrived structure which gives the impression of form without actually achieving it.

Nevertheless, it is highly unlikely that *Huckleberry Finn* could have been written without the exploration of character and of village life represented in *Tom Sawyer* or without the stimulation provided by Mark Twain's return to the river country in 1883 and his writing of *Life on the Mississippi,* which supplies not only the background for the major portion of the book, but specific characters and events as well. There is evidence that Twain probably desired a more formal structure for *Huckleberry Finn* than that finally accomplished. He gave great pains to the beginning and the ending of the book, apparently attempting to whip it into more conventional form. Clearly he did not (at once, at least) recognize the epic form provided by his materials, for the book falls easily into three principal divisions: the first, an introduction of the characters who are to supply our attitudes toward American life of the epoch depicted—the Widow Douglas, Pap Finn, Tom, Huck, and Jim; the second, the quest, as represented in the river episodes and in Huck's constantly shifting relationships to Jim, to the two river rogues, the Grangerfords, and the Wilkses; finally, the merging of the two principal thematic concerns (reality and imagination in Huck and Tom; the moral problem in the relationship of the two boys to Jim) in the events at the Phelps's farm.

The character of Huck stands midway between two extreme positions. There is the Widow Douglas with her genteel concepts of morality, social decorum, and simple goodness, and there is Tom with his more or less refined ideas of life as reflected in the romantic fiction of the day. Both represent ways of life more demanding than those to which Huck is accustomed, and both are utilized by the author as a means of highlighting the essential rightness of Huck himself. On the other side, Huck has Jim, the Negro, with his primitive knowledge and the more artificial limitations of his personal slavery, and he has his father, a horrifying example of the possible evil extreme of his position. Here is represented the essential ambivalence of American life, the pull of culture and sophistication on the one side, of natural goodness and evil on the other. Huck's pilgrimage is to bring him into contact with many variations of the qualities represented in these characters, but they remain as guides and norms by which the reader is able to gauge the variations as represented by the river outlaws, the two vagabonds, the Grangerford family, the Wilkses, and the Phelpses. The river journey becomes a kind of loose allegory in which Huck Finn is brought into contact with roguery, gentility, and simple goodness, all upon separate levels and all commented upon simply and shrewdly through the irony of understatement as represented in Huck's picturesque Pike County speech. His report of attending church with the Grangerfords, for instance, is a modification of Tom's experience in the opening of *Tom Sawyer,* accomplishing more in a single paragraph than the first book did in a full chapter:

Next Sunday we all went to church about three miles, everybody a-horseback. The men took their guns along, so did Buck, and kept them between their knees or stood them handy against the wall. The Shepherdsons done the same. It was pretty ornery preaching— all about brotherly love, and such-like tiresomeness; but everybody said it was a good sermon, and they all talked it over going home, and had such a powerful lot to say about faith and good works and free grace and preforeordestination, and I don't know what all, that it did seem to me to be one of the roughest Sundays I had run across yet.

There is the suggestion at the end of the book that Huck has ended where he began, transferred merely from the gentility of the Widow Douglas into the simple goodness of Aunt Sally; but though he remains a rebel against society (as what outstanding citizen does not), we can be certain that the condition of his dead father and of Injun Joe, even the innocent vagabondage of Muff Potter, are not for him. His determination to strike out for the Indian Country, while consciously it may have meant only that Mark Twain was thinking in terms of another book, suggests the kind of life for which Huck's talents were best suited: the life of the frontiersman, the "mountainman," the pioneer. The test of Twain's characterization is the manner in which other characters can be projected, set into the whole mythical pattern of society. Tom Sawyer might well have become Mark Twain himself (though it is a testimony of Twain's ability that we are never able to recognize him in that role—the autobiographical figure), for we can imagine him growing up into a rebellious, but on the whole, stable citizen, perhaps into one of the independent journalists of our frontier days or, like Mark himself, into an artist.

The problems Huck has to contend with follow the pattern of most first-rate fiction. They are first of all moral: the dilemma of Jim's freedom, the demands of Jim as a human being who, despite the fact that he had been treated well by the widow, naturally desires the right to live his life as a freeman with his own family, desires, in short, a privilege given the Injun Joes, the Muff Potters, and the Pap Finns, but denied the Negro. The concept ingrained in Huck by his training in the near-South demanded that he betray Jim (his friend) in obedience to the social code operating against the slave.

". . . I got aboard the raft, feeling bad and low, because I knowed very well I had done wrong, and I see it warn't no use for me to try to learn to do right; a body that don't get *started* right when he's little ain't got no show—when the pinch comes there ain't nothing to back him up and keep him to his work, and so he gets beat. Then I thought a minute, and says to myself, hold on; s'pose you'd 'a' done right and give Jim up, would you felt better than what you do now? No, says I, I'd feel bad—I'd feel just the same way I do now. Well, then, says I, what's the use you learning to do right when it's troublesome to do right and ain't no trouble to do wrong, and the wages is just the same? I was stuck. I couldn't answer that. So I reckoned I wouldn't bother no more about it, but after this always do whichever come handiest at the time.

Here is the strongest conflict between loyalty and duty, and other conflicts are arranged between forms which suggest artificial (civilized) demands, such as church-going, loyalty to such unworthy friends as the rogues of the river, and loyalty to a code which would require him to betray his friend, and the more real (natural) demands of friendship, the religion of the woods and rivers, and genuine family obligations. In short, the conflict is between some concept of real virtue as demanded by action and the sterile virtue of forms from which all meaning has been drained. It is a tribute to the work as a novel that the social and moral problems are so closely related. Upon another level, however, there is the examination of outmoded social forms which have been preserved through the reading of romantic literature, and we have these depicted in the imagination of Tom Sawyer (culminating in the elaborate and unnecessary ritual of freeing Jim when he is already a free man), as well as in the feud between the Grangerfords and the Shepherdsons, the revival meetings, and the frontier entertainments provided by the Duke and the Dauphin.

The journey of Huck and Jim on the raft is merely the central action in a series of events which, as Constance Rourke has pointed out, carry us not only over an actual countryside, but also, symbolically, through an amazing portion of American mythology: tales of outlawry and the discovery of buried gold, or runaway slaves, southern feuds, southern gentility, river pirates, and crude impostures. The characters in all of these events were well known in folk-tales and had been adapted in cruder form by humorists of the school in which Mark Twain developed, as well as by novelists who had gone before. "Cooper, Bird, Simms, Thompson of Vermont, and Kennedy of Maryland [plotting] out every area of the older America, viewing almost every significant passage in the American past, used a scope that roughly approached the epical scale." Huck's contact with life beyond the village of St. Petersburg is an initiation and a test, not the dramatic test it might have become had his author (less wisely) had him actually free Jim, but a more subtle and a human one—one which, perhaps, marks the distinction between the idyllic and the social novel. Huck does not demand, as the social reporter would have done, a conversion of all to his point of view. He recognizes the virtue in Tom's imagination, in the Widow Douglas' morality, and in the Phelps's goodness, and the events of the novel demand no more than this. The success of his trial consists in this recognition, and no more.

Huckleberry Finn is an epic of childhood, set in the fluid period of America's youth, for it is not the childhood of Huck and Tom alone that is embodied, but the childhood of a nation. The adult life of America from the beginning has been static, set in those molds of European culture which the colonists transferred to our shores. The epic form mirrors national growth in the trials of our heroes, and this is one reason why the heroes of American epic fiction have invariably been either the primitive (youthful) males of the novels by Ernest Hemingway and John Steinbeck or the boyhood figures of Thomas Wolfe and James T. Farrell. Beyond that we must resort to allegory, as in Hawthorne and Melville, or to the novel of manners as in Howells and James. The epic is idyllic, and Mark Twain, with remarkable insight, called *Tom Sawyer* an idyl of boyhood. *Huckleberry Finn* is more than that: it is an idyl of America's boyhood, the nearest thing we have to a national epic—perhaps as near as we can hope to come.

Stephen Crane:
Author in Transition

I renounced the clever school in literature. It seemed to me that there must be something more in life than to sit and cudgel one's brains for the clever and witty expedients. So I developed all alone a little creed of art which I thought was a good one. Later I discovered that my creed was identical with the one of Howells and Garland and in this way I became involved in the beautiful war between those who say that art is man's substitute for nature and we are most successful in art when we approach nearest to nature and truth.

This statement, written by Stephen Crane at the beginning of his career (1892), may have had much to do with the frequent early classification of his work as "naturalistic." We know better today, but what do we know? We know that later critics, impressed less by *Maggie: A Girl of the Streets* than by *The Red Badge of Courage* and the later short stories, called him impressionist. We know that recent criticism, impressed by Crane's use of certain highly charged metaphors, labels him symbolist.

The use of such categories reflects the critic's need for classifiction in the final disposition of an author, but there is a sense in which the most important authors defy such pigeon-holing. Stephen Crane is one of these. His short career, lasting less than ten years, was marked by change. Crane was a transitional figure. He participated in "the beautiful war" between cleverness and truth for a while, but, as an artist he was never wholly committed to it. There is as much difference between *Maggie,* published the year in which he made the statement above, and the short story "The Blue Hotel," written in 1898, as there usually is in works written by two altogether different authors. *The Red Badge of Courage* (1895) and "The Open Boat" (1897) stand somewhere between the two, containing qualities of each, but representing in themselves identities apart from each other and from the preceding and following works.

There is, however, an aspect of Crane's work where he changed very little. All his fiction, regardless of technique, dealt with nature as a force affecting his characters. In *Maggie,* which is the most anomalous of his major works, not the most characteristic, as the early critics seemed to believe, nature is a force thwarted by social evil, where natural impulses lead not to happiness, but to misfortune. In *The Red Badge of Courage,* natural forces compete within the person of the hero as well as in the conflict of opposing armies. In "The Open Boat," man is confronted by nature directly and close at hand, the power of nature naturally *and* symbolically portrayed. In "The Blue Hotel," it is the uncontrollable urge of fear, set against an implacable nature, that determines the events of the story.

In Crane's life, as in his works, there is a certain consistency within inconsistency. As a young student, journalist, and author, he felt the need to rebel against prevailing social and literary attitudes. As a literary rebel, he should surprise no one by seeing himself engaged in a dispute between opposing literary armies. Because he considered the establishment of his own creed as a choice between extremes (as in actual warfare), it would be surprising had he not gone to an extreme in formulating it in his early years. It would have been equally surprising, had he not followed this by plunging into life as a reporter of man's greed and misery, associating by choice with Bowery bums in soup kitchens and flop houses, becoming a defender and friend of drunks and prostitutes, viewing this life as the real thing. Crane appears consistent in his regard for the life of the American West, conceiving of it as a land of action and traveling across it to experience the "real" life of cowboys, bandits, and revolutionaries. He sought to learn the truth about war by visiting battlefields in Cuba and Greece.

Yet Crane was at home in literary discussions of a much cleverer sort than his rejection of "the clever school" would indicate. He became friends with Henry James, Joseph Conrad, and Ford Madox Hueffer, whose concerns with literary matters were anything but simple. Socially, too, his home in England, where he spent the last years of his life, was a far cry from the New York slums and the western plains. He lived in Brede Place, an ancient and pretentious English house, taking pride in its aristocratic traditions, taking pleasure, too, in such social amenities as dressing for dinner, perhaps from an unconscious urge to make the manner conform fittingly to the background.

The inconsistency in Crane's writing can best be exemplified by calling attention to the fact that, while Crane believed that true art should derive from the artist's own experience, many of his works, including his most famous novel, came before he had had any personal experience of the kind depicted. Also, when he did write from experience, he showed himself not reluctant to modify the factual events wherever necessary to serve his aesthetic ends.

R. W. Stallman explains Crane's inconsistency by saying Crane wanted it both ways, which may have been true in the later period and in his private life, but such an explanation tends to make Stephen Crane's career, short as it was, too static. It seems likely that the first significant change to be traced in his writing began during the composition of *The*

Red Badge of Courage. Beginning it, as he admits, as a pot-boiler ("something that would take the boarding school element—you know the kind?"), Crane became interested in the subject and had to do it, as he explained, "in my own way." The question here would seem to be, what was his *own way?*

Certainly the way of *The Red Badge of Courage* is not the way of *Maggie: A Girl of the Streets,* for his first novel had been an attempt to achieve a kind of reportorial objectivity of the kind Garland used to portray the struggles of the frontier farmer—a method pursued for the sake of "nature and truth." *Maggie* portrayed scenes of poverty and low life with a detail that now impresses us only mildly, but that shocked the usual reader of the 1890's. The youthful Crane undoubtedly considered it an exposé of society's ills. We know he was aware of its shock value, for he spoke of its effect upon "Mr. Podsnap" and "Mrs. Grundy." It remains an early example of the kind of novel that Virginia Woolf described (in writing about Arnold Bennett) as leaving the reader primarily with the feeling that he should sit down and write out a check for some worthy cause.

In *The Red Badge of Courage,* "the cause" has almost wholly disappeared; or, rather, has become transformed into "the subject." If we ask ourselves how this occurred, we shall undoubtedly be asking a question that Crane, consciously or unconsciously, asked himself, particularly during the several times he studied, revised, and rewrote his manuscript. Taking his materials more lightly than he did in his first novel, he may, in the beginning, have played down any evidence of "a cause," for there is no sign anywhere that he intended to write an anti-war novel, as he had written an anti-society novel in *Maggie.* With his sensitivity to his material become acute (for he was not a born hack), Crane discovered his subject, which was not *war* but *nature*—war being merely the occasion for the work, not the theme of it. The two armies Crane saw not so much as social aggregates as he saw them as accumulations of natural forces in opposition.

To make this point clear, Crane described the two armies in beast imagery: the army "stretches out on the hills, resting"; it "awakened and began to tremble with eagerness"; a river "purled at the army's feet"; the opposing army's campfires are portrayed as "red, eyelike . . . set in the low brow of distant hills." They are like two monsters confronting each other, and, indeed, Crane likens the regiment to "one of those moving monsters wending with many feet."

In such an atmosphere Crane placed his characters, a small company of almost nameless soldiers who not only have to take into consideration the power of nature that surrounds them but must also consider "nature" within—their own at times uncontrollable urge to run or rage to fight. In the midst of such forces, they depict subtle emotional attachments "born of the smoke and danger of death."

Crane's attitude towards nature was not too different from Mark Twain's, but their manners of utilizing it to create fiction (except in the late stories of each) were entirely different. Twain introduced nature through the various frontier myths in order to define his characters. Crane used his characters, with their varying attitudes, as a means of defining the role nature plays in determining human events. Left alone, Huck Finn would have been able to adjust easily to the natural life. It was only when he listened to the contradictory voices of society that he became confused. No character in Crane's works ever begins by understanding nature; he comes gradually to such understanding. He is as much a "characteristic" as he is a character, given such names as "the Easterner," "the cowboy," "the correspondent," "the oiler," and "the cook." Even Henry Fleming, the protagonist of *The Red Badge of Courage,* is seldom named, and his companions are known mostly as "the tall soldier," "the loud soldier," or according to their rank in the army.

Henry Fleming is known mostly as "the youth," and it is through his eyes that we see the events of the novel, through his developing consciousness that we are made to feel the impact of those events; and we both see and feel them in terms of nature. Henry runs away from his first battle, then discovers that behind the lines "Nature has gone tranquilly on with her golden process in the midst of so much devilment." When he does later stand up and fight, he realizes "that he had been a barbarian, a beast." With the war over, he sees again that "He had been an animal blistered and sweating in the heat and pain of war," *but* "He turned now with a lover's thirst to images of tranquil skies, fresh meadows, cool brooks—an existence of soft and eternal peace."

The suggestion is that it was not nature that was in upheaval, threatening man, but man in confusion, blaming nature. When the men gave themselves naturally and wholeheartedly to the battle, either they were killed or they became heroes: "The imperturbable sun shines on insult and worship." But they do gain a new knowledge of themselves and respect for their comrades. After the final battle, Henry Fleming "felt a quiet manhood, nonassertive but of sturdy and strong blood. He knew that he would no more quail before his guides wherever they should point. He had been to touch the great death, and he found that, after all, it was but the great death. He was a man."

On this point, Crane became more specific in his next important work, "The Open Boat." Four men who have been shipwrecked find themselves in a small boat on a heavy sea, closely and intimately confronting the great force of nature— the waves that "were most wrongfully and barbarously abrupt and tall." In the midst of danger, there is here, as there was in the war, "a subtle brotherhood of men . . . established . . . it dwelt in the boat, and each man felt it warm them." When they encounter difficulties in reaching shore because of the heavy rollers, the spokesman of the tale (the correspondent) cries to himself: "If I am going to be drowned—if I am going to be drowned—If I am going to be drowned, why, in the name of the seven mad gods who rule the sea, was I allowed to come thus far and contemplate sand and trees?"

His thrice-repeated cry, so much like an incantation, leads him to the following contemplation:

When it occurs to a man that nature does not regard him as important, and that she feels she would not maim the universe by disposing of him, he at first wishes to throw bricks at the temple, and he hates deeply the fact that there are no bricks and no temples. Any visible expression of nature would surely be pelleted with his jeers.

Then, if there be no tangible thing to hoot, he feels, perhaps, the desire to confront a personification and indulge in pleas, bowed to one knee, and with hands supplicant, saying, "Yes, but I love myself."

A high cold star on a winter's night is the word he feels that she says to him. Thereafter he knows the pathos of the situation.

The pathos is that nature does not care, and all that is left is for man to care for himself.

Three of the men in the story do reach shore safely, but a fourth, the oiler, drowns in the surf.

It seemed that instantly the beach was populated with men with blankets, clothes, and flasks, and women with coffee-pots and all the remedies sacred to their minds. The welcome of the land to the men from the sea was warm and generous; but a still and dripping shape was carried slowly up the beach, and the land's welcome for it could only be the different and sinister hospitality of the grave.

For the drowned oiler there was, pathetically, none of the ceremony accorded the survivors. But nature was not to blame. The man had been simply too exhausted, or too unlucky, and such is the danger man runs when he finds himself pitted against nature. Yet there were rewards in the comradeship of the struggle and in the hospitality of the welcome given the survivors, even in the beauty of nature viewed from a respectful distance. As it had been with Henry Fleming after the war, so it was for the men after their ordeal.

When it came night, the white waves paced to and fro in the moonlight, and the wind brought the sound of the great sea's voice to the men on the shore, and they felt that they could then be interpreters.

With the knowledge that nature was powerful, but indifferent to the plight of man, Crane had achieved a general definition of nature and of man's relation to it. He had also hinted at a relationship between man and man, portraying it as a form of ceremony, as something *sacred* to men's minds; but he had shown it as something secondary to the struggle, almost accidental. He had also hinted at the part chance plays in man's relationship with nature, but again he had not dealt with it in detail, had not himself, perhaps, discovered how great a part he really conceived it to be. These were to be the separate concerns of his last two important works, "The Bride Comes to Yellow Sky" and "The Blue Hotel."

It would be too much to say that "The Bride Comes to Yellow Sky" is a small "comedy of manners"; yet, if it is not, we have no traditional name for such a story. True, these are not the "manners" of Henry James, for James, when he portrayed the American westerner, showed him as one with few manners. In the West, however, where Crane's story is set, certain forms were in the process of development that, simple though they might be, smoothed the way for social intercourse. In fact, it would not be saying too much to suggest that where the usual institutions of society were so few, manners (or something like manners), had often to bear the full weight of preserving public order. Crane calls it humorously Man's "duty to his friends, or of their idea of his duty," and he centers his short comedy about an incident involving two violations of a code of duty. The first occurs when Jack Potter, the town marshal, leaves Yellow Sky and, without notifying his fellow townsmen, gets married. As Crane tells us:

. . . such was Potter's thought of his duty to his friends, or of their idea of his duty, or of an unspoken form which does not control men in these matters, that he felt he was heinous. He had committed an extraordinary crime. Face to face with this girl in San Antonio, and spurred by his sharp impulse, he had gone headlong over all the social hedges.

The second violation is in Potter's relation to Scratchy Wilson, the simple former badman, who is a wonder with a gun. When Scratchy is sober, we are told, "he wouldn't hurt a fly," but when he is under the influence of spirits, he sets out with guns blazing in search of a fight. He plays with the town as if it were a toy, terrorizing it and disrupting its order: storekeepers lock their doors and housewives pull closed their shutters. At such times, it is the marshal's duty to confront Scratchy, to get the drop on him and lock him up until he becomes sober. This time, however, when Scratchy goes on his spree, Potter has not yet returned from San Antonio, so at least the citizens believe. After Scratchy has amused himself by shooting at a dog, putting a few bullets into the saloon door, and shooting up the house of his best friend, he goes in search of the marshal. Potter arrives, not from his house as was expected, but from a side street, up from the railway station with his bride. At first Scratchy is furious, thinking Potter has attempted to sneak up on him; then, when the marshal tells him he has no gun, he is incredulous. "Don't tell me no lie like that. There ain't a man in Texas ever seen you without no gun," he says. Potter replies: "I ain't got a gun because I've just come from San Anton' with my wife. I'm married." For Scratchy this revelation is like "a glimpse of another world." He lowers his revolver. The code of Yellow Sky, and particularly the relationship between Scratchy and the marshal, did not allow for so unforeseen an event. Stephen Crane leaves no doubt about how we are to understand it. Scratchy, he says, "was not a student of chivalry; it was merely that in the presence of this foreign condition he was a simple child of the earlier plains." Lacking the proper "form" to complete his "play," Scratchy must retire from the game, but in retiring he is no different from Jack Potter when he decided to propose to the girl in San

Antonio. He was conforming to an unspoken form. That Crane presents his action as a game does not minimize the seriousness of his concern with manners. In fact, by preserving a comic tone and the exaggeration of comedy, he emphasizes the significance of social definition; for if we are to say what the story is about, we must say that it is the tale of a childlike man confronting a new, and more complex situation than his simple code allows for. Scratchy Wilson differs only in degree from James's Christopher Newman, but he is a far cry from the characters of Crane's *Maggie,* whose predatory lives reflect only the pathos of squalor or the cheating forms of a false sophistication.

Despite the rightness of the ending of "The Bride Comes to Yellow Sky" as Crane wrote it, it must have occurred to the author that the incident could have ended otherwise. If the rage of Scratchy had been less play, more the result of a genuine emotion, Scratchy might very well have shot Jack Potter. So far as theme is concerned, the story could as easily have depicted the breakdown of a code of manners as it does the operation of "an unspoken form." Whether such a possibility occurred to Crane or not, the theme of such a breakdown is embodied in his later story, "The Blue Hotel."

"The Blue Hotel" opens with a character known only as "the Swede" and two other strangers as they leave the transcontinental express train at a small Nebraska town during a snowstorm. The three men engage rooms in a nearby family hotel, then settle down to an evening of waiting in the hotel's public parlor. It is evident at once from the peculiarity of the Swede's actions that he is a "badly frightened man." What he fears, we soon surmise, is the unfamiliarity of the surroundings, this unfamiliarity heightened by the storm outside and by the presence of men he does not know. These men are the two strangers, called by Crane only "the Easterner" and "the cowboy," and the hotel landlord and his son. The Swede appears to believe himself in the West of legendary badmen, and he soon begins to feel that the others have designs upon him, that he will be robbed or beaten or killed. When he announces that he will leave, his fellow travelers have no regrets, for the Swede has been obstreperous in speech and act; but the landlord considers it his duty as host to pacify his guest. He takes him to his room and gives him a drink of whiskey. He extolls the town of Roper, saying there will be "a line of ilictric street-cars" here by spring, and "there's a new railroad goin' to be built down from Broken Arm to here." He enumerates the four churches, describes the "big brick school house" and the factory. "Why," he says, "in two years Roper'll be a met-tro-pol-is." He shows the picture of his "little girl that died." He tells the Swede that his oldest son is a lawyer.

Meanwhile, in the public room, the other men have been discussing the Swede. The Easterner says: "it seems to me this man has been reading dime novels, and he thinks he's right out in the middle of it—the shootin' and stabbin' and all." "But," the cowboy says, emphasizing what the landlord had been attempting to tell the Swede, "This ain't Wyoming, ner none of them places. This is Nebrasker." "Yes," the landlord's son adds, "an' why don't he wait till he gits *out West?*"

When the Swede returns to the room, the whiskey and the landlord's words seem to have calmed him. He leaves the room for a glass of water, and the landlord confirms the Easterner's guess: "It was only that he was from the East, and he thought this was a tough place." When the landlord's son insists that he still thinks the Swede "too fresh," his father reprimands him:

"I keep a hotel," he shouted. "A hotel, do you mind? A guest under my roof has sacred privileges. He is to be intimidated by none. Not one word shall he hear that would prejudice him in favor of goin' away. I'll not have it. There's no place in this here town where they can say they iver took a guest of mine because he was afraid to stay here."

Nevertheless, the son, Johnnie, is right. The Swede is too fresh; but even when the Swede claps the landlord too heartily on his injured shoulder, the landlord's code prevents him from taking offense. When the Swede proposes a game of cards, an entertainment he has formerly rejected, the two travelers and Johnnie unenthusiastically sit down with him. They have played only a short time when the Swede accuses Johnnie of cheating. In the altercation that follows, Johnnie challenges the Swede to a fight. Although the others try to dissuade the two men, they finally go outside the house to do battle. Here the Swede's fears revive when he realizes that the others all want Johnnie to win, but the landlord, still true to the code, insists that it will be a fair fight.

In the fight that follows, the Swede finally wins. Weary, but flushed with victory, he now prepares to leave the hotel. Even the landlord raises no more objections. The Swede has put himself outside the small society of the hotel now finally through an arrogance in victory that alienates even his considerate host. As he makes his way through the blankness of wind and snow, the author-narrator (the Easterner) takes the occasion to comment:

He might have been in a deserted village. We picture the world as thick with conquering and elate humanity, but, here, with the bugles of the tempest pealing, it was hard to imagine a peopled earth. One viewed the existence of man then as a marvel, and conceded a glamour of wonder to these lice which were caused to cling to a whirling, fire-smitten, ice-locked, disease-stricken, space-lost bulb. The conceit of man was explained by this storm to be the very engine of life. One was a coxcomb not to die in it.

The Swede makes his way to a saloon. In the room are a bartender and four men playing cards, one of them a professional gambler. The gambler, we are told, holds his position in the town by a rigidly defined code, as elaborate as that held by the landlord. He was allowed to fleece unwary travellers and boastful farmers, but he was considered by the men of the town as an admirable and trustworthy person. The Swede comes among these men, full of pride in his victory, further elated at having found asylum from the storm. He attempts to get the men to drink with him. Because of his arrogant manner, they all refuse. Finally, he attempts to force the gambler to take a drink, grasping him by the throat and dragging him from his chair. The gambler pulls a knife and stabs the Swede, piercing, as Crane says, "this citadel of virtue, wisdom, power . . . as easily as if he had been a melon." Where the man fell, his eyes seemed "fixed upon a dreadful legend that dwelt atop of the cash-machine: 'This registers the amount of your purchase.' "

The story does not end here, although there have been readers who maintained that it should. The most recent is R. W. Stallman, who has written most forcibly on the subject:

This point marks the legitimate end of the story. Crane spoiled the whole thing by tacking on a moralizing appendix. The off-key tone is at odds with the tone of the preceding part, and the theme that his beginning prepared for stands at odds with the trumped-up theme announced in the totally irrelevant and non-ironic conclusion.[1]

Mr. Stallman's objection could be more easily examined had he stated clearly what he thought the theme to be that Crane had prepared us for. Given the broadly ironic clue of the cash register, we might say that the story illustrates how man's actions determine the kind and amount of punishment he is to receive. But this would be contrary to all that Crane had said about his characters in the past, even earlier in the same story, where he speaks of men as lice, peopling an extremely unpleasant globe. In his earlier stories, he had shown man "as a marvel," exactly because he had found a means to exist in a universe that appeared uncaring. It might be that Mr. Stallman finds a successful irony in the story at this point by seeing the legend on the cash register as meaning exactly the opposite of what it says; but, again, there seems little in the story to justify such a reading, and the method itself would be contrary to Crane's normal use of such symbols.

In the ending that Crane supplied, such questions are resolved, and the conclusion is achieved with a more telling

[1] *Stephen Crane: An Omnibus* (New York, 1952), pp. 482–483.

irony than if the story had merely ended with the Swede's death. In the final section, Crane shows us the Easterner and the cowboy meeting at a later date, when they discuss the light sentence given the gambler for killing the Swede. They speculate on various things that might have been done to prevent the death. The Easterner says: "The Swede might not have been killed if everything had been square." "Might not have been killed?" exclaims the cowboy. "Everything square? why, when he said that Johnnie was cheatin' and acted like such a jackass? And then in the saloon he fairly walked up to get hurt?" The cowboy's conclusions are just about what any reader's would be at this point in the story, but they reduced the Easterner to a rage because he knew better. With a reversal as neatly ironic as anything he had ever written, Crane has the Easterner reply: "Let me tell you something. Listen! Johnnie *was* cheating."

With this bit of information, the whole meaning of the story has taken on another dimension. It was not merely the Swede who was responsible, who had failed out of simplicity, ignorance, and fear; it was the Easterner, who knew but had not the nerve to say that Johnnie was cheating; it was even the hotel keeper, who allowed the fight to go on against his better judgment; above all, of course, it was Johnnie, who even more wilfully than the Swede had violated one of the simplest of all codes by cheating in a game played "for fun." As the Easterner says: "We are all in it. We, five of us, have collaborated in the murder of this Swede."

It is clear now that the machine did lie. It did not register the true amount. But a machine that even makes such a claim represents a reflector of man's confidence. The true machine is the universe—nature; and we already know what this machine registers concerning man—nothing. The story is about man's struggle for some identity in the face of nature's indifference. What motivates the struggle is man's conceit. His method of conducting it is to seek the protection of the code that binds him to his fellowmen. Johnny and the gambler, although they violated one code, were protected by another. The code protected the cowboy because he was too stupid to know what had happened; it protected the Easterner because he was too shrewd to admit he knew it had been violated. The Swede was insensitive to the code that bound the others, so he confronted them as he confronted the storm, fearfully but defiantly. Ironically, he was right to have feared for his life, but for the wrong reason. No one had designs on him, least of all nature. It was ignorance that killed him, ignorance of the manner by which men cling together for protection against both the inner and the outer nature. His ignorance of the code dislocated the social structure, which dislocation, like a chain reaction, affected all of those social atoms—men—with whom he came in contact. Events exploded in the Swede's death and the gambler's crime. As the Easterner rightly surmises, the events that followed the fight at the blue hotel might have been predicted, for they were as logically determined (and as machine-like) as the pressing of a number on the cash register.

If this seems a pessimistic view of nature, it is not only the logical end of Crane's concern with the subject, it is the logical end of America's concern. When Hawthorne and Melville questioned Emerson's view of nature as the benevolent image of the Over-Soul, they revealed an ambiguity in nature that begged closer inspection. Stephen Crane's examination showed nature to be as unmotivated as a machine with which man had come only accidentally in contact. Man's villainy and his virtue were solely the responsibility of society. Social relationships were governed by codes of conduct that man could violate only at his own—and his fellows'—peril. Henry Fleming of *The Red Badge of Courage,* the correspondent of "The Open Boat," Scratchy Wilson, and the Swede are all exemplars of this discovery in increasing degrees of complexity.

Crane's subject, then, was not so much "nature" as man's relation with his fellows. In his treatment of these relations, he probably moved as near to the interests of Henry James as he had been near the interests of Howells and Garland at the beginning of his career. In method, too, he moved from the rugged "veritism" of *Maggie* to the ironic symbolism of "The Blue Hotel." Yet he did not become another James, as he had never been completely won to the naturalists. What he did was suggest the proper means of bridging the two extremes between the naturalists' too intense interest in life at the expense of art and Henry James's interest in forms at the expense of nature. And he did, even more than Garland or James, anticipate the future interests of American letters. Hemingway's examination of the worlds of violence and the codes that governed them appears, at times, little more than an extension of Crane's work. William Faulkner's last man, he with the "puny inexhaustible voice, still talking" in the face of imminent destruction, is an image that Crane would have understood and approved. Almost single-handedly, in an era of declining greatness and vapid gentility, Crane not only kept the tradition of honest investigation alive, he made it meaningful for generations to follow.

Ezra Pound and
Contemporary Criticism

To THE YOUNG POET or scholar, who is still educated during his early years in the romantic traditions of the
nineteenth century, the ideas of contemporary criticism are
exciting, almost as exciting perhaps as they were to the young
poets of the years preceding the First World War who read
Blast, and later read Ezra Pound's contributions to *Poetry,*
the *Little Review,* the *Dial* and *Exile,* who as exiles in London, Paris, Vienna, or Rome met Pound or talked about him,
or read about him in *The Criterion* or *Hound and Horn.*
T. S. Eliot is the literary figure best known to the young
poets today, and too few of them realize the tremendous debt
owed by Eliot and others of the modern school—Williams,
Tate, Ransom, Bishop, Macleish, and even Yvor Winters—to
Ezra Pound's early writing. Even Eliot himself, as recently as
September, 1946, had written that he still considered Pound's
critical writings "to be almost the only contemporary writing
on the art of poetry that a young poet can study with profit."[1]

As Mario Praz has shown,[2] many of the ideas explored in

[1] *Poetry: A Magazine of Verse,* LXVIII, No. 6, 331.
[2] "T. S. Eliot and Dante," *Southern Review,* Winter, 1937.

modern literary criticism were first expressed by Pound in his *Spirit of Romance* (1910). Later volumes include *Pavannes and Divisions* (1918), *Instigations* (1920), *Imaginary Letters* (1930), *How to Read* (1932), *A. B. C. of Reading* (1934), *Polite Essays* (1937), and *Culture* (1938). Pound's prose also includes a volume on music, *Antheil* and the *Treatise on Harmony* (1924), and a book upon the sculptor Gaudier-Brzeska, in addition to two books on economic theory.

The bulk of Pound's criticism is concerned with actual studies of the poetic works themselves. Probably the most rewarding of these is his study of Dante in *The Spirit of Romance,* closely followed by his treatment of medieval romance in the same volume. His interest in modern French poetry, first published in the *Little Review* in 1918, republished in *Instigations,* did much to arouse an interest in the French symbolists among American and British poets of the 1920's. A long section in *Instigations* probably represents the first attempt in English to consider the form of the novel by a close analysis of Henry James's novels in a fashion only recently applied by such practitioners as Cleanth Brooks and Robert Penn Warren to the short story. As an early rebel against narrowly regional or national concepts, Pound admired James for his emotional intensity and because he felt that James had attempted to break down the international barriers of the nineteenth century, against which he himself had struggled. "No other American was," Pound said, "of sufficient importance for his change of allegiance to have constituted an international act."

Pound's criticism aimed at a reinvigoration of writing by breaking down the old categories and re-examining the past for new models. It demanded a view of history and of traditional literature radically different from that which prevailed among scholars and artists of his time. He believed that the critical act demanded a direct and close concern with the specific work under consideration, not with the author's life or with his historical background. He called upon teachers to adopt responsible attitudes toward the teaching of literature as language charged with meaning and emotion, not as "cenotaphs" of past cultures only.

The true artist, Pound believed, reported life accurately, not only to scholars and critics, but to all of society. The purpose of art was to reconcile humanity to the act of continued living, to ease the mind of strain, and to supply what he calls "nutrition of impulse." Such general statements might be twisted, as they were by Marxists of the thirties, to mean that Pound's view of poetry proposed merely a romantic escape from life, especially when the highly individual personality of the man himself is taken into account, but Pound's preoccupation with the problems of technique, while it led him often into making what now appear to be ridiculous formulations, kept his criticism at a level of practicality which is more often than not amazing in its quality of perception, particularly in the light of our development since. It is important to remember that many of the attacks which have been made against Pound have been directed principally at his eccentric style, his personality, his later economic theories, or his general statements.

This does not mean that everything Pound wrote is to be swallowed whole. As is true with most innovators, there is a naiveté about many of his theories which the development of the great body of twentieth-century criticism has removed, while at the same time appropriating much that was valuable to itself, too often without adequate acknowledgment or even recognition of its source. Pound was the innovator—the prophet. The foremost among his successors, such men as Eliot and F. R. Leavis, have made adequate and gracious acknowledgment, have indeed refined and even modified many of the central ideas by supplying their own examples, drawing their own conclusions, and exerting their own emphasis. In justice to Ezra Pound, this fact should be made clear, for it is the only fact which is really important. The argument as to whether Eliot or Pound is the *major* voice in twentieth-century criticism is as academic as the question, which Eliot dismisses in a paragraph, as to whether Pound will finally be known primarily as a critic or as a poet.

Pound conceived of poetry as "a sort of inspired mathematics, which give us equations for the human emotions."[3] Its practice demands the precision of a Dante, which raises the important and the unimportant details alike to the level of immortality. The problem of personal belief is dismissed: "The sceptical age hungers after the definite, after something it can pretend to believe. The marvelous thing is made plausible, the gods are humanized, their annals are written as if copied from a parish register; their heroes might have been acquainted with the author's father." He cites Provençal poetry as an illustration of the proper use of nature as background for action, but it represents also an equation, a "metaphor by sympathy" for the mood of the poem. A system of belief, whether the chivalric world of Provençal verse, Greek mythology, or Christian religion, is a means merely of "exteriorization of the sensibility." Genuine religion, as opposed to the "Mosaic or Roman or British Empire type," seems to be concerned not with dogmatic truth nor with ethics of the usual sort, but its aim seems to be to stimulate confidence in the "life force."

Such ideas do not constitute a philosophy of poetry any more than they construct a systematic theology, but their relevance to contemporary criticism, with its concern for "the myth" and the objectification of emotion, is obvious. Yeats's problem, Pound believed, resulted from a mistaken belief that so narrow a culture as Irish nationalism would provide materials for a new sacred book. Usable myth is the creation of a great culture only: "Pisistratus, Li Po, the Japanese emperor who reduced the number of Noh dramas to about 450; the hackneyed Hebrew example; in less degree the Middle Ages, with the matter of Britain, or France, or Rome le Grant."

[3] Cf. Eliot's "objective correlative" theory as expressed in his "Hamlet and His Problems," 1919. Pound's statement was made before 1910 and appeared in *Spirit of Romance*. Cf. also Praz "T. S. Eliot and Dante" cited above.

Pound's approach to poetic theory was made naturally enough through his interest in language, though he made it clear that he did not wish his early studies to be considered as philological works. If we may say that a preoccupation with economic theory has dominated the last twenty years of his career, it is equally true that the early years were influenced by his study of foreign literature as a graduate student and as an instructor of languages, both before and after he went abroad in 1908, and by his concern with problems of translation as well as of original composition. "Great literature," he wrote, "is simply language charged with meaning to the utmost possible degree." Pound's concept of "meaning," however, has little to do with the didactic content of nineteenth-century verse. It is indissolubly bound to a concept of form objectified and realized, as the drawing of a circle is the realization of the abstract idea of a circle, as well as of the abstract mathematical formulation—to draw from one of Pound's own examples. He divides poetry into three classifications which he calls Melopoeia, Phanopoeia, and Logopoeia. The first is concerned primarily with poetry as music, "wherein the words are charged, over and above their plain meaning with some musical property, which directs the bearing or trend of the meaning." Such a quality is not translatable, except briefly and rarely, and limits the enjoyment of such verse to those who can read it in the original or to those who, failing to understand the meaning of the words themselves, can catch its quality when hearing it read aloud in a language they do not understand. Phanopoeia "is a casting of images upon the visual imagination" as in dramatic action or in metaphor, and this can usually be rendered effectively in translation. The third, Logopoeia, Pound calls "The dance of the intellect among words," taking into consideration special usages of languages to provide an ironic play of ordinarily unrelated words, one against another. It is this quality, he says, which belongs wholly to poetry and provides an aesthetic content unavailable through plastic art forms or in music. It cannot be translated directly, but only by finding a derivative or an equivalent for the author's state of mind may it be transmitted through another language.[4]

The problem of Ezra Pound's translations is extraneous, or, at most, illustrative, except as it concerns Pound's interest in problems of translation—which are critical problems (Pound has, of course, been called the greatest of all English translators). Such problems served, however, to focus attention upon the very problems which the most recent verse before 1910 had neglected. Whatever revolution is represented in Victorian or Georgian verse in England or in late nineteenth-century verse in America (from Whitman to Masters), with the exception of Hopkins and Yeats in England and Dickinson in America, had constituted a revolution, not of technique, but of subject matter. Imagism was a step in the direction of increased concern for technical understanding, but it is a mark of Pound's greatness as a critic that so meagre a step did not satisfy him. An examination of older forms from Confucius and the Greeks forward and including the French *symboliste* school gave him his clue:

Different languages—I mean the actual vocabularies, the idioms—have worked out certain mechanisms of communication and registration. No one language is complete. A master may be continually expanding his own tongue, rendering it fit to bear some charge hitherto borne only by some other alien tongue, but the process does not stop with any one man. While Proust is learning Henry James, preparatory to breaking through certain French paste-board partitions, the whole American speech is churning and chugging, and every other tongue doing likewise. . . . The man who does not know the Italian of the duocento and trecento has in him a

4 These concepts appeared in *How to Read*, and F. R. Leavis in his essay "How to Teach Reading" in *Education and the University* (1943) attacks them vigorously and intelligently as inadequate discussions of the problems raised. It is just here, however, that both the value and the limitations of Mr. Pound as critic reside. The innovator poses the problems for others to sift and evaluate. It seems to me, too, that Mr. Leavis is misreading Pound when he suggests that Ezra Pound calls for one of these qualities (melopoeia, for instance) to be studied apart from the others or apart from individual poems. Such a practice would be contrary to everything Pound wrote in regard to the critical act.

painful lacuna, not necessarily painful to himself, but there are certain things he doesn't know, and can't; it is as if he were blind to some part of the spectrum.

Certain readers may feel that such an awareness for language has been carried too far, and too directly, in the *Cantos*. But in Pound's critical writing it brought him directly to the problem of how language operates, as well as leading him to the principal sources outside his own tongue.

Eliot once wrote that the first half of the twentieth century would eventually become known as "The Age of Ezra Pound." This is undoubtedly an exaggeration of fact, but as a metaphor it will do. Pound lead in the reintroduction of Dante to the present age and in the recognition of the late nineteenth-century *symboliste* poets. He introduced the concept of literary history as a continuing or ever-recurring present, thus not only piercing the walls of pragmatic scholarship, but reviving the works of Homer, Catullus, Propertius, Ovid, Dante, and the Provençal poets.

It is dawn at Jerusalem while midnight hovers above the pillars of Hercules. All ages are contemporaneous. It is b.c., let us say, in Morocco. The Middle Ages are in Russia [1910]. The future stirs already in the minds of the few. This is especially true of literature, where the real time is independent of the apparent, and where many dead men are our grandchildren's contemporaries, while many of our contemporaries have already been gathered into Abraham's bosom.

Except for Pound's unique style, such a statement might have come from Eliot's "Tradition and the Individual Talent," and it and other comparable statements undoubtedly had a great deal to do with Eliot's views.

Pound pioneered in the revival of Stendhal and James, and in the recognition of such contemporary authors as James Joyce, D. H. Lawrence, and Eliot. Through his early interest in imagism, his later preoccupation with the Chinese character studies of Ernest Fenollosa, and his feeling "that poetry ought to be as well written as prose," he undoubtedly had a great deal to do with the trend away from the lyrical and sentimental traditions in English and American verse. During his period with Eliot in London, he wrote,

that at a particular date in a particular room, two authors . . . decided that the dilutation of *vers libre,* Amygism, Lee Masterism, general floppiness had gone too far and that some counter-current must be set doing. . . . Results: Poems in Mr. Eliot's second volume, not contained in his first ['Prufrock' *Egoist,* 1917], also, 'H. S. Mauberly.'

Perhaps his greatest contribution, however, and one which has exercised the most complete shift of emphasis in twentieth-century criticism and in the teaching of literature, was his insistence that scholars and critics focus their attention upon the works themselves. "My opinion of critics," he once wrote,

is that: the best are those who actually cause an amelioration in the art which they criticize. The next best are those who most focus attention on the best that is written (or painted or composed or cut in stone). And the pestilential vermin are those who detract attention *from* the best, either to the second rate, or to hokum, or to their own critical writing.

Pound believed that "All teaching of literature should be performed by the presentation and juxtaposition of specimens of writing and NOT by discussion of some other discusser's opinion *about* the general standing of a poet or author." His own method in his examination of James's novels was, briefly, as follows: first, a brief review of the principal characters and the action; second, a quotation from sections of the work; third, interpretations, a critical raising of questions, and an estimation of the value of method and content.

While we may account for Ezra Pound's interest in literature as such through his training in languages, his interest in Fenollosa's ideographic writing, and his translations, we can no more account for his perceptual genius than we can explain occasional acts of foolishness perpetrated by that genius. Both are, in part at least, results of his fearless originality, for he continually thought of himself as an experimentalist. That he achieved as much as he did in his criticism is no doubt due to the corresponding strong respect which he held for tradition, as John Crowe Ransom has pointed out,[5] and which supplied a rein and a corrective. Still, there was enough of the bohemian "original" in Pound to lead him to excesses of language and of personal behavior which prevented his ever being taken quite as seriously as he desired by contemporary society. There have, however, been recent signs of a revival of his reputation. There have also been signs of an increasing stodginess in our critical writing, a resting upon laurels of which Mr. Pound and others of his generation are perhaps more deserving. It may not be too far-fetched to consider the possibility of Ezra Pound effecting a second revolution within a single lifetime, through the rediscovery of what was written so many years ago. His definition of experimental writing is one which every young poet might well keep in mind: "Experiment aims at writing that will have a relation to the present analogous to the relation which a past masterwork had to the life of its time."

Pound's career has steadily aimed at what has popularly become known as "a correction of taste," and there is justification for the raising of Dante to the level which Shakespeare occupied during the nineteenth century, if for no other reason than to suggest to the ordinary student the possibility of values outside the English tongue. There is a like justification for introducing to American teachers of literature an awareness of world literature, for as Pound wrote in *Polite Essays:* "Homer, Villon, Propertius, speak of the world as I know it, whereas Mr. Tennyson and Dr. Bridges did not," and several generations of American schoolboys (including Pound's own generation) had focussed upon Tennyson at the expense of literature exceedingly more pertinent and valuable to them.

[5] *Saturday Review of Literature*, Jan. 19, 1935.

It seems finally that Pound's reputation as a critic will rest upon those measures of "correction" which he introduced, rather than upon any total or systematic view of literature. Artists he considered "the antenna of the race," the "registering instruments; and if they falsify their reports there is no measures to the harm that they do." To critics and teachers, he said, the teaching or evaluation of literature in general terms or in terms not directly relating to the work of art itself is "inexcusable AFTER the era of 'Agassiz and the fish'—by which I mean now that general education is in a position to profit by the parallels of biological study based on EXAMINATION and COMPARISON of particular specimens." These two points, considering the influence they have had upon our concept of the creative process, the critical act, and upon the educational theories of this age, are quite enough to assure him a position of eminence in the history of criticism in the twentieth century.

Personal History and the
Four Quartets

T. S. ELIOT'S *Four Quartets* has been seen as predominately a religious poem. This is not wholly true although religious concepts are at the center of it and religious imagery makes up a large part of the whole. It would be more exact to say that the philosophic concerns of our time, aesthetic and social, as well as religious, stand at its center. One aspect of the work which has been neglected is the unusual amount of "personal history" which it incorporates. I say "neglected" because although it has not escaped observation, it has not been sufficiently considered in any of the discussions which I have seen.

To begin with, each of the four long poems is titled by a place name. The first, Burnt Norton, is an old house in Gloucestershire, known to the poet and providing the rose garden from which its central imagery, reflecting the present in terms of the past and the future, has been obtained. The second, East Coker, is the Somerset village from which the poet's ancestors emigrated to America. The third, The Dry Salvages, refers to three small islands off the coast of Cape Ann, in Massachusetts, where Eliot's forefathers settled; this section also contains an image of the Mississippi River in Missouri, where the poet grew up. The fourth, Little Gidding, refers to a village in Huntingdonshire, where Nicholas Ferrar retired, and to the Ferrar chapel, which has come down in history as a symbol of high-church Anglican devotion of the kind preferred by Eliot.

Thus there can be seen a kind of personal development—almost a tracing of self—from the present of "Burnt Norton," which is the most abstract of the four poems, but which appears to reflect a contemporary experience in a rose garden, back into a memory of the past in "East Coker," progressing through memories of Eliot's own American background in "The Dry Salvages," up to a consideration of his personal resolution in "Little Gidding." Too much must not be made of this, it is true, for fear of diminishing the development of other themes in the poem. Personal history must not be seen as apart from these, but rather as an additional light to be shed upon them or, perhaps, as a means of holding them together in a dramatic framework, to provide a unified point of view. For instance, in the first poem there is the emphasis upon the problem of time—the moment when the poet's memory is confronted by a consideration of both the past and the future. In the second the problem is mostly spatial—the changing landscape of the native village, the rising and falling of houses, the disappearance of eminent men, the shifting panorama of dancers who disappear under a hill. The third, while it progresses in personal time, moves backward in general time. Eliot's forebears moved from East Coker to Massachusetts, and then to Missouri, but in moving into a more primitive natural scene, they moved backwards in racial time. The time here is not measured by modern means, but by the ground-swell of the earth itself; man is still more subject to the "strong brown god"—the pagan god of the river. It is the story of a history that is not "mere sequence," but has a pattern of its own. The knowledge here is of a primitive relationship with nature which still exists in the present. The fourth presents Little Gidding (the Church), but not as an absolute solution:

> There are other places
> Which also are the world's end; some at the sea's jaws,
> Or over a dark lake, in a desert of a city—
> But this is the nearest, in place and time,
> Now and in England.

But the church is, for the poet, the nearest, in this place and this time, now and in England.

The construction of this long poem is intricate and formal, but it is not modeled upon any particular tradition. It is probably the most personal of all Eliot's poetry. Its metrical form is, as Miss Helen Gardner has pointed out, less dependent upon earlier English forms than are such poems as "Prufrock" and *The Waste Land*. It reflects the idiom of the present more than it does a traditional "poetic" diction, and thus seems to reflect the achievement of the kind of language which Eliot meditated in his *The Music of Poetry* in 1942:

> I believe that any language, so long as it remains the same language, imposes its laws and restrictions and permits its own license, dictates its own speech rhythms and sound patterns. And a language is always changing; its development in vocabulary, in syntax, pronunciation and intonation—even in the long run, its deterioration—must be accepted by the poet and made the best of. He in turn has the privilege of contributing to the development and maintaining the quality, the capacity of the language to express a wide range, the subtle gradation of feeling and emotion; his task is both to respond to change and make it conscious, and to battle against degradation below the standards which he has learnt from the past.

As Miss Gardner states it: "Mr. Eliot approaches the problem of how the greatest thoughts can be expressed naturally, that is with the ring of the living voice, by concentrating on the problem of how we may 'call a servant or bid a door be shut.' If we can discover a poetic rhythm in the most commonplace speech, this rhythm may then be capable of refinement and elevation so that it may accommodate the greatest thoughts without losing naturalness." Eliot considers the problem again in the fifth section of "East Coker," where he says:

Personal History and the Four Quartets

So here I am, in the middle way, having had twenty years—
Twenty years largely wasted, the years of *l'entre deux guerres*—
Trying to learn to use words, and every attempt
Is a wholly new start, and a different kind of failure
Because one has only learnt to get the better of words
For the thing one no longer has to say, or the way in which
One is no longer disposed to say it. And so each venture
Is a new beginning, a raid on the inarticulate
With shabby equipment always deteriorating
In the general mass of imprecision of feeling,
Undisciplined squads of emotion. And what there is to conquer
By strength and submission, has already been discovered
Once or twice, or several times, by men whom one cannot hope
To emulate—but there is no competition—
There is only the fight to recover what has been lost
And found and lost again and again: and now, under conditions
That seem unpropitious. But perhaps neither gain nor loss.
For us there is only the trying. The rest is not our business.

There is a greater regularity and a greater precision in the
Four Quartets than there was in the earlier poems, but the
thematic musical method of *The Waste Land* has not been
discarded. The symbolic use of lines from poems in older
traditions is still utilized, though less obtrusively. The whole
poem is still bound together by central themes which are
modified and developed as the poem progresses. I have suggested the historical, chronological development, against
which is counterpointed the concerns with Time, Space,
Nature, and the Church. It has also been pointed out that
each of the four poems is concerned with one of the four
elements of tradition: *air* in "Burnt Norton," *earth* in "East
Coker," *water* in "The Dry Salvages," and *fire* in "Little Gidding." There is also the circular pattern, which is the pattern
of music—the return to the point of departure—to the initial
statement. As Eliot stated it in "Little Gidding":

> We shall not cease from exploration
> And the end of our exploring

Will be to arrive where we started
And know the place for the first time.

Adopting our chronological—historical—interpretation, we can here suggest that Eliot has reversed the journey made by his forebears from England to America. In an aesthetic sense, this parallels the unending struggle of the artist to control experience, which is always new experience, but which always brings us back to the old problems. Ideologically, though the terms change and demand our attention, they are seen finally as a restatement of ideas ever-present but ever incapable of a final solution. Eliot prefaces the *Four Quartets* with epigraphs taken from an older literature, as he does most of his poems, and the author in this case is Heracleitus. The first quotation, in translation, reads: "But though the Word is common, the many live as though they have a wisdom of their own"; the second: "The road up and down is one and the same."

The second quotation is most pertinent to our purpose. It can be seen in the ambiguity of Eliot's paradoxes, and may be stated somewhat as follows: Though what the poet says about experience is true, it is also not-true; and the not-true is as true as experience. Such a view represents neither perversity nor pragmatism in the poet. It represents, rather, a recognition of the impossibility of ever achieving a final and absolute truth; it represents a scepticism similar to that of a Melville or a James. On the level of objective experience, it might be stated in terms of the poem as saying: Although T. S. Eliot's grandparents left England for America, they were destined to return, for their grandson returned. The statement that they returned is true, but it is also not-true; yet the phrase that they returned, which is not-true, is as true as the actual experience. Such an experience—and such an attitude toward that experience—projects us onto another level of consideration, more abstract, but still tied to the concrete image: One may be confined by time and by space, yet symbolically unconfined. If the symbolic reference is abstract enough and undefined, we have an ideological resolution of the paradox, as we had in Emerson, where the Over-Soul was indefinite and in-exhaustible, therefore capable of resolving all contradictions. But Eliot was not satisfied with such a resolution. In terms of his figure, the resolution is still represented in a concrete image, the image of the poet himself who retraced his elders' journey; therefore, the attempt at resolution is bound to fail—except in degree: the poet returned and he did not return. *Four Quartets* is a study of the degree in which the poet represents the return, as well as of the degree in which he does not. The impossible resolution, Eliot defines as "the still point," which is a point in time as well as in space:

> At the still point of the turning world. Neither flesh nor
>   fleshless;
> Neither from nor towards; at the still point, there the dance is,
> But neither arrest nor movement. And do not call it fixity,
> Where past and future are gathered. Neither movement from
>   nor towards,
> Neither ascent nor decline. Except for the point, the still
>   point,
> There would be no dance, and there is only the dance.
> I can only say, *there* we have been: but I cannot say where.
> And I cannot say, how long, for that is to place it in time.
> The inner freedom from the practical desire,
> The release from action and suffering, release from the inner
> And the outer compulsion, yet surrounded
> By a grace of sense, a white light still and moving,
> *Erhebung* without motion, concentration
> Without elimination, both a new world
> And the old made explicit, understood
> In the completion of its partial ecstacy,
> The resolution of its partial horror.
> Yet the enchainment of past and future
> Woven in the weakness of the changing body,
> Protects mankind from heaven and damnation
> Which flesh cannot endure.

The experience of "Burnt Norton," the first of the four poems, represents both an actual experience, a walk from a house into a garden, and it represents an intellectual experience in relating objects of the house and garden into a pattern of images concerned with the problem of time: the passageway leading to the garden, the door, the singing of birds in the garden, the rustle of dry leaves, the drained pool, the hidden voices of laughing children. The metaphysical problem concerns the meaning of time, "Time past and time future." "To be conscious," the poet says, "is not to be in time":

> But only in time can the moment in the rose-garden,
> The moment in the arbour where the rain beat,
> The moment in the draughty church at smokefall
> Be remembered; involved with past and future.
> Only through time time is conquered.

To put it another way, only through his involvement with actual facts—and facts in time are historical facts—does man prevent the descent "into a world of perpetual solitude." The image of the children is an attempt at definition. The children are hidden, except for their laughter, which comes from the foliage. They will reveal themselves only when there is a past and a future, a memory and a hope, "Caught," as Eliot says, "in the form of limitation/Between un-being and being." The movement is toward form, toward association in human form, and toward the final goal of love:

> The detail of the pattern is movement,
> As in the figure of the ten stairs.
> Desire itself is movement
> Not in itself desirable;
> Love is itself unmoving,
> Only the cause and end of movement . . .

"East Coker" opens with a portrayal of change: "Houses rise and fall, crumble, are extended/Are removed, destroyed, restored, or in their place/Is an open field, or a factory, or a bypass." The poem begins with a statement, which is a reversal of the motto on Mary Stuart's chair of state, which the poet makes to read: "In my beginning is my end.[6] It is the meditation of the poet, who has reached middle age and is now ruminating upon his beginnings in this village where his ancestors once lived. As he says:

> The knowledge imposes a pattern, and falsifies,
> For the pattern is new in every moment
> And every moment is a new and shocking
> Valuation of all we have been.

The tone of this section is affected by the subject of decay—its mood somber and concerned with thoughts of death:

> O dark dark dark. They all go into the dark,
> The vacant interstellar spaces, the vacant into the vacant,
> The captains, merchant bankers, eminent men of letters,
> The generous patron of art, the statesmen and the rulers,
> Distinguished civil servants, chairmen of many committees,
> Industrial lords and petty contractors, all go into the dark . . .

The speaker admonishes himself to wait without hope, "For hope would be hope of the wrong thing," to wait without love, "For love would be love of the wrong thing." Yet, he says, there is faith; "But the faith and the love and the hope are all in the waiting." "As we grow older," he says, "The world becomes stranger, the pattern more complicated/Of dead and living." The laughter in the garden, which he remembers, echoed ecstacy, but it pointed to the agony of birth and death:

> Our only health is the disease
> If we obey the dying nurse
> Whose constant care is not to please
> But to remind of our, and Adam's curse,
> And that, to be restored, our sickness must grow worse.

[6] This section ends with the original motto: "In my end is my beginning."

The end of the poem affirms the restlessness which took his forebears away from East Coker, for "We must be still and still moving/Into another intensity/For a further union, a deeper communion/Through the dark cold and the empty desolation,/The wave cry, the wind cry, the vast waters/Of the petrel and the porpoise."

"The Dry Salvages," the third poem, concerns itself with an examination of that other "intensity," which is upon our special level the movement to America. America, however, becomes a symbol for a further journey, the investigation of a still deeper past—the past of primitive forces and our early nearness to nature. While it is concerned with this past partly in terms of modern psychological theory, the poet does not fall into the error of that modern thought which examines the past only in order to disown it, to show how man has evolved—has progressed. He says:

> It seems, as one becomes older,
> That the past has another pattern, and ceases to be
>   a mere sequence—
> Or even development; the latter a partial fallacy
> Encouraged by superficial notions of evolution,
> Which becomes, in the popular mind, a means of
>   disowning the past. . . .
>   I have said before
> That the past experience revived in the meaning
> Is not the experience of one life only
> But of many generations—not forgetting
> Something that is probably quite ineffable:
> The backward look behind the assurance
> Of recorded history, the backward half-look
> Over the shoulder, towards the primitive terror.

We are concerned now with a time that is half-magical: the river as "a strong brown god," "keeping his seasons and rages, destroyer, reminder/Of what men choose to forget." The rhythm of the river Eliot remembers as being present in the

nursery bedroom, where it was felt probably with more intensity than by the "dwellers in cities," who believed they had
tamed the god with their bridges and barges and dikes.

The river and the sea are to him reminders of an earlier
creation, just as they were to Melville. "The river is within us,
the sea is all about us." The river's blind force recalls the
primitive urges, the uninhibited libido, the unconscious natural man which still exists within modern man; the sea en-
closes him and defines him in terms of his earliest history,
containing in itself reminders of that time in the forms of
primitive life which it still contains. The time of the sea is the
time of the buoy-bell of the treacherous rocks, which rings not
only with the rhythm of the sea, but with a rhythm of the
ground swell of the earth itself. Such concepts carry us back to
the poems preceding *The Waste Land,* where Eliot considered
the relationship between prehistory and history, such images
as "Christ the tiger," in "Gerontian," or the relationship of
ancient ritual to modern Christian belief. They also carry us
forward into the relationship of psychology and belief in such
later works as *The Family Reunion* and *The Cocktail Party.*

Again, Eliot affirms the urge which causes man to travel—to
explore as his ancestors were part of the exploration of a new
continent. He repeats the advice of Krishna to Arjuna on the
field of battle. It is not, he says, "farewell,/But fare forward,
voyagers." He then offers a prayer to an image of the Virgin,
which stands on the promontory, to all those whose business
has to do with the sea—a sea which like Captain Ahab's is not
only the actual sea, but the mythical sea of historic memory. It
is the sea in which man is bound to venture, but doomed also
to destruction. As Eliot expresses it:

> . . . right action is freedom
> From past and future also.
> But for most of us, this is the aim
> Never here to be realized;
> Who are only undefeated
> Because we have gone on trying.

Or, as he had stated it a few lines earlier:

> But to apprehend
> The point of intersection of the timeless
> With time, is an occupation for the saint—
> No occupation either, but something given
> And taken, in a lifetime's death in love,
> Ardour and selflessness and self-surrender.

Only the saint engages in "right action" and is freed from past and future, and this finally is no action, for it is something which comes of itself as a result of the qualities of love, ardour, selflessness, and self-surrender. These are the conditions of sainthood, but neither the poet nor his ancestors were saints; he is involved in history, racial and personal, and it is only in time that the proper definition can be achieved.

The final poem "Little Gidding" is a return to the present of Eliot's own conversion to Anglo-catholicism, which I suggested earlier represents not necessarily a complete solution to the problem of the poet's self-definition within the corpus of modern life, but, as the poem states it, "the nearest in place and time,/Now and in England." "Here, the intersection of the timeless moment/Is England and nowhere. Never and always." "If you came this way," the poet tells us:

> Taking any route, starting from anywhere,
> At any time or at any season,
> It would always be the same: you would have to put off
> Sense and notion. You are not here to verify,
> Instruct yourself, or inform curiosity
> Or carry report. You are here to kneel
> Where prayer has been valid. And the prayer is more
> Than an order of words, the conscious occupation
> Of the praying mind, or the sound of the voice praying.
> And what the dead had no speech for, when living,
> They can tell you, being dead: the communication
> Of the dead is tongued with fire beyond the language of
>   the living.

The specific "here" is the Nicholas Ferrar chapel at Little Gidding. "Little Gidding," as Miss Helen Gardner describes it,

"is a place of dedication, to which people came with a purpose. It was not the ancestral home of the Ferrars, but a house which old Mrs. Ferrar had bought and to which the family retired during the plague of 1625. In the next year Nicholas Ferrar 'grew to a full resolution and determination of that thing and course of life he had so often wished for and longingly desired. And that week before Whitsunday gave himself to a very private retirement, both in his thoughts and in his person, and was observed to fast much, eate sparingly and sleep little, and on Whitsun Eve he was up all night in his study.' On trinity Sunday he went with his tutor to see Laud, and was ordained deacon, refusing all his life to proceed to the priesthood, and returned to Little Gidding to share his goods with his family and lead that life of ordered devotion and good works which made this remote Huntingdonshire village famous throughout England." For the Anglican Church, Miss Gardner says, "Little Gidding remains 'a symbol perfected in death.' "

For Eliot, I suspect, it remains a symbol of the particular kind of Anglican worship which he prefers, for Nicholas Ferrar, was a high-church Anglican, and the chapel at Little Gidding represented the nearest a good Anglican could come to re-establishing the ceremonial forms frowned upon by many worshippers in the Church of England of the seventeenth century.

With this view we are confronted with an additional irony contained in the motto beginning and ending "East Coker": "In my beginning is my end," "In my end is my beginning." The dissent of the poet's ancestors represented a first step away from high-ceremonial church observance, but this first step was also, paradoxically, the first step toward a return. What does this mean beyond the statement of Heracleitus that "The road up and down is one and the same?" There is no answer except the fact of the return, "So, while the light fails/On a winter afternoon, in a secluded chapel/History is now and England."

We shall not cease from exploration
And the end of our exploring
Will be to arrive where we started
And know the place for the first time.

There are many things which could be said about this poem
in order to approach a complete reading, and many of them
have been said elsewhere. What is important to us here is how
the poet has managed to combine these elements of personal
experience and personal history with the general theme of a
possible existence where time and space intersect and become
a world unlimited by either time or space. It is important, too,
to see how such paradoxes are resolved; or, rather, the degree
to which Eliot admits a solution. For the poet, the hidden
children represent a hint of the future, and the poet himself,
who is the child of his voyaging ancestors, represents also the
future; the long river is both the voyage of the ancestors and
the long voyage backward into historical and racial memory:

At the source of the longest river
The voice of the hidden waterfall
And the children in the apple-tree
Not known, because not looked for
But heard, half heard, in the stillness
Between the two waves of the sea.

The waterfall, which is the source of the river, is heard but is
hidden; the children in the apple-tree are but half-heard in
the stillness between moments filled with distracting sounds.
The important time is "here, now":

Quick now, here, now, always—
A condition of complete simplicity
(Costing not less than everything)
And all shall be well and
All manner of thing shall be well
When the tongues of flame are in-folded
Into the crowned knot of fire
And the fire and the rose are one.

There is a note here of what a psychologically-inclined reader might term "guilt" toward a parent betrayed by the child, but in another sense, such "guilt" may be seen only as a recognition of responsibility to history. And history is Heracleitus as well as religious dissent. What appears to be a simple note of hope at the end of the poem, in the lines "And all shall be well and/All manner of thing shall be well," becomes finally a statement of the need of faith and love in the developed imagery of "the fire" and "the rose."

Even so, such an ending may strike some readers as unnecessarily inconclusive and unjustified, but Eliot does not attempt a complete reconciliation or resolution. Inbedded in the poem are the contrasts between a world which looks only into the future and one which might conceivably look only to the past. T. S. Eliot does not accept either extreme: "The word is neither diffident nor ostentatious." It is not an "easy commerce of the old and the new." It is "The common word exact without vulgarity,/The formal word precise but not pedantic." Exactly where the point is—"the still point," as he calls it—we shall never know in a history or a life-time, but the experience of life, and the experience of the poem, is to narrow the field of possibility, to assist in the definition.

Ernest Hemingway:
The Failure of Sensibility

Too OFTEN CRITICS have been content to accept Ernest Hemingway's attitudes at their face value. Thus, when he writes that all men die like animals, he is put down as a materialist or a naturalist. When he says as he does through the character of Jake Barnes in *The Sun Also Rises,* that all love becomes finally a matter of sex, or through Frederic Henry in *A Farewell to Arms* that the life of man is no more than the struggle of ants on the burning log of a camp fire, the inference is only too plain: he is indeed the spokesman for the lost generation. When he says that morals are what you feel good after, he is put down as an impressionist and a pragmatist.

Just recently, however, his critics have begun to suspect something quite different. Malcolm Cowley, for instance, in referring to his first novel states that "It is a less despairing book than the critics like to think, with their moral conviction that drinkers and fornicators are necessarily unhappy." What Mr. Cowley fails to recognize, apparently, is that this is not alone the dilemma of the critics. It has all along represented

142

the dilemma of the author himself. Mr. Hemingway explains in a short and curious little essay entitled "A Natural History of the Dead" that "The first thing you found out about the dead was that, hit badly enough, they died like animals. Some quickly from a little wound you would not think would kill a rabbit. . . . Others would die like cats . . . that crawl into the coal bin with a bullet in the brain and will not die until you cut their heads off." This certainly represents an ideology of despair in Hemingway, yet there are innumerable examples in his books to contradict this view. Perhaps the most notable is the death of Catherine Barkley in *A Farewell to Arms,* notable because in this case the author is attempting to portray the futility of her death. There is Manuel, the old bullfighter in "The Undefeated." There is Ole Andreson in "The Killers," and there is the stoical Indian who commits suicide because he cannot bear his wife's suffering in "Indian Camp." Though these stories all preceded or were roughly contemporary with "A Natural History of the Dead," these characters do not die like animals. They are all fair examples of human decorum in the face of death.

The first apparently conscious attempt of Mr. Hemingway to reconcile ideology and sensibility appeared in the third novel, *To Have and Have Not,* but the importance of the change was generally overlooked at the time, because the critics' chief concern was for what the Marxists were calling "social consciousness" in fiction. What no one seemed to realize was that this book was a re-examination of the problem presented eight years earlier in *A Farewell to Arms,* with the principal character affirming a kind of lukewarm socialism in place of the nihilism of Frederic Henry. It was a failure on almost every other count. It was badly organized and weak in characterization, and it substituted the tough hero—Harry Morgan—for the sensitive Jake and Frederic of the earlier books. The chief female character, Marie, Harry's wife, is a parallel with, almost a parody of, Frederic Henry's position in the preceding novel. Marie finds no consolation in her husband's death, because she is too old to remarry and certainly unable to find a second husband with a "talent for the bed" as great as Harry's.

The most important point concerning *To Have and Have Not* is that in it the author was struggling for an acceptable form of affirmation for the first time. The attempt was repeated in the play *The Fifth Column*, with Hemingway obviously unable to come to terms with Marxism.

A more satisfactory solution, however, is achieved in the novel, *For Whom the Bell Tolls*. In it, Robert Jordan is made to say:

He fought now in this war because it had started in a country that he loved and he believed in the republic and that if it were destroyed life would be unbearable for all those people who believed in it. He was under Communist discipline for the duration of the war. Here in Spain the Communists offered the best discipline and the soundest and sanest for the prosecution of the war. He accepted their discipline for the duration of the war because, in the conduct of the war, they were the only party whose program and discipline he could accept.

This is, in fact, a rejection of Marxism as well as defeatism, an admission that the conflict of *The Fifth Column*—between personal love and political duty—has been resolved. Communism is merely an expedient for the winning of the war. More important, however, is the suggestion of some greater affirmative value: He fought in this war because it had started *in a country that he loved* and *he believed in the Republic.* If after this statement anyone can still doubt that Mr. Hemingway has reversed himself since *A Farewell to Arms,* let him compare the above statement with the remarks given to Frederic Henry ten years earlier:

I was always embarrassed by the words sacred, glorious, and sacrifice and the expression in vain. We had heard them . . . and had read them, on proclamations that were slapped up by billposters over other proclamations, now for a long time, and I had seen nothing sacred, and the things that were glorious had no glory and the sacrifices were like the stockyards at Chicago if nothing was done with the meat except to bury it.

It is not only that the explicit statement indicates a changed point of view on the part of the author. The shift from a negative to an affirmative philosophy demands a shift in the resultant action. Thus, while Frederic Henry deserts the Italian army, Robert Jordan continues a mission which he knows to be hopeless. He continues despite the knowledge, uncertain though it is, that he is to die as a result of that mission. He continues despite the confusion in command, which was almost as disorganized as the retreat at Caporetto and which was one of the motives for Frederic's desertion. He continues despite a love affair in every way similar to the attachment of Frederic to Catherine, and just as in the first affair, the philosophical change is even clearer when we are directly concerned with the relationship between Robert Jordan and Maria. "Is it all right for me to love Maria?" Hemingway has Robert ask.

Yes, himself said.
Even if there isn't supposed to be any such thing as love in a purely materialistic conception of society?
Since when did you ever have any such conception? himself asked. Never. And you never could have. You're not a real Marxist and you know it. You believe in Liberty, Equality, and Fraternity. You believe in Life, Liberty, and the Pursuit of Happiness. . . . You have put many things in abeyance to win a war. If this war is lost all of those things are lost.

But we must realize that Ernest Hemingway has not been, from the beginning, primarily interested in political ideology. To deny the materialism is a long step toward answering the questions he had asked in the relationship of Jake and Brett Ashley, or Frederic and Catherine, but it is again simply a denial, not a solution. This is suggested by Maria, a Spanish girl raised in the Neo-Platonic tradition of Roman Catholicism. "But we will be one now and there will never be a separate one," she is made to say early in the book. "I will be thee when thou art not there." Robert Jordan apparently accepts this, for at the end of the book, when he is wounded and when the only possibility of the party's escaping lies in their leaving him behind, he talks with her:

> *"Guapa,"* he said to Maria and took hold of her two hands. "Listen. We will not be going to Madrid—"
> Then she started to cry.
> "No, *guapa,* don't," he said. "Listen. We will not go to Madrid now but I go with thee wherever thou goest. Understand?"
> She said nothing and pushed her head against his cheek with her arms around him.
> "Listen to this well, rabbit," he said. He knew there was a great hurry and he was sweating very much, but this had to be said and understood. "Thou wilt go now, rabbit. But I go with thee. As long as there is one of us there is both of us. Do you understand?"

This is the end of despair and futility—the end of the "lost generation." It was no accident that Ernest Hemingway took the title for this novel from a seventeenth-century devotion of John Donne or that he quoted a section of the devotion in his preface, for there is more of Donne in *For Whom the Bell Tolls* than the critics have imagined. Both authors were gifted with a highly developed sensitivity, making them doubly aware of the diversity of nature and of human experience. Both were conscious of the breakdown of institutional humanism—the conflict of science and the church—and both were particularly concerned with those mysteries for which an expanding knowledge of natural science was unable to supply the answer. As though to erase any doubt as to his final solution, the twentieth-century author has Robert Jordan consider the problem again while he is awaiting death at the hands of the fascists.

> Try to believe what you told her. That is the best. And who says it is not true? Not you. You didn't say it, anymore than you would say the things did not happen that happened. Stay with what you

believe now. Don't get cynical. The time is too short and you have just sent her away. Each one does what he can. You can do nothing for yourself but perhaps you can do something for another.

Mr. Hemingway might very well have been talking to himself as he wrote those lines.

II

Upon the appearance of *For Whom the Bell Tolls* in 1940, the reviewers, with their customary enthusiasm, hailed it as a masterpiece. Mr. Howard Mumford Jones, writing in *The Saturday Review of Literature,* went so far as to state that "Manner has been replaced by style, and the mere author has died out in the artist." More considered evaluations since then have either evaded the comparison or have come out strongly for the view that it is inferior to *The Sun Also Rises* and *A Farewell to Arms.* Alfred Kazin is most perceptive when he states, in his critical volume *On Native Grounds:* "Yet *For Whom the Bell Tolls* is among the least of Hemingway's works. . . . And if one compares this work of his ambitious conversion, with its eloquence, its calculation, and its romantic inflation with the extraordinarily brilliant story of this period, 'The Snows of Kilimanjaro,' it is clear that the attempted affirmation of life in the novel, while passionate enough, is moving only in itself, while the concentrated study of wastes and death in the story is perfectly dramatic, perfectly Hemingway's own."

Mr. Jones' statement is most curious because it states the superiority of the novel on the grounds that most critics have used to condemn it, namely upon the basis of style. Most critics would agree, I suppose, that Hemingway's early style represents the triumph of his work, and that the novel is unsuccessful because it attempts to go beyond the sparse understatement, the "premeditated casualness," as one critic has called it, of the earlier works.

The argument goes something like this: The Hemingway

style, with its short, crisp sentences, its ironic contrast between understatement and violent action, is perfectly suited to bear the weight of brutal action in the bull ring, the big-game hunt, and the prize ring, but is incapable of sustaining the long passages of description and meditation to be found in *For Whom the Bell Tolls*. While there is some truth in this argument, it represents a superficial attitude toward the problem of style. If we examine the passages already quoted from *A Farewell to Arms* and *For Whom the Bell Tolls*, we will discover that the failure of the passage from the latter does not come as a result of an attempt to wrestle with ideology in terms of simplicity or complexity of language. It is true that the quotation from the later book does have a slightly more complicated structure, but we could revise the selection from *A Farewell to Arms* to approximate the later passage, thus:

I was always embarrassed by the words sacred, glorious, and sacrifice and the expression in vain, *because* I had heard them . . . and had read them, on proclamations that were slapped up by billposters over other proclamations, now for a long time, and *because* I had nothing sacred, and the things that were glorious had no glory and the sacrifices were like the stockyards at Chicago if nothing was done with the meat except to bury it.

It will be seen that the insertion of the italicized subordinating conjunctions do little to weaken this passage. Its strength lies in the shocking force of its imagery. Yet there are few sentences more complicated than this in *For Whom the Bell Tolls*. Even in the passages of meditation, Hemingway adopts a rhetorical device already familiar from the earlier works: he has the speaker cross-examine himself, and if this manner seems stilted and sometimes artificial it is more noticeable in *For Whom the Bell Tolls* only because it is slightly more common. *For Whom the Bell Tolls* is a longer book than its predecessors. It is a more pretentious work. True, its pages seem more crowded, and its paragraphs are longer, and the picture is obscured slightly by the device which the author uses in an attempt to catch the idiom of its Spanish dialogue. I do not feel, however, that this feature represents the failure of Ernest Hemingway's style. The same charge could be made against the style of his two latest short stories, at least one of which represents the high point in Mr. Hemingway's method. His failure in the novels is, indeed, a stylistic failure, but not superficially. It is a failure of that insight—that sensitivity—which is part and parcel of his style.

The reader may well ask what is meant by insight or sensitivity. I mean that perceptivity or natural awareness of the artist for the variety and range of sense objects surrounding him in nature and which he consciously or unconsciously organizes or synthesizes into an artful pattern or form. Thus the creation of a *meaningful* (ideological) image or the formation of a *meaningful* order of events from the raw material of nature is the result of the artist's sensibility in operation. Speaking of Hemingway's sensibility, Cleanth Brooks and Robert Penn Warren, in their book *Understanding Fiction,* say:

The short simple rhythms, the succession of co-ordinate clauses, and the general lack of subordination—all suggest a dislocated, an ununified world. Hemingway is apparently trying to suggest in his style the direct experience—things as seen and felt, one after another, and not as the mind arranges and analyzes them.

The weakness of Hemingway, from the beginning, has been that he has attempted—at some place or another in every novel—to pause and comment upon the material—to force it to his own ideological end—to moralize. That this tendency has not been noticed and condemned is due primarily to the manner in which it has been done, through a series of sharp—often shocking—images that were successful in themselves though not integrated with the work: life as a baseball game where each error is punished by death or compared to the struggle of ants on a burning log, condemned because the "Messiah" is too lazy or too insensible to do anything about it, the comparison of a hero's death with the slaughter of animals at the stockyard. Hemingway's sensibility, like John Donne's, has always worked upon an immediate, objective level, which translates ideas into terms of concrete things. Donne's imagery is, upon a superficial glance, even more impious and shocking: the flea becomes the God-head, the church is depicted as a prostitute, or man's sick body is likened to a flat map. To choose an example near to one facet of Hemingway's subject in *For Whom the Bell Tolls,* we can point to the use of the compass in "A Valediction: Forbidding Mourning." Speaking of the separate souls of the two lovers who must part, Donne says:

> If they be two, they are two so
> As stiff twin compasses are two.

This is exactly the point Hemingway wishes to make in the problem confronting Robert and Maria:

> Dull sublunary lovers' love,
>   Whose soul is sense, cannot admit
> Absence, because it doth remove
>   Those things which elemented it.
>
> But we by a love so much refined
>   That ourselves know not what it is,
> Inter-assurëd of the mind,
>   Care less eyes, lips, hands to miss

But it is a point so completely foreign to the explicit statement in the early Hemingway, that when he comes to stating it, his muse (to make use of a conception still valid except in terminology) fails him. Robert can only assure Maria that, "I will go with thee." He cannot rise above the simple statement: "As long as there is one of us there is both of us."

This is illustrated even better in the passage where Robert Jordan is attempting to justify the affirmative value which he has discovered in the continuation of his mission. The objectification is on so simple and so conventional a level that it lacks conviction, and perhaps this is the reason so few critics have even admitted its presence. He fought in a war because *it had started in a country that he loved* and *he believed in the Republic.* This argument might have come from the platform of any patriotic orator, and it is a failure, not because it is an affirmative value, not because it is a patriotic sentiment, but because it is conventional and trite. When he says, "You believe in Liberty, Equality, and Fraternity. You believe in Life, Liberty, and the Pursuit of Happiness," the author is attempting to rely only upon generalities which, admirable as they may be as a statement or even as symbols of democracy, are not sharp enough to carry the emotional weight put upon them. And rather than summing up with a striking image, as he does in the passage cited from the early novel, he ends with the puerile statement: "You have put many things in abeyance to win a war."

I do not mean to suggest that Ernest Hemingway's failure is entirely a matter of imagery. I have mentioned his well-known use of understatement. Its effectiveness is still evident in the final novel in such passages as the one where Robert Jordan is awaiting the arrival of the fascists at the end of the book. Robert has sent Maria, Pilar, and the others on, and he has lain in ambush, hoping to delay the enemy, hoping to get himself killed quickly. The tension of the scene is held in the casual manner in which the author soliloquizes about their coming. "Robert Jordan's luck held very good because he saw, just then, the cavalry ride out of the timber and cross the road." The fact that Hemingway can state the arrival of the enemy as an example of Robert Jordan's luck holding is an illustration of the effectiveness of the use of understatement in moments of crisis. But the irony operates within a small frame. It refers, perhaps, as far back as Jordan's separation from Maria, but it does not, as it is capable of doing in the short stories, pick up and charge the whole narrative with meaning, as it does, for instance, in the case of Manuel, the bullfighter, at the end of "The Undefeated."

"I was going good," Manuel insists just as he is about to die, and the reader agrees with him. He was indeed "going good," but not in the ordinary sense. The spectators had not thought he was "going good." They had thrown cushions into the bull ring, and one of these cushions was, indirectly, the cause of his death. In "The Killers" it is the constant interplay between the world of normality and the "unreal" world of the gangsters that is highlighted by the irony of understatement. Mrs. Bell, the maid at Mrs. Hirsh's boarding house, represents the normal world on its simplest level. She it is who, in talking about Ole Andreson, the man who is awaiting the arrival of the killers, says: "He's been in his room all day. . . . I guess he don't feel well. I said to him: 'Mr. Andreson, you ought to go out and take a walk on a nice day like this,' but he didn't feel like it." This speech elucidates the whole relationship between Nick and the world of the Killers; it suggests all the relationships in the story—the various levels between Mrs. Bell's unconscious normality and Ole's complete awareness and acceptance—all of which have their representations in other characters.

But these short stories are focused upon relatively small, isolated worlds with clearly defined codes. Though the interpretation is complex, the references are simple. The reader is left with two primary objections: 1. Too much dependence upon the method of understatement leaves him with a feeling of having been tricked or cheated. This accounts for those readers who have complained that Ernest Hemingway's style was "forced" or "unreal." 2. Too limited a background gives the impression that the author is concerned only with the sensibilities of simple people, which accounts for the accusation that Hemingway is interested only in the values of a primitive society.

On the other hand, there is at least one example of an almost perfect integration. In the story "The Short and Happy Life of Francis Macomber" these objections are overcome by the use of a third, and more common, type of irony—that which is inherent in the action itself. To use an expression of T. S. Eliot, Ernest Hemingway has, in this story, found the "objective correlative" for the conveyance of emotion and theme. The scene is laid in Africa, where an American sportsman has just shown himself to be a coward on the hunt. The body of the story is concerned with the subtle relationships between Francis Macomber and his wife which are thrown out of balance by the act of cowardice. Margot, the wife, feels herself freed of restraint by his violation of their unspoken code, and she is untrue to him. When he redeems himself by standing up to a charging water buffalo, she, under a pretense of shooting the animal, sends a bullet into his brain.

But a simple statement of the action does not suggest the careful and intricate weaving of it by the author, the subtle ironies which combine and reinforce the final irony of Francis Macomber's death—another example of victory in the face of death. "That was a pretty thing to do," the guide said in a toneless voice. "He would have left you too." Ernest Hemingway has not only found the objective correlative, he has allowed it to carry its proper burden in the story even though it contradicted the views expressed in "A Natural History of the Dead." This is true also of "The Snows of Kilimanjaro" where the author not only does not refute the obvious theme of his story, but where he uses a highly self-conscious symbolism to reinforce it. While I consider this story one of Hemingway's best, I do not share Mr. Kazin's enthusiasm for it. The story is technically more complex than most, but it is spoiled for me by the conventionality of its leading symbol: the White-capped mountain as the House of God.

Which brings us again to the problem presented in *For Whom the Bell Tolls:* whether Ernest Hemingway has succeeded finally in freeing himself from a conception which he was unable to integrate with the material supplied him by his sensitivity, and if he has, why has he not succeeded in writing his masterpiece in this final novel? The first half of the problem has, I believe, been solved. The answer to the second lies inherent in the comparison with John Donne. While the seventeenth-century poet began with a doubt similar to Hemingway's and while his work exhibits a similar self-searching, he ended with a recognition that the mystery was real and absolute and could be expressed as an art object:

> Betray, kind husband, thy spouse to our sights,
> And let mine amorous soul court thy mild dove,
> Who is most true and pleasing to thee then
> When she is embraced and open to most men.

The paradoxical image he recognized as the most that could be said concerning divine mystery. Also, his sensitivity seemed to be functioning at its highest point of awareness when confronted by such a mystery. We get the shocking, almost irreverent, image of the church, the bride of Christ, becoming a mild, innocent prostitute courted by all men. The crowded imagery of the lines, the paradoxical resolution suggest a certainty-within-uncertainty, a conclusion tinged with irony, which is the objectification of the emotion Donne obviously wished to convey. It is not merely that he, like Plato's poet, is singing hymns of praise to God. He is suggesting the subtle relationship between the poet—between man and God.

Hemingway's sensitivity, too, has presented him with such paradoxes. Mr. Cowley has suggested one of them in his discussion of *The Sun Also Rises:* There are some positive values suggested in the novel, despite Jake Barnes' belief (as stated) that his impotency is the final, degrading blow. "It always gets around to that," he tells Brett Ashley, who apparently accepts this judgment, for almost the entire novel is concerned with her experimentation with sex. Yet her final act is one of restraint. "You know it feels rather good deciding not to be a bitch," she tells Jake after giving up the young bullfighter.

The familiar theme of death is, similarly, a kind of paradox —even Catherine's statement of it: "I'm not afraid," she tells Frederic, "I just hate it." But the chiefly paradoxical nature of the incident lies in the fact that Catherine does not die like an animal. She hates it, but she is not afraid to talk about it, and she seems almost more concerned for Frederic than for herself. Likewise, though more completely, the death of Francis Macomber is an exemplification of the paradoxical idea that man achieves his greatest success through death.

I do not mean to say that, except in the instance of "The Short and Happy Live," Ernest Hemingway was consciously attempting to portray death as anything other than what he explicitly says it is in "A Natural History of the Dead." The paradox is not conscious, as it was with Donne, but results, rather, from the conflict between his ideology, on the one hand, and his sensitivity, which, on the other, could not force his materials into the mould prepared for it. The early novels are successful partly because of this conflict and partly despite it. They are not completely successful, and Ernest Hemingway himself must have been aware of this by the time he came to write *To Have and Have Not*.

I have suggested that part of this failure lay in the inability of the author's style to encompass a form so large and inclusive as that of the novel. His greatest successes, particularly in the early works, were with the short story. This is as true of *For Whom the Bell Tolls* as it was of the first two, but it is not the whole story. In *For Whom the Bell Tolls* there is, in addition, a failure of that sensibility which had served him so well in the early books. At that time he was more or less certain in his point of view, though it did, as we have seen, conflict with the objective portrayal of natural experience. By the time we come to the final novel, the solution is pat. Robert Jordan did not believe in Marxism, he believed in democracy. But what is democracy? It is life, liberty, and the pursuit of happiness. This is the answer of the rhetorician, the public orator, or the moralist, it is not the method of the artist. What about religion? He did not believe in materialism; he accepted a form of mysticism similar to that of John Donne. Notice:

Listen, one thing. Do you remember? Pilar and the hand? Do you believe that crap? No, he said. Not with everything that's happened?

No, I don't believe it. She was nice about it early this morning before the show started. She was afraid maybe I believed it. I don't though. But she does. They see something. Or they feel something. Like a bird-dog. What about extra-sensory perception?

Ernest Hemingway's conversion seems to have been a struggle, not so much against doubt as a struggle for complete acceptance of the affirmative aspects of democracy and Christianity, and this seems somehow to have made him susceptible to general phrases of belief rather than to the striking objective portrayal of which he is capable. There is but a single figure of speech in the above passage. It refers to Pilar's claim for supernaturalism, and it could be restated something like this: She sees something or feels something, like a bird dog. Contrast this with the striking example already cited from *A Farewell to Arms:* The death of a hero in war is like the stockyards at Chicago if nothing was done with the meat except to bury it.

It is the difference between the expression of those two ideas which I would term the failure of sensibility in Ernest Hemingway. It illustrates, I believe, the fallacy of a more or less popular theory today that to clothe oneself in an affirmative ideology is enough to assure the "responsibility" of the artist. Rather, if we examine the evidence of novelists from Tolstoi to Aldous Huxley, I believe we can convince ourselves of the opposite. The artist has a greater responsibility to his sensibility in relation to his materials than he has to any body of abstract knowledge. The ideology is not imposed upon the material, it grows out of it, and any attempt to impose it results in artistic failure.

This is not to say that Ernest Hemingway is a failure in the usual sense of the word. The measure of his failure lies only in comparison with the very best writers in the genre—perhaps with Dostoievsky and Henry James. He has written a few of the best short stories of our age. His present limitations would incline me to prefer that his future work would be done in the field of the short story, but these are limitations no greater than have been overcome by other artists. Our greatest hope lies in the fact that he has never, despite appearances to the contrary, relaxed his self-searching. But this is not ground for hope alone. It is a test of the "responsibility" of a writer who has become the chief target for all charges of "irresponsibility."

A Farewell to Arms

E RNEST HEMINGWAY'S first three important works were *In Our Time,* a collection of curiously related short stories; *The Sun Also Rises,* his first serious and successful novel; and *A Farewell to Arms.* All three deal with the same subject: the condition of man in a society upset by the violence of war. The short stories, while complete (almost idyllic) within themselves, take on an added dimension when viewed against the animal-cruelty of the connecting war scenes. *The Sun Also Rises,* although set in the postwar period, is conditioned by the wartime disability of its principal figure, Jake Barnes. But the setting for *A Farewell to Arms* is the war itself, and the romance of Frederic Henry and Catherine Barkley, their attempt to escape the war and its resulting chaos, is a parable of twentieth-century man's disgust and disillusionment at the failure of civilization to achieve the ideals it had been promising throughout the nineteenth century. While the relation of one story to another in *In Our Time* is more or less arbitrary, while the meandering action of the ex-patriots' excursion into Spain in *The Sun Also Rises* is at most emblematic, the sequence of events in *A Farewell to Arms* is ordered and logical to an extreme which (outside of Henry James) is the exception in the American novel.

A Farewell to Arms

As a matter of fact, the physical form of *A Farewell to Arms* more nearly resembles the drama than it does the majority of American works of fiction. It is composed of five separate books, each composed of a series of scenes, and each scene broken into sections which might be likened to stage direction and dialogue. Thus, in section one we have the introduction of all major characters, the general war setting, and a statement of the problems involved; in section two, the development of the romance between Frederic and Catherine; in section three, the retreat at Caporetto and the decision of Frederic to escape the chaos of war; in section four, the supposed escape, the rowing of Frederic and Catherine across the lake into Switzerland; and in section five, the hope of sanctuary which, through a reversal reminiscent again of the drama, comes to a climax in the ironic scene of Catherine's death while giving birth to their child.

As Robert Penn Warren has pointed out (*Kenyon Review:* Winter, 1947), *A Farewell to Arms,* while not a religious book in the usual sense, depends upon a consciousness of the religious problems of our time. Its subject is the search for truth— for ethical standards to replace those which seemed impossible under the wartime conditions which it depicts. The use of the Christian religion is not, however, confined to the conventional uses of the ordinary religious novel, in which the characters are evaluated according to their acceptance or rejection of orthodox views. Rather, it is ironically implied, for instance, that Catherine, who is repeatedly portrayed as one with no orthodox religious sense, is really on the side of the priest, whose orthodoxy is beyond question. It is implied, too, that the priest's religious sensibility, like the sensibility of all of the participants in the novel's action, is heightened by the events of the war. After the difficult summer, during which Frederic was confined in the hospital, all of the men in his group have been softened. "Where are all the good old priest-baiters?" Rinaldi asks. "Do I have to bait this priest alone without support?" Frederic could see that the baiting which had gone on earlier did not touch the priest now. In talking with the priest he makes a distinction which is important to our interpretation of all the characters: even the priest is now not only technically a Christian, he is more like Our Lord. "It is," Frederic says, "in defeat that we become Christians."

On the other hand, it is not merely the humility of defeat, but the result of active participation (a firsthand acquaintance with the objective facts instead of the abstract theories of warfare) which makes all the difference. Outward forms divorced from action do not suffice, as when the soldier under Frederic refuses to believe that the Austrians were going to attack, because, as he said, "What has been done this summer cannot have been done in vain." Frederic thinks:

I was always embarrassed by the words sacred, glorious, and sacrifice and the expression in vain. We had heard them, sometimes standing in the rain almost out of earshot, so that only the shouted words came through, and had read them, on proclamations that were slapped up by billposters over other proclamations, now for a long time, and I had seen nothing sacred, and the things that were glorious had no glory and the sacrifices were like the stockyards at Chicago if nothing was done with the meat except to bury it. There were many words that you could not stand to hear and finally only the names of places had dignity.

When the words became separated from the acts they were meant to describe, then they meant nothing; the slaughter of war was less than the slaughter of animals in the stockyard. The names of places had dignity because the places still had some objective reality. Likewise, the acts of Rinaldi when he is practicing his craft, of Dr. Valentini (but not of the incompetent physicians), have dignity because they are done surely and skillfully—to some purpose. The early stages of Frederic and Catherine's courtship were like moves in a chess game or a game of bridge; later it became something different, so different that even the outward form of marriage could make no difference. Catherine asks: "What good would it do to marry now? We're really married. I couldn't be any more married."

A Farewell to Arms

Even the war, when Frederic was no longer participating, "seemed as far away as the football games of someone else's college." No activity has meaning unless the participant is emotionally involved; this is the real test, like the names of places. There is Christianity and there are true Christians. There is incompetence and competence. There is marriage and there is true love. In a story in *In Our Time,* we have the picture of a bullfighter who is defeated and derided by the crowd, but he is really "The Undefeated" (the title of the story), because he is only outwardly not inwardly defeated. As we have seen, in "The Short Happy Life" even death does not defeat Francis Macomber, for it is in death that he triumphs.

But what is the real distinction between the failures—the defeated—and the genuine men and women in the novel—what critics have come to call "the initiated"? Rinaldi (who is one of them) says to Frederic at the time when Frederic returns to the front: "You puncture me when I become a great Italian thinker. But I know many things I can't say." Frederic, when he is talking to the priest after his return from the hospital, says: "I never think and yet when I begin to talk I say the things I have found out in my mind without thinking." There are times when Catherine "feels" immoral, but most of the time she "feels" that her love is sanctified. The peasants and the defeated soldiers have wisdom because they are not misled by the empty forms. Hemingway seems to be saying, like William Wordsworth, that such men are by circumstance closer to reality—and thus to wisdom. In the book which followed *A Farewell to Arms—Death in the Afternoon* —Hemingway says, "Morals are what you feel good after." Brett Ashley in *The Sun Also Rises* decides to give up a love affair because it makes her *feel* good "deciding not to be a bitch." The test of morals is the unadulterated sensibility— the sensibility not misled by the empty forms of patriotism, religion, and love: the sensibility of Rinaldi when he does not attempt to be a great Italian thinker; the sensibility of Dr.

161

Valentini, who knows at once what is to be done and does it without quibble and consultation; the sensibility of the peasants; the sensibility of Catherine, who learns from her love for Frederic that it is all right, who says: "Everything we do seems so innocent and simple. I can't believe we do anything wrong." Even the sensibility of Frederic, which is the developing moral sense of the novel, is superior to Rinaldi's because it has greater scope—the surgeon is happy only when he is working. "I know more than you," Rinaldi says, and Frederic agrees with him. "But you will have a better time. Even with remorse you will have a better time."

It is this limiting quality in Frederic's character which points to the principal problem of the novel. Rinaldi calls it remorse. Frederic cannot completely escape the forms of his early training, though he makes a systematic progress throughout the book. Before he was wounded he had attempted to accept Catherine's philosophy that death is the end, but his experience seemed to prove otherwise, for in her antireligious position Catherine is as orthodox as the priest. Frederic says: "I felt myself rush bodily out of myself and out and out and out and all the time bodily in the wind. I went out swiftly, all of myself, and I knew I was dead and that it had all been a mistake to think you just died." This is Hemingway's mysticism which triumphed in *For Whom the Bell Tolls* and which was at its lowest ebb in his curious little essay "A Natural History of the Dead." Frederic does not love God, but he is afraid of him in the night sometimes. Because he does not "belong," he and Catherine cannot find sanctuary in the church the evening they are waiting for the train, though an Italian couple does. Yet Frederic is much more anxious about the absence of the marriage ceremony than Catherine, and when the child is born dead he is disturbed because it had not been baptized. The limitations of Frederic's religious sensibility (a symbol for the religious sensibility of our time) are depicted in two scenes, the first in his failure to visit the home of the priest at Abruzzi, where "You would like the people and though it is cold it is clear and dry"; the second is the incident at the church:

> There were streetcar tracks and beyond them was the cathedral. It was white and wet in the mist. We crossed the tram tracks. On our left were the shops, their windows lighted, and the entrance to the galleria. There was a fog in the square and when we came close to the front of the cathedral it was very big and the stone was wet.
> "Would you like to go in?"
> "No," Catherine said. We walked along. There was a soldier standing with his girl in the shadow of one of the stone buttresses ahead of us and we passed them. They were standing tight up against the stone and he had put his cape around her.
> "They're like us," I said.
> "Nobody is like us," Catherine said. She did not mean it happily.
> "I wish they had some place to go."
> "It mightn't do them any good."
> "I don't know. Everybody ought to have some place to go."
> "They have the cathedral," Catherine said.

Catherine and Frederic have a hotel room (the "lost generation"), while the Italian soldier and his girl have the cathedral; the priest has his cold, clear, dry country; the atheists have their houses of prostitution. The priest's country appeals to Frederic, and he is sorry he did not visit it while he was on leave:

> I had wanted to go to Abruzzi. I had gone to no place where the roads were frozen and hard as iron, where it was clear cold and dry and the snow was dry and powdery and hare-tracks in the snow and the peasants took off their hats and called you Lord and there was good hunting. I had gone to no such place but to the smoke of cafés and nights when the room whirled and you needed to look at the wall to make it stop, nights in bed, drunk, when you knew that that was all there was, and the strange excitement of waking and not knowing who it was with you, and the world all unreal in the dark and so exciting that you must resume again

unknowing and not caring in the night, sure that this was all and all and all and not caring.

Here is the symbol of Frederic's predicament, a key passage, since it represents the religious contrast. The priest's religion is his clear, cold country; Catherine's religion is her love, which, as Count Greffi says, "is a religious feeling," or, as Catherine tells Frederic: "You're my religion. You're all I've got." Frederic is the modern hero, lost between two worlds, the world of tradition and certainty which he cannot wholly relinquish, and the exciting but uncertain world of the twentieth century, where you only occasionally find something substantial to look at to make everything stop whirling, where you live for the moment, giving yourself up to sensations, for it is through the senses that you discover truth: the strong man giving equal odds to his weaker opponent, the boxer, the hunter, the bullfighter, the soldier, and the lover; the strong man aware that the only order in the universe is that which he himself can supply, but aware, too, that such order is transitory, that perhaps the highest possible values consist in pure sensation which seeks out new order and a stoicism which transcends physical defeat.

II

At the beginning Frederic wavers between reason and sensibility, between formal religion and "true" Christianity, between the empty forms of love and true love. He has been thrust into a world of violent action in which choice is eventually to become necessary. An English critic has called Frederic "a curiously passive hero," but this is true only in the sense that Thomas Mann's Herr Friedemann was passive. The Hemingway hero is, theoretically, passive, because he is allied to nature through his unreason, but his particular dilemma usually has all the appearances of active seeking.

Frederic's relationship to Catherine in Book I is like a game where you pretend to be playing for stakes, but do not know what the stakes are. At the end of the section Frederic is wounded, but not seriously. It is the first hint that what he had called "the picturesque front" was capable of becoming something else. It is a foreshadowing of the retreat at Caporetto.

In Book II the action takes place in the American hospital at Milan, and almost at once we know that the formal relationship (love like a bridge game or a game of chess) has ended. Frederic thinks:

> God knows I had not wanted to fall in love with her. I had not wanted to fall in love with any one. But God knows I had and I lay on the bed in the room of the hospital in Milan and all sorts of things went through my head but I felt wonderful . . .

We are introduced to the incompetent doctors and to the professional patriots like Ettore. Frederic, although he cannot reject Ettore as completely as Catherine, does reject his own decoration, because he knows that he is not a hero. The silver metal repeats the pattern of the empty form. A new action is suggested in this book by Catherine's fear of death. She is afraid of the rain, she says, and when pressed by Frederic for an explanation, admits that it is because she sometimes sees herself dead in it. Frederic is unbelieving. "And sometimes I see you dead in it," she adds. "That's more likely," Frederic says. "No it's not, darling. Because I can keep you safe. I know I can. But nobody can help themselves." Here is one of the secrets of the passivity of Hemingway's characters. Later in the section, when Catherine admits that she is going to have a baby:

> "You aren't angry are you, darling?"
> "No."
> "And you don't feel trapped?"
> "Maybe a little. But not by you."
> "I didn't mean by me. You must be stupid. I meant trapped at all."
> "You always feel trapped biologically."

"Biologically," in the Hemingway world, covers just about everything; there is nothing you can do about life but accept it with stoicism. This is an anticipation of the final scenes in the novel, but Frederic, fortunately, did not realize how final the trap was:

Poor, poor dear Cat. And this was the price you paid for sleeping together. This was the end of the trap. This was what people got for loving each other.

In this book, however, the threat is taken only seriously enough to provoke discussion of death and the conditions of man's dying. Frederic has quoted the line, "The coward dies a thousand deaths, the brave but one"; Catherine replies: "The brave dies perhaps two thousand deaths if he's intelligent. He simply doesn't mention them."

There is an indication that Frederic is very little different from Catherine in his fear of death. They are in a café and it is raining. He quotes Andrew Marvell: "But at my back I always hear/Time's wing'd chariot hurrying near." He wants to talk facts. Where will the baby be born? Catherine refuses (stoically) to discuss it. "Then don't worry, darling," she tells him. "You were fine until now and now you're worrying."

The tone of this section suggests death, but the reader does not know, any more than do Catherine and Frederic, whose death it is to be. Frederic returns to the front, where there are rumors of a new attack by the Austrians. Catherine awaits the time when she will have her baby. Both are, in a sense, trapped—trapped by the war, by their love, and (though they are unaware of it) by death.

At the very beginning of Book III we are introduced to the town of Caporetto. Frederic "remembered it as a little white town with a campanile in a valley. It was a clean little town and there was a fine fountain in the square." This is where the summer fighting has ended. One of Hemingway's most constant symbols of the goal which his heroes seek is—to utilize the title of one of his stories—"A Clean, Well-Lighted

Place." War has undoubtedly destroyed the "clean little town," but this is just an additional indication of war's ugliness. Caporetto is the point where the Austrians succeed in breaking through and turning Frederic's "picturesque front" into a machine of destruction. There are only isolated examples of decency and order in the retreat; the whole atmosphere is one of anarchy and confusion.

Malcolm Cowley has likened Frederic's plunge into the river to escape execution as a baptism—a symbol of Frederic's entering the world of the initiated, but this is true only in so far as it refers to his decision (his rebirth) concerning the war. The chapters preceding, where Frederic returns to the front and meets his old comrades, indicates both how much he had learned through his stay at the hospital (the baptism of love) and how much the members of his company have learned through the difficult fighting of the summer (their baptism of fire), but the final consecration does not come until later when Frederic is confronted by love and death at the same time. The retreat does, however, represent a major phase in his initiation. Frederic is in the position of the fat gray-haired little lieutenant colonel whom the carabinieri were questioning at the bridge:

The questioners had all the efficiency, coldness and command of themselves of Italians who are firing and are not being fired on.
"Your brigade?"
He told them.
"Regiment?"
He told them.
"Do you not know that an officer should be with his troops?"
He did.
That was all. Another officer spoke.
"It is you and such as you that have let the barbarians onto the sacred soil of the fatherland."
"I beg your pardon," said the lieutenant-colonel.
"It is because of treachery such as yours that we have lost the fruits of victory."
"Have you ever been in a retreat?" the lieutenant-colonel asked.

The military police are firing but are not being fired on. They are like religious persons who have never been tempted, condemning the sinner who has succumbed; the police have the hollow shell of patriotism, using such phrases as "the sacred soil of the fatherland" and "the fruits of victory," but it is punctured by the lieutenant colonel's simple question: "Have you ever been in a retreat?" The carabiniere's brave words have no relation to the reality of the situation, while the condemned man's question goes right to the heart of it. Frederic rationalizes his own situation as follows:

You had lost your cars and your men as a floorwalker loses the stock of his department in a fire. There was, however, no insurance. You were out of it now. You had no more obligation. If they shot the floorwalkers after a fire in the department store because they spoke with an accent that they always had, then certainly the floor-walkers would not be expected to return when the store opened again for business. They might seek other employment; if there was any other employment and the police did not get them.

Anger was washed away in the river along with any obligation. Although that ceased when the carabiniere put his hands on my collar. I would like to have had the uniform off *although I did not care much about the outward forms* (my italics). I had taken off the stars, but that was for convenience. It was no point of honor. I was not against them. I was through. I wished them all the luck. There were the good ones, and the brave ones, and the calm ones, and the sensible ones, and they deserved it. But it was not my show any more and I wished this bloody train would get to Mestre and I would eat and stop thinking. I would have to stop.

The fighter obeys the rules until they are suspended or no longer enforced; then he gets out of the ring (cf. Margot Macomber in "The Short Happy Life"). With the retreat at Caporetto, the Austrian front ceased to be "the picturesque front"; it is no longer subject to the traditional rules of "honorable" warfare. Frederic, too, for the time being ceases to be the "curiously passive hero." He cannot escape the war until he escapes from Italy with Catherine, and to escape is to struggle.

Yet according to the standards of Frederic Henry's world, such a decision is in itself dangerous. His reasoning is too pat, his assurance too great. The determination to struggle becomes a kind of "tragic flaw"—a brash modern pride which tempts fate as the occupants of Stephen Crane's little boat tempt the seven mad gods of the sea. Hemingway hints at this in the beginning of Book IV. In the hotel at Stresa, where Frederic went to find Catherine, the barman asks him questions about the war.

"Don't talk about the war." I said. The war was a long way off. Maybe there wasn't any war. There was no war here. Then I realized it was over for me. But I did not have the feeling that it was really over. I had the feeling of a boy who thinks of what is happening at a certain hour at the schoolhouse from which he has played truant.

The war is not over. Even after the successful effort to leave Italy and enter Switzerland, the war (which is really a symbol for the chaos of nature—the biological trap) catches up with Frederic and Catherine. It is significant that Frederic's reason tells him he can escape—that he *has* escaped; his sensibility suggests that he is only playing truant. Frederic felt like a masquerader in his civilian clothes. That is to say, in the modern sense, all happiness is a form of truancy. The months in Switzerland were idyllic. Even the snow came late, almost as though Frederic had ordered nature's cooperation.

The trap is sprung in Book V. Catherine's confinement is difficult, and the birth when it does come is finally performed through a Caesarean operation. The child is born dead. Catherine herself dies soon afterward. Yet, though it is Catherine who dies, *A Farewell to Arms* is not her tragedy. Unlike Francis Macomber and unlike Manuelo in "The Undefeated," she does not *become* admirable in her dying; she *remains* admirable according to the rules of decorum which Hemingway has set up:

> The nurse opened the door and motioned with her finger for me to come. I followed her into the room. Catherine did not look up when I came in. I went over to the side of the bed. The doctor was standing by the bed on the opposite side. Catherine looked at me and smiled. I bent down over the bed and started to cry.
> "Poor darling." Catherine said very softly. She looked gray.
> "You're all right, Cat," I said. "You're going to be all right."
> "I'm going to die," she said; then waited and said, "I hate it." I took her hand.
> "Don't touch me," she said. I let go of her hand. She smiled. "Poor darling. You touch me all you want."
> "You'll be all right, Cat. I know you'll be all right."
> "I meant to write you a letter to have if anything happened, but I didn't do it."
> "Do you want me to get a priest or any one to come and see you?"
> "Just you," she said. Then a little later, "I'm not afraid. I just hate it."

Catherine had had the perception of death early, but it had come to Frederic only since learning of the doctor's fears. During the operation he thought she was dead: "Her face was gray." Catherine knows intuitively that she is going to die. Frederic senses it, but his reason will not allow him to accept it, as she does, as ". . . just a dirty trick."

> I knew she was going to die and I prayed that she would not. Don't let her die. Oh, God, please don't let her die. I'll do anything for you if you won't let her die. Please, please, please, dear God, don't let her die. Dear God, don't let her die. Please, please, please don't let her die. God please make her not die. I'll do anything you say if you don't let her die. You took the baby but don't let her die. That was all right, but don't let her die. Please, please, dear God, don't let her die.

Frederic's hope that he could prevent her from dying is as illusory as his belief that he could escape the war by signing a separate peace. In a sense, Frederic is a depiction of the narrator's figure in "The Open Boat," who, when he realizes that there is no tangible thing to hoot, feels the desire to confront a personification and indulge in pleas. It isn't until he has accepted the terrible reality of Catherine's death that he is truly initiated: "It was like saying good-by to a statue." This is the biological trap—sprung. Catherine has been right from the beginning. Early in the novel, in speaking of her English lover who was killed in France, she says: "I thought perhaps he couldn't stand it and then of course he was killed and that was the end of it." "I don't know," Frederic said. "Oh, yes," Catherine emphasizes. "That's the end of it."

These are the limits, then, as circumscribed by nature: death is the end of life. After death there is only the lifeless statue. It was this conclusion (or something like it) which caused Gertrude Stein to say of Ernest Hemingway that he belonged to the "lost generation," lost because the comfortable morality of the nineteenth century had been denied them after 1914. Frederic Henry attempts to believe in the validity of warfare, but even the peasant soldiers under him know better. When he puts his trust in religion or in his love for Catherine he is also defeated. He reasons it out as follows:

That was what you did. You died. You did not know what it was about. You never had time to learn. They threw you in and told you the rules and the first time they caught you off base they killed you.

In "The Short Happy Life of Francis Macomber" the emphasis was upon man's final victory over death. That view is represented here in the stoical death of Catherine, but the emphasis is upon futility. In a striking image which represents the key scene in the novel, we have Frederic thinking about an experience he has had:

Once in camp I put a log on top of the fire and it was full of ants. As it commenced to burn, the ants swarmed out and went first toward the centre where the fire was; then turned back and ran toward the end. When there were enough on the end they fell off into the fire. Some got out, their bodies burnt and flattened, and went off not knowing where they were going. But most of them went toward the fire and then back toward the end and swarmed on the cool end and finally fell off into the fire. I remember thinking at the time that it was the end of the world and a splendid chance to be a messiah and lift the log off the fire and throw it out where the ants could get off onto the ground. But I did not do anything but throw a tin cup of water on the log, so that I would have the cup empty to put whiskey in before I added water to it. I think the cup of water on the burning log only steamed the ants.

The relationship of this parable to Catherine's predicament is unmistakable. For her there is likewise no messiah to come to the rescue. Death is the end of it, and the only value in death is man's knowledge of it. In Ernest Hemingway's novels, those who live well die like heroes. They are the initiated. But the initiation of Frederic Henry comes gradually. He learns about war, love, and finally death. Catherine's death is the final stage in his initiation.

III

If this conclusion is true, we might ask: "Why the title: *A Farewell to Arms*"? The title suggests in its obvious implications that the author saw his subject as concerned primarily with the war. In that case, we might say either that we are wrong in our conclusions or that the author was wrong in his selection of title. This raises the question of Ernest Hemingway's method—his style. Hemingway's sensibility, when it is functioning at its highest point, has always worked upon an immediate objective level which translates ideas into terms of concrete things: life as a baseball game where each error is punished by death or compared to the struggle of ants on a burning log, the comparison of a hero's death with the slaughter of animals at a stockyard. In each case we are aware of the double implication, the idea and the image; and the emotional force of the idea is intensified by the shock supplied by the image. This is the more complicated form of Hemingway's noted "understatement." At the time of Catherine's operation, while the doctor has gone to make his preparations, Frederic is left to administer the anesthesia. He has been told that the correct amount would register upon the dial at number 2, but when Catherine is in extreme pain, he says, "I turned the dial to three and then four. I wished the doctor would come back. I was afraid of the numbers above two." The statement "I wished the doctor would come back" is understatement. The use of the machine-image suggests Catherine's immediate danger. Another author might have examined in great detail both Catherine's illness and the emotion which Frederic was experiencing at that time; but from the simple, quiet statement, reinforced by the dial registering the numbers above two, we get the full force of Frederic's terror in a few strokes.

That Hemingway was aware of this quality is evidenced by the statement which he once made that what he was attempting to get was a "fifth dimension" in his prose; not the ordinary dimensions of exposition and description, but the full quality of the emotional experience. This is not an unusual characteristic of a work of art; it is merely Ernest Hemingway's means of explaining his own intention; but it suggests the caution a reader should exercise in taking the author's words or sentences at their most obvious level of meaning. Perhaps this is true also of the title, *A Farewell to Arms.* Someone has suggested somewhere that the "Arms" referred not to the war, but to the arms of Catherine; thus suggesting that what the novel was about, really, was Frederic's loss of his love. This is as limited an interpretation as that which sees the novel as only a "war novel." A more valid interpretation would see the title as completely ironic. Frederic has attempted to escape from the obligations which life imposes. He did not wish to fall in love, but he did. He attempted to escape the war, but he felt like a schoolboy who was playing truant. His life with Catherine in Switzerland and the life which they anticipated after the war were relatively devoid of conflict. Catherine and Frederic had said farewell to the life of action and struggle, but ironically their greatest test—the attempt to save the life of Catherine—came at the very moment when they seemed to have achieved a successful escape.

What the novel says, finally, is that you cannot escape the obligations of action—you cannot say "farewell to arms"; you cannot sign a separate peace. You can only learn to live with life, to tolerate it as "the initiated" learn to tolerate it.

Faulkner's *Light in August:*
A View of Tragedy

WILLIAM FAULKNER, like Herman Melville in *Billy Budd* and Ernest Hemingway in *The Old Man and the Sea,* finds a significant image for our time in the Christian agony of the death and resurrection. Melville used it because he believed that the atheism of the French Revolution had provoked a "crisis for Christendom," perhaps even delivered a death blow, while itself going down to defeat, but that it provoked an infusion of new breath "to belly philosophy's flattened sails," come from some source of primitive innocence to be crucified by authority and revived by art. Hemingway stresses the limitations of the flesh, set against the indomitable spirit of the Old Man. In the resulting conflict, he suggests victory in defeat, a theme that had been portrayed in at least two of his earlier works: "The Undefeated" and "The Short Happy Life of Francis Macomber." William Faulkner utilizes the myth of death and regeneration in three novels. Underlying the events of Easter Week in *The Sound and the Fury* is the concept of degeneration-regeneration, decadence and a suggested re-birth in Southern society. In *The Fable,* admittedly an allegory, the surface story is controlled and illuminated by the underlying image of innocent Man crucified by authority in an attempt to preserve Truth. In *Light in August,* Faulkner utilizes the concept in its most comprehensive and enlightening form.

William Faulkner's principal subject in all his fiction has been the rise and decline of Southern society. At its best, this society contained energy, honesty, and beauty; yet even at its height it embodied the seeds of failure in its history of human injustice in dealings with the native Indians and its Negro slaves. The weakness of this society consisted, in part, in its very aristocratic ideals, which denied the possibility of change, and the drama of most of Faulkner's works results from this attitude; an attitude of arrogance towards the inevitable movement of time; a pride in the society it had created, which is both admirable and tragic, but doomed.

Modern life, as Faulkner sees it, is characterized by change, but marked by the absence of the old virtues, a loss of personal responsibility and a lack of individual skill or pride in skill. It is mercantile rather than agrarian, thus removed from nature. It is greedy in its utilitarianism, confused by an absence of real values.

At its most general, then, Faulkner's problem is one of permanence and change. It presents a contrast between a view of life as static, therefore putting little emphasis upon time, and a view that sees life as in constant flux. Above all, it is a view that sees man, on the one hand, separated from nature, viewing nature as something created for his own use; on the other, viewing man in an existence close to nature, respecting the force and power of nature and acknowledging his responsibility and subjection to it.

Faulkner has been accused, at times, of weighting his fiction in favor of an aristocratic South, and such critics have seen him as urging a return to the past and the past values. In one respect this may be true, for Faulkner has no such distrust of the world of the past as that which motivated Ernest Hemingway's Frederic Henry to distrust even the old words. Yet whenever one of his characters attempted to remain in the world of past values, the result was, at its worst, pathetic, at its best, almost tragic. Through attempting to hold such a belief, a character might be driven to alcoholism, to insanity, suicide, and even murder.

Yet regardless of the sympathy with which Faulkner presented such characters, regardless of the effectiveness with which the reader might be moved by the events, both characters and events were celebrating a way of life that was dead or dying; they were not prefiguring a world that lived or promised to live. Even in the hopefulness of the by now famous short story, "The Bear," we are more impressed by a sense of an *end* of something than we are by a suggested *beginning.* Such is not true of *Light in August,* where the expiatory figure of Joe Christmas, combined with the innocent faith of Lena Grove, provide a moving and eloquent (though not uncomplicated) image of sacrifice and regeneration.

The background of the novel, as is usual with Faulkner, is the legendary town of Jefferson, with a few of the familiar names appearing briefly, but containing on the whole a singular cast of characters, the most important of whom are not from Jefferson at all—whose lives cross there momentarily to fulfill the purposes of the narrative. More important than the characters, for our present purpose, despite the skill with which the author presents them, are the meanings that we derive from them as they take their places in the expertly woven tapestry of ideas.

The story is told with Faulkner's familiar shifts in time, so that the narrative begins at a point very near its end, but continually shifts into the past to supply background events in the lives of many characters, all of whom are to become involved, in one way or another, with the climactic scenes of death and regeneration that provide a climax. The two principal characters, Joe Christmas and Lena Grove, never meet, although their lives intersect to provide the central images of crucifixion and resurrection. Joe is the baffled figure of one who is at once "everyman" and "noman," because he is white with Negro blood, the doomed object of Man's (and particularly, here, Southern Man's) curse. Lena is the husbandless mother, who plods perseveringly from Alabama to Mississippi (and throughout the events of the novel), with the unerring and implacable sureness of purpose of nature itself.

Yet the contrasts in the novel are not between Joe and Lena, who combine to represent Man's totality, as they are between Woman and Man, between intuition and knowledge, between Negroes and whites, between the present and the past. Lena symbolizes the enduring present that will in the future prevail. Joe Christmas is the agonizing present that is doomed to suffer and die amidst the horror of not knowing what or who he is. Lena is primarily presented as a vague, phantom-like creature, performing her symbolic journey toward the future, while Joe comes nearer than any other fictional character since Captain Ahab or Milly Theale to becoming a genuine hero. Despite his symbolic function, Joe Christmas comes close to rising, as the tragic hero must rise, above any definition (even that of undefinition), and he fails finally to achieve heroic stature only because of the author's overriding image of him as Christ-like.

Nevertheless, the searching journey of Joe Christmas to discover his identity and purpose, from the moment he is left a foundling on the doorstep of an orphan's home until his end by shooting and emasculation at the home of the Reverend Hightower thirty years later, represents more than initiation, for it is a defining of the stuff of tragedy, even if it does not become itself tragic. When a man carries the mixed blood of two races, in the indiscernible manner that makes him suspect to both, the author seems to be saying, he is bound to become a scapegoat—the sacrificial offer—for the expiation of the guilt of both; yet it is only through such ceremonial horror that the curse can be removed and the rebirth occur.

Joe's wandering is not only through the worlds of black and white, but also through a world of men and women. At the orphanage, he unwittingly becomes a witness of an act of sexual aberration by two of the attendants and is immediately caught between the interests of the girl, who would have him removed by revealing her suspicions that he is part Negro, and of an old man, whom Joe does not know is his grandfather, who has devoted these years of his life to concealing Joe's Negro blood. Instead of being sent to a Negro orphanage, Joe is put out by adoption to a Scotch-Presbyterian farm family and takes the name of Joseph McEachern. There for many years he suffers the tension of being pulled between the puritanical piety and severity of his foster father and the womanly indulgence of his foster mother. In a nearby town, he experiences sex for the first time with a generous waitress-prostitute, but is mocked as a "hayseed" by the girl's employer, who also complains of the girl's generosity in a situation that he sees purely as a business arrangement. When Joe's affair in town is discovered by his foster father, the two fight, and Joe strikes him over the head with a chair. He leaves the McEacherns, taking with him the savings of his foster mother (knowing that she would have given them to him if he had not stolen), not knowing whether or not he had killed McEachern.

For the next fifteen years, Joe traveled to all parts of the country, living now as a black, now as a white, now married, now unmarried, not caring whether he was inside or outside the law. Eventually he arrived at a house near the outskirts of Jefferson, where he took up quarters in an abandoned outbuilding and began an affair with the spinster owner of the house, who was the descendant of an abolitionist family from the North that had moved South to assist the Negroes. In this affair, Joe achieves a kind of apotheosis in that he finally proves his manhood by feminizing the masculine Miss Burden; but the moment of apotheosis becomes also the beginning of Joe's doom, for Joanna Burden makes their relationship a means of expressing her white man's guilt. When their relationship ends with Joanna's "change of life," she reverts to her masculine role, finally repeating the demands of the pious McEachern when she insists that Joe get on his knees and pray with her for forgiveness. Joe refuses, and she attempts to shoot him with a faulty old revolver that misfires. In desperation, Joe slashes her with his razor. Then begins the furious chase that is to end finally with his surrender, then in an attempt to escape again, then in his final capture, emasculation, and death.

It is at the moment that Christmas murders Joanna Burden that Lena Grove enters Jefferson. She had heard that the father of her unborn child was working in a planing mill in Jefferson, having neglected his promise to send for her and marry her when he found work, and she has come with full and unquestioning faith, not only that he would be pleased to see her, but that he would be anxious to marry her before the baby is born. In fact, her former lover has been employed at the mill, but he has changed his name, so that she does not know that he had been engaged with Joe Christmas in the sale of bootleg whiskey or that he is at the moment in the same town with her, attempting to get the one thousand dollar reward for Joe's capture. She is taken in hand by Byron Bunch, the foreman of the mill, a serious and pious young man, who guesses the identity of the person she is seeking, but who refrains for several days from telling her, because he knows her lover, once named Burch, now Brown, is in the custody of the sheriff. He does, eventually, install her in the cabin where Brown and Christmas had formerly lived, and with the aid of his friend and counselor, the Reverend Hightower, finally sees the baby born safely. He also brings Brown to her, but Brown stays only long enough to realize what is expected from him, then disappears from the country altogether.

The relationship of Byron Bunch and the Reverend Hightower is significant. They are at once similar and different. Hightower had come originally as the minister of a local congregation in Jefferson, because the town had been forever imprinted in his mind as the scene of his grandfather's heroic action during the Civil War, when he had come as one of a daring band of horsemen to burn the stores of the occupying General Grant. Hightower's obsession with the past amounted to a kind of madness that tinctured his religion and drove his wife to debauchery and death. His wife's death lost him his ministry, but made it impossible for him to live anywhere except Jefferson, where he stayed on, doing good whenever it became necessary, but absorbed by his dreams of the past. His Southern past, like Joanna Burden's Northern past, led to debauchery and death, parallel in many ways, but differing as Hightower was male, Joanna, female. Byron Bunch, on the other hand, had singularly little past and no particular attachment to any place; but he was a steady and honest worker, and he had a firm sense of moral responsibility.

It is these two men, the one a representative of the static idealism of the Southern past, the other a suggestion of moral sensibility that foretells the future, who are given the care of Lena and the birth of the child, a labor of necessity for one because of his code, of love for the other because of his sense of moral rightness.

At the same time, another contrasting relationship enters the novel in the late stages, this one composed of the reappearance of Joe Christmas' grandfather, along with his grandmother, whom we meet for the first time. Here, again, the contrast is in terms of masculine and feminine characteristics, as it was with the McEacherns. Old Doc Hines, the grandfather, had attempted to disguise Joe's Negro blood, not for Joe's sake, but for the sake of the *idea* of blood supremacy. The grandmother, from the beginning, had accepted Joe for *what he was,* her daughter's child, and she had grieved his loss ever since her husband had taken him away to the orphanage. The old couple happened to be living in the town where the chase for Joe ended—where he had chosen to allow himself to be captured. They recognized him at once as their lost grandchild, but the old man is at the fore of those who would immediately lynch Joe for his murder of Joanna Burden, while the old woman encourages Joe to try to escape. Ironically, it is the grandmother's encouragement that leads to Joe's violent end, similar to that which her husband and the mob demanded. Thus, Joe is destroyed by the feminine power of love, in the manner advocated by the masculine force of hate.

As the grandmother had, inevitably, become involved with Hightower and Bunch in her attempt to find someone who would help her free Joe, she also happens to be present when the birth of Lena's child occurs. In her old woman's mind, weary with the events of the day, she gets the two events mixed, so that she imagines that the mother is her daughter, Milly, the mother of Joe, and that the newborn child *is* Joe. Thus William Faulkner resurrects Joe Christmas in the person of Lena's child, who has been born, as Hightower thinks, from "The good stock peopling in tranquil obedience to the good earth; from these hearty loins without hurry or haste descending mother and daughter."

So, in the person of Joe Christmas is the guilt propitiated, while in the symbol of Lena's child a new innocence is born. But it is not quite as simple as that either, for the "good earth" of Lena's world is the world of evil. It is in the masculine world that the dream of something higher exists, even if the dream is a mistaken one, as it was with Doc Hines, McEachern, Hightower, and the masculine side of Joanna Burden. Byron Bunch, when he undertakes to become Lena's guide, at first in search of Brown, then as Lena's unmarried husband, has already had his purity corrupted; indeed, the corruption began the moment he fell in love with her and, in order to protect her, was forced for the first time in his life to lie. So it is that in the novel Joe Christmas is more often spoken of as the devil than as the Christ. If he is the Christ, he is the Christ who was required to take on flesh and submit to the devil's torment, and that is what he is called finally. Faulkner has Hightower refer to him as "poor man," subject to "poor mankind."

Because Joe is a symbolic hero, not an actual one, the meaning here, as in the Christian allegory, is that the tragedy of Joe is the tragedy of mankind—or society; for, as Joanna Burden's father tells her in relating the story of how her grandfather and brother had been murdered by Colonel Sartoris for aiding the Negroes:

Faulkner's Light in August: *A View of Tragedy*

Your grandfather and brother are lying there, murdered not by one white man, but by the curse which God put on a whole race before your grandfather or your brother or me or you were even thought of. A race doomed and cursed to be forever and ever a part of the white race's doom and curse for its sins.

And as Joanna tells Joe Christmas:

I thought of all the children coming forever and ever into the world, white, with the black shadow already falling upon them before they drew breath. And I seemed to see the black shadow in the shape of a cross. And it seemed like the white babies were struggling, even before they drew breath, to escape from the shadow that was not only upon them but beneath them too, flung out like their arms were flung out, as if they were nailed to the cross.

It would be a mistake to take Faulkner's images as referring to the Negro problem only, for everyone including Faulkner knows that if there had been no racial problem in the South, the problem of Man's evil would still have existed. He would have found other means to express his limitations, as indeed he has elsewhere than in the South. Ironically, it is often the impulse to achieve the highest kind of good in a society that results in the greatest evil, and implicit in such an irony is the terrifying paradox of tragedy. The Greeks called it *hubris;* perhaps our word is arrogance: the arrogance of the man who believes he can draw inspiration from the heavens, not from the earth. In portraying such a concept, William Faulkner, if he has not achieved tragic dimensions in *Light in August,* has at least affirmed the tragic view.

Implicit in tragedy, however, is the hope, even the faith, that evil can be overcome by good, if not permanently, at least momentarily. Society, like the individual, is born in innocence, educated into knowledge, and decays to death; but neither society nor the individual experiences this process in isolation —only the hero. If the Greeks saw their heroes as splendid, but terrifying, individuals, defying the gods; we see them as born in innocence, but already bearing the cross of society's violation of that innocence—its violation of nature. The conditions of Greek culture and our own are different, but the effects of tragedy are similar. The great educating force on a society is its literature, on its individual members, its heroes; and if Ralph Waldo Emerson was right in saying that the great artists and the greatest heroes were those who read nature truly and recorded it for posterity, then Faulkner (regardless of how much he differs from Emerson) is right too when he says that it is only through man's coming to know nature, as Sam Fathers, and Ike McCaslin, and Dilsey, and Lena Grove were one with nature, that a regeneration of society can be accomplished.

When we have come to see this, when we recognize that the struggle between the demands of nature and the demands of our dreams are as terrifyingly real as a former society saw its struggle between its gods and its human institutions, then we shall have learned to *feel* the struggle. We shall have achieved the tragic sense. Something like this is what William Faulkner's portrayal of the agony of Joe Christmas and the innocent faith of Lena Grove seems to be saying to us.

The American Short Story

THE "SHORT STORY" is the most recent of all literary forms. It is the only mode in which American writers were privileged to participate from the very beginning. An American author was the first to use the term "short story" to describe his collection of prose tales. It was an American writer who attempted the first significant definition. Over the past century and a half, Americans have produced a body of work in the short story form that is probably unsurpassed by any other national literature.

Before the middle of the nineteenth century the short prose narrative was usually known as a "tale." We have examples of tales from ancient cultures that go back as far as the eighth century B.C. We have a collection, *Tales of the Magicians,* that dates from 4000 B.C. We have the individual legends of early Greece, from which most of the great epics and tragedies were constructed. We have the short narratives of the *Old Testament.* We have the parables of the *New Testament.* By the end of the Middle Ages, we have two supreme literary examples of tale telling, Boccaccio's *Decameron* and Chaucer's *Canterbury Tales.*

All of these early examples were, however, either part of a larger whole or their purpose was other than literary. When they were not, strictly speaking, literary productions, as the Greek legends, they became subject matter for works of literature. When they were written as parts of a related series, as in Boccaccio and Chaucer's works, they depended upon the larger "frame" for their total meaning and they revealed medieval man's vision of the small work of art as a mere detail within a grander structure.

The world of Greece and the universe of the Middle Ages were relatively small, so that man loomed large in both of them, though smaller than the gods and "a little lower than the angels." Only in art could man rival heaven, so his vision of art was generally on a grand scale. As the universe increased in size and complexity during the Renaissance, the stature of man diminished. No longer was the principal need the adoration of a known world, but the examination of an unknown one. The English Renaissance marked the end of the great tragedies and the rise of the personal lyric. By the beginning of the nineteenth century, even the "decoration" of verse was called into question. The prose narrative came to rival poetry as a means of expressing man's vision of himself in relation to his world.

Such changes did not occur without a struggle, and simply to name them does not take into account the complex problems that arose not only in literature but in society. Nevertheless, it is a fair summary of the shift from the condition of relative certainty, in which the primary need was for ceremonious affirmation, to an attitude of uncertainty, where mankind felt the need to investigate and define the conditions under which he existed. Some of the earliest important prose works, such as Cervantes' famous *Don Quixote,* aimed at the ridicule of conventional and outworn ideals; others, such as the novels of Defoe and Smollett, began an almost systematic examination of man in nature; still others, such as Richardson's, Fielding's, and Austen's works, examined man in relation to his society. Eventually, novelists even penetrated the minds of their characters, exposing and surveying the hidden depths of the unconscious.

For the most part, however, the novel performed best when viewing nature from the outside, either from the point of view of the author, who stood as spectator apart from the action, or from the point of view of one of the characters, somewhat closer to the scene, but still separate from it. As a method of investigation, it represented what might be called the "telescopic view." As a view, it paralleled the method of the science of its day. The novelist selected what were considered permanent elements of society, set his characters into motion against them, and drew conclusions from the resulting action.

Such a method has its limits in science as well as in fiction, so that when the microscope and the X ray reveal to scientists a universe of being beyond the limits of man's ordinary perceptions, fiction, too, shifted its method and its aim, discovering a means of focusing its attention upon those inward motives and impulses, even as the instruments of science focused upon a small segment of the unseen world of outer nature.

It is probably no accident that the beginnings of the modern short story paralleled this rise in interest in the psychological motives for action or in the psychological results of past events. Although the beginning of the short tale had represented little more than an objective recounting of picaresque adventure, some authors, by utilizing the atmosphere of "Gothic" settings, had hinted at mysteries that might be explored, perhaps even unconsciously suggesting that the supernatural world of medieval romance might represent a clue to the inner workings of the mind. One such author was an American, Washington Irving, who in his most important tales of adventure portrayed, not ancient castles in far countries, but Dutch-American settlements in the Hudson River Valley of the New World, and treated them with a gentle humor that was typically American; he also made telling comments upon his characters' motives and aspirations. Yet Irving's tales did preserve the traditional coloring of the conventional tales from other lands.

In this respect, Irving was not so much a founder of the American short story as he was a forerunner of it. His intentions were too unclear, even to himself, to make a strong impression on those who followed. Two other Americans, Nathaniel Hawthorne and Edgar Allan Poe, must be given almost equal credit for making the sharpest break with the traditions of the short prose narrative as "tale" and the clearest beginning of what we call the "short story," and their influence upon later authors is undeniable. Hawthorne not only affected Poe himself but he left his mark upon the writings of Herman Melville and Henry Janes, who were to follow. Poe's most significant influence was to be delayed and to return to a later generation of American authors through the impression he made upon a generation of French poets, novelists, and short story writers at the end of the nineteenth century.

The first significant volume of American short stories was Nathaniel Hawthorne's edition of *Twice-Told Tales,* published in 1837. But it was not only the original publication of these stories that was important, it was also the reaction of Edgar Allan Poe to them when he reviewed them in *Graham's Magazine* in 1842, for the review gave rise to the first serious attempt to define the short story.

Poe's definition was brief. He said that the tale should strive to achieve "a certain unique or single *effect*" and that every word and every action should contribute to the working out of this "one pre-established design." He added that such an accomplishment could constitute one of the highest achievements of art. Hawthorne (possibly in reply to Poe's review) added that such stories should be in the style of a man of society (by which I take him to mean not high society but his *own* society) , and that they might serve "to open intercourse with the world."

In its general statement of serious purpose and in its outline, Poe's definition served to set the short story form on a course from which it has never since deviated. By his example, Hawthorne suggested possibilities for the short tale that had been overlooked by writers before him and that have seldom been excelled since. It remained, however, for another American, Henry James, to add emphasis and detail to what had concerned Hawthorne and Poe.

Early in his career, James wrote: "To write a series of good little tales I deem ample work for a lifetime." In his writings, he showed that the short story form could be used for serious literary intents. So far as can be discovered, James was the first author to use the term "story" to describe his own short prose narratives. In his criticism, James advised the writer of fiction to "write from experience and experience only," then added: "try to be one of the people on whom nothing is lost." He stressed the matter of form in fiction, but as an organic whole, encompassing as much as possible of life, not a simple arrangement of selected events:

In proportion as in what [fiction] offers us we see life without rearrangement do we feel that we are touching the truth; in proportion as we see it with rearrangement do we feel that we are being put off with a substitute, a compromise and convention. It is not uncommon to hear an extraordinary assurance of remark in regard to this matter of rearranging, which is often spoken of as if it were the last word in art . . . Art is essentially selection, but it is a selection whose main care is to be typical, to be inclusive. For many people art means rose-colored windowpanes, and selection means picking a bouquet for Mrs. Grundy. They will tell you glibly that artistic considerations have nothing to do with the disagreeable, with the ugly; they will rattle off shallow commonplaces about the province of art and the limits of art till you are moved to wonder in return as to the province and the limits of ignorance. It appears to me that no one can ever have made a seriously artistic attempt without becoming conscious of an immense increase—a kind of revelation—of freedom. One perceives in that case—by the light of a heavenly ray—that the province of art is all life, all feeling, all observation, all vision.

Henry James wrote finally that "the deepest quality of a work of art will always be the quality of the mind of the producer." Such an axiom, he added, "for the artist of fiction, will cover all needful moral ground." Like Poe and Hawthorne before him, Henry James showed, in his own stories, how the short story could, by its inner penetration, open vistas of the mind as dazzling as any panorama in even the longest novel.

D. H. Lawrence, soon after he had first become acquainted with the works of American authors, wrote:

The American art-speech contains a quality that we have not calculated. It is a suggestive force which is not relative to us, not inherent in the English race. This alien quality belongs to the American continent itself.

Although we might disagree with the reasons Lawrence gave for this statement, we cannot quarrel with the statement itself. The most singular quality in the works of important American writers is what we have come to call "the American style." Such a style developed early in our history, and it resulted despite a close language tie with Great Britain; American experience did differ from that of England, and the principal difference was the difference of the continent itself.

Whereas in England and Europe the forms and manners of an earlier time continued to retain much of their authority, in America in the seventeenth and eighteenth centuries the settlers had to face a new continent, where the old traditions were often ineffective. America's early history represents a search for new forms. In such a society, the great need was for definition, not only in the large general sense of a national philosophy but in a more immediate, personal sense. The American settler, isolated in scattered villages and on farms, was face to face with nature and with the fact of himself facing it.

One of the means by which our ancestors accommodated themselves to their primitive environment was by the invention of tales concerning themselves and their relation to the place where they had settled. The earliest of these stories were told by itinerant peddlers, who traveled from place to place, providing news and entertainment by recounting events that had allegedly happened to them in their wandering. In time, the tellers so embellished their "news" that it became an elaborate comment on frontier society. In the beginning, the tales outlined the qualities of shrewdness, simplicity, and energy that were recognized as necessary qualities for survival. In time they became an almost mythical means by which the native American came to recognize his own character. Eventually, Americans had what amounted to an oral tradition of "tall tales" by which they had not only reconciled themselves to the hardships of settlement but they had also created a typical *voice* (or style).

As American settlers pushed westward, their tales accompanied them and were enlarged and altered to meet the new circumstances of the American continent. By the nineteenth century these folk tales had become so much a part of the social fabric that a group of writers arose to exploit them in the pages of the popular press. American newspapers were so filled with tales of the adventures of such mythical heroes as Davy Crockett and Mike Fink, besides a host of local celebrities, raised to legendary levels, that their exploits encompassed, as Constance Rourke has pointed out, almost every aspect of American life.

By the middle of the century, a burgeoning of such writing took place, a burgeoning that a later American humorist likened to the lyrical productions of the Elizabethans in England, when England was "a nest of singing birds." The authors of these works were lyrical-humorists, celebrating the American character and American life, adopting such pseudonyms as Josh Billings and Artemus Ward to chant their humorous praises in the pages of *The Jolly Joker* or *Merryman's Monthly*.

It has been said that the accents of the mythical Americans created in the legends and expressed through the "masks" of the native humorists can be heard in the more vigorous and rustic phrases of Emerson, Hawthorne, and Thoreau. They can be recognized, whole and complete, but with a certain sophistication, in the tales and novels of Mark Twain. Varieties of the Yankee character can be found in the works of Melville and Henry James. Melville noted the American quality of Hawthorne and gave it appropriate expression after he had read the early stories. He admonished American readers: "The smell of your beeches and hemlocks is upon him; your own broad prairies are in his soul; and if you travel away inland into his deep and noble nature, you will hear the far roar of his Niagra."

Yet so much should not be made of the unique qualities in American writing that we lose sight of its place in the general literary tradition. American humorous writings did not aspire to the level of art. They did not, in themselves, influence or inspire serious writers. They did, however, present, in the exaggerated form of popular comedy, both the typical voice in which the American spoke and a cast of characters drawn from a wide area of American life. They demonstrated, too, the effect a new continent could have upon the society that settled it—reflecting a life in nature, preoccupied with coming to terms with nature.

The principal philosophic interest of the nineteenth century was nature. The most important literary subject was the relation of man to nature. In America both interests were particularly pertinent. In Europe, the interest in nature was as great as in America; the expression of that interest was more eloquent. But in most of Europe, nature had been tamed. The early Romantics of Germany, France, and England tended to look upon nature as mostly benevolent. Literary works that dealt with the subject of nature portrayed scenes of pastoral or haunting beauty. There was an element of the Romantic philosophy that demanded that nature be seen in this light, and so it was, and so must the domesticated nature have seemed to those who described it.

In America such ideas had their force, particularly in New

England, where life had become almost as settled and civilized as in the old countries. Even the Indians appeared to James Fenimore Cooper as "noble savages." Ralph Waldo Emerson's nature is, for the most part, as idyllic as Wordsworth's. Henry D. Thoreau believed that nature would provide all the necessities if man would but submit to its benevolent demands. Our natural philosophers believed that by studying nature's demands and accommodating ourselves to them, an era of complete happiness could be obtained. Our social philosophers sought the means by which such ideals could be achieved.

The first serious questioning of these assumptions occurred, perhaps not altogether accidentally, concurrent with the rise of the short story form in America. Nathaniel Hawthorne's early tales examined much past and contemporary life in New England and discovered a dramatic conflict between man's view of himself as an innocent child of nature and the real facts of history or contemporary events. For him the noble savages of Cooper became symbols of evil. The haunting beauty of Cooper's forests became the dark woods that were the devil's abode. Edgar Allen Poe showed little interest in contemporary nature, but the landscapes that he borrowed from his Gothic forebears were inhabited, not by vigor and energy, but by decay. He applied natural science in his fiction, not to give examples of a trend toward Utopia, but as a means of fathoming mystery. Herman Melville found the life in nature a struggle, heroic but doomed, against the unknown forces of evil. Like his contemporary, Mark Twain, he saw the society that arose in the primitive West as vigorous, but chaotic, innocent and gullible.

What these early discoveries meant was that American fiction, and particularly the American short story, had found its subject. What these American authors were doing, in effect, was questioning the materialistic consequences of the romantic attitude toward nature of their time and in terms of their place, which was the American continent. Hawthorne presented as the greatest evil, the denial of evil, because it re-

sulted in arrogant self-assurance—what he called the harden-
ing of the heart. Poe emphasized the ideal of beauty that was
not an image of the natural world, but a reflection of some
higher, "celestial" sensibility.

It is important not to underestimate the significance of these
two attitudes in American fiction. Hawthorne's views were
immediately influential in the development of Herman Melville and Henry James, and, through them, on a whole line of
American short story writers, including Mark Twain and Bret
Harte. Edgar Allen Poe's primary influence was to be delayed
and indirect, but not insignificant, for he spoke eloquently to
a whole generation of French writers of the late nineteenth
century, and through them to another generation of American
authors in their own time, when the subjects of Hawthorne
and Melville merged with Poe's sensibility (as transmitted
through Gautier, Flaubert, and the Russian Chekhov) to affect
the short stories of Ernest Hemingway, William Faulkner, and
Katherine Anne Porter.

Influence is, of course, a tenuous effect and one difficult to
define. Perhaps a statement of "influence" can be accepted
only when it is acknowledged, as it was in the case of Hawthorne's influence upon Melville and James; or, as was the
case in Poe's effects upon the aims and methods of Charles
Baudelaire. Oftentimes, what appears to be an influence
represents no more than the acceptance of common attitudes
or of similar methods, when such matters are "in the air."
There is, I think, no direct influence of Hawthorne upon
Mark Twain, Bret Harte, and Stephen Crane. The most direct
influence upon Twain's writings was his apprenticeship in the
school of native humorists. Yet he rose above their crudities
almost exactly in the degree that he rejected the pastoral-
romantic view of nature and in the seriousness with which he
examined the condition of man in America or the American
in relation to the rest of the world. What Hawthorne called
"heart" Mark Twain called "common-sense," and both used it
as a measure of man's worth.

Melville and James accepted Hawthorne's rejection of innocence as an ideal, and each strove to discover what elements of
the past supported their values, what elements of the present
could be accepted as vital and needful. Both accepted Hawthorne's view of the importance of evil and his concept of evil
as a humanizing force. Both rejected forms and manners that
had lost their function in modern society. They rejected, too,
the materialism of the present, but saw in the natural honesty
of many moderns a "moral sensibility" (to quote Henry
James) more effective than traditional systems of moral
values.

By the end of the nineteenth century, with the completed
writings of Hawthorne, Poe, Melville, James, Twain, and Bret
Harte, the first great period of the American short story had
come to an end. Hawthorne had examined the effects of sin
and innocence on the American character, particularly as they
were to be found in his Puritan forebears. Poe had created
situations of horror and mystery, where his macabre effects
tested the stability of the human mind, or he posed mental
problems that suggested the mind's infinite possibilities. Melville had looked into the past as well as the present, contrasting evil and innocence, revealing beauty in decay, utility in
innocence, discovering monotony and sterility in much of
modern life, injustice and wanton cruelty in much of the past.
Henry James raised questions concerning the nature of reality,
and his stories had revealed the true and the false, as they
were expressed particularly in social manners and in art. In
posing American vitality against European sophistication, he
had suggested a wide range of relative moral positions. Mark
Twain and Bret Harte had utilized their experiences in the
American West to illustrate the advantages of innocence and
"common-sense" over social pretensions and romantic ideals.

In all of these writers, the American "voice," or what D. H.
Lawrence called the American art-speech, had spoken with
varying degrees of effectiveness. All of them had delved into
the American background and the American character, with
the apparent aim of definition and understanding. All had

based their works, more or less, upon the subject of nature and the condition of modern man. They had written with a consistency of aim and a degree of excellence that had not heretofore been approached in American writing. Above all, they had established the short story in what Poe had said it was capable of achieving: the rank of the highest achievements of art.

With the beginning of the twentieth century, the short story had become an established form. What changes took place occurred only because of the changing times. Perhaps the most significant events were the rediscovery of Henry James and Herman Melville by American authors following the First World War and the discovery of Poe through the French authors whom he had influenced. James and Melville had lost their popular following at the end of their careers, but their works were uncovered by the war generation, whose disgust with the excessive gentility of much of the writing done at the turn of the century matched their resentment against their elders' views on morality and politics. With the example of Henry James's finely wrought stories (James himself was an admirer of the French craftsmen of his day) and the short stories that Melville completed at the end of his career, American authors were preparing to enter a second stage, rivaling the first in skill and energy, although not differing significantly from it.

If I choose Stephen Crane to mark the beginning of the modern American short story, I do so with the realization that all of his works were completed in the nineteenth century. However, Crane is a transitional figure. His works owe a debt to Mark Twain, with roots in the tradition of native humor, and to Henry James, with whom he became friends late in his brief career, who confirmed him in the "impressionistic" method with which he had accomplished his best work and who, as a literary craftsman, aroused his great admiration. More than this, Crane's interests combined two divergent strands that were to appear importantly in the American short story of the twentieth century.

Early in his career, Crane wrote:

> I renounced the clever school in literature. It seemed to me that there must be something more in life than to sit and cudgel one's brain for the clever and witty expedients. So I developed all alone a little creed of art which I thought a good one. Later I discovered that my creed was identical with the one of Howells and Garland and this way I became involved in the beautiful war between those who say that art is man's substitute for nature and we are most successful in art when we approach the nearest to nature and truth.

What Crane characterizes as the "clever school in literature" were the writers of "the genteel tradition" that flourished at the close of the century, most of its writers forgotten and properly so. He may also have had in mind a group of self-styled "aesthetes" and "bohemians," who were a cut above the genteel authors, but who, in their posturings and in their writings about art, aped the worst features of the French *Symbolistes*. The best among these were Ambrose Bierce and Lafcadio Hearn. Their opposite was the rising school of Realists, which included William Dean Howells, Hamlin Garland, Frank Norris, and, later, Jack London. Their realism consisted, for the most part, in telling what they considered to be the truth about society in a language as vigorous as that spoken in real life. Under their influence (or the influence of his creed), Crane wrote his Bowery tales, including the short novel *Maggie: A Girl of the Streets,* not his best works but superior in language and rendition to much writing that passed itself off as "realistic." The aim of such writing was to portray characters trapped by the unnatural conditions of modern society, thus exposing the truth about social justice in a repressive society.

From the beginning, however, Crane's method distinguished him from the followers of Howells and Garland. In his short stories particularly, his vision refined certain aspects of the natural scene until they took on an added, transcendent significance. Objects like the waves in "The Open Boat" or actions like the quarreling of the belligerent Swede in "The Blue Hotel" took on meanings over and above their usual roles in any natural scene or course of events. Crane's style, too, became less "natural," more exaggerated in its simplicity, as in "The Bride Comes to Yellow Sky" and "The Upturned Face."

What remained constant in Crane was his subject—his preoccupation with the part nature plays in human events. He saw nature first as a force that man tried to control through social institutions, but one which they, because of their basis in social inequality, were powerless to contain. He came to see nature, finally, as an indifferent force, to which man must learn to accommodate himself, first as an individual, then in society.

These two views of nature, although not unrelated, tend to put value upon different literary techniques. The first, with its emphasis upon social institutions, can be best adapted to its subject through the larger form of the novel. The second, concerned first of all with the individual's relation to nature, is best suited to the short story or to the very short novel. It was for this reason that William Dean Howells was more successful in his novels than in his short stories. Hamlin Garland's stories appear slight and slipshod by themselves but take on an added measure of importance when seen as part of the larger sequence of his work, which encompasses the primitive society of the border states. Likewise, Theodore Dreiser might, in his relation to Crane, be seen as incorporating the values of Crane's initial attitude, not his second, so that Dreiser's more important work was done in the novel form. Sherwood Anderson, although he saw nature as a positive force, was successful in a few short stories because he saw that force primarily in its relation to individuals, but he was often unsuccessful because he could not always find an adequate image (or symbol) to express the power he believed to reside in nature, and so lapsed into sentimentality.

The most important modern writer to follow Crane in his second line of development was Ernest Hemingway, whose acknowledged American masters were Mark Twain and Crane. In Twain, Hemingway believed America had first found its real voice. In Crane, he found not only a further development of that style but an attitude toward nature that seemed real and vital. Like Crane, Hemingway chose as subjects for his stories those moments in the life of the individual that present a violent physical crisis. Like him, too, he adopted the concept of the "code" as a means of confronting those crises. He may even have taken a hint from Crane's use of simple sentences and curt speech to develop his own method of understatement. In fact, so much does Hemingway's writing in his short stories seem an extension of what Crane had done in his short career that it is difficult not to make too much of Crane's influence.

However, other authors had a share in shaping the young Ernest Hemingway. During his apprentice years, he came under the tutelage of Ford Madox Ford, and through him learned of Henry James and Joseph Conrad, as well as Stephen Crane. Through Ford, he also met Ezra Pound, the American poet, of whom he once wrote: "He spawned a whole generation of poets." Through these two tutors he was introduced to the generation of French authors that had so affected James, and in them he was most impressed by the concept of the *mot juste*, economy and accuracy in the choice of words. What appears likely, under the circumstances, is that Hemingway, unlike many other contemporary American writers of the time, was less attracted to James's preoccupation with "manners," which may have seemed to him outdated after the First World War, than he was to Crane's portrayal of the "code" of behavior in the face of an indifferent nature. There seems little doubt that Crane's more simple and direct style and his vigorous treatment of violent subject matter had more appeal for him than James's more genteel subject and manner.

Yet Henry James did set the tone for a great deal of the work that was to be done following the rediscovery of his stories and novels in the 1920's, at a time when most of the significant "modern" authors were just beginning their careers. In fact, it might be said that part of the vitality of the American short story in our time comes from the need of our authors to consider both the subject matter revealed by such writers as Melville, Twain, and Crane and the attitude and method represented by James. Certainly this appears to be true in the case of two important representative figures, F. Scott Fitzgerald and William Faulkner.

F. Scott Fitzgerald, along with Ernest Hemingway, has for a good many years now been considered a spokesman for the "lost generation," that group of writers that grew up and began their labors at the time of the First World War. Meaningful as that title may be in discussing the background of the works of these authors, it is too limited to special social effects to serve a larger critical purpose. However, it does have value if we see it as merely a local manifestation of an attitude of rebellion that had existed in the best American writing from the beginning. Insofar as their rebellion reflected disillusion with the past, these authors made common cause with those earlier writers who portrayed the decay of Western traditions in the art and society of Europe; insofar as it viewed contemporary society as a kind of wasteland, it was in agreement with Hawthorne, who had surveyed a world of evil, and with Melville, who saw the years since the French Revolution as "the crisis of Christendom," a period of drabness and sterility, inevitable but depressing in its utilitarian waste of values and in its hypocritical greed.

F. Scott Fitzgerald's "sad young men" sought meaning and beauty in a world that could provide them only a momentary sensation. Ernest Hemingway's heroes sought certainty by discovering and adapting themselves to "a clean well-lighted place"—to the limited provisions of the code. The need for change was implicit, but the possibilities seemed limited. Such an attitude was a reaction to the idealism and the optimism of the past, as well as a representation of the sterility of the present, but it offered little hope for the future. Perhaps such hope is beyond the limited range of the short story, perhaps it is beyond the range of literature itself, perhaps it belongs rightly only within the range of philosophy or politics. Perhaps the short story, like the microscope, can be engaged only with diagnosis, not with the cure. Nevertheless, the most significant of our literary works at least hint at more than analysis, and perhaps the most important evidence of our day resides in the work of William Faulkner.

Faulkner, growing up in the American South, found himself deeply preoccupied with the subject of change in modern society. Of a generation that still felt the effects both of the destruction of an old society and the rise of a new, his short stories reflect a pervading sense of loss as well as a concern for what has superseded the old world of pre-Civil War manners and custom. In a sense, the posing of these two worlds provides a contrast similar to James's contrast between Americans and Europeans. Faulkner presents, in his short stories and novels, a postwar Southern society that is made up almost equally of characters who cling futilely to the ideals of prewar life in the South and characters who have accepted, or come to terms with, the present. In addition, he hints at an overriding judgment, based on natural virtue, that will "endure" and "prevail."

Based on injustice, the old world of Faulkner's fiction did create a society noted for its beauty and its culture. Based on concepts of liberty and utility, the modern world does emphasize greed and opportunism. Yet the old was decadent and doomed; the new does contain a certain healthy vitality. Faulkner's series of examinations of these worlds seems to be asking, What of value can be salvaged from the past?, What must of necessity be accepted in the present? Poised between two conflicting ways of life, his world of fiction is peopled by grotesques and marked by violence, but Faulkner's "human comedy" exaggerates in order to point up the futility of man's struggle against nature, to indicate the inevitability of man's survival in a world that he has done all he can to make, but which he can only momentarily (and sometimes tragically) alter.

Like William Faulkner, other Southern authors have also been impressed by the particular problems represented in their region, by the availability of its recent history almost as a "myth" for the presentation of contemporary moral problems. Katherine Anne Porter stresses the difference between the romantic dream of a colorful past and the reality behind the dream. She portrays the movement of a society in flux, depicting the futile struggle to preserve the past in the present. She emphasizes the meaningfulness of knowledge, which is the loss of innocence, the gaining of insights into the reality of change, which is corruption and death. Robert Penn Warren, likewise, stresses the significance of a recognition of evil, seeming above all to sense the dangers of innocence. Innocence he portrays as a lack of moral awareness, a breeder of irresponsible and violent events.

The lesson of these Southern authors has not been lost upon the youngest generation of American authors. Sensing in them a wisdom discovered by Hawthorne, Melville, and James, few young American writers seem willing to deny the importance of knowledge or to take their craft less seriously than their forerunners. Yet reacting against what appears to be too great an emphasis upon evil, they appear often to yearn for a more positive attitude, as though attempting to recall the optimism of Twain at his most benevolent. Even Eudora Welty, herself a Southerner, treats the Southern predicament as a kind of gentle joke that history has played upon the middle-class inhabitants of that region. Walter Van Tilburg Clark, raised in the Far West, does not appear unaware of the importance of evil in nature and society, but he seems more genuinely impressed by the sense of life that the struggle for existence in nature engenders, fraught as it is with danger not only to the individual but to society. J. F. Powers, a Midwesterner and a Catholic, portrays ironically the struggles of the modern clergy to effect a compromise between the demands of life today in America and the demands of their ancient clerical code. Flannery O'Connor and R. V. Cassill, from the South and Midwest respectively, see the absence of moral standards and social justice in contemporary society, but approach their subjects and their situations with an understanding sympathy. In most contemporary portrayals, the emphasis is upon the need for readjustment without betraying the essential spirit of the traditions of the past.

The optimism vaguely apparent in these young writers is more apparent in the short stories of John Steinbeck, who, although of the generation of Hemingway and Faulkner, reminds us that it is still part of our American inheritance to celebrate the innocent awareness of a life that is lived close to nature. Although Steinbeck occasionally lapses into sentimentality, as did Sherwood Anderson, he does at best portray a kind of primitive joy that is as genuine as the more sophisticated emotions that result from an examination of evil.

But a comparison between Steinbeck and Faulkner at their best would not suggest so much a difference of kind as a difference of emphasis. Evil in Faulkner is often allied to nature. Evil in Steinbeck is allied to manners and institutions that have lost their effectiveness. Yet even in Faulkner, nature often represents life at its most effective, while in Steinbeck, what appears to be natural life, turns out upon closer inspection to be highly mannered.

Perhaps the principal importance of such revelation is to suggest that from the beginning of its history the American short story has been presented with a dramatic and significant subject matter, and that the importance of the American story, as a literary form, has resulted from an honest preoccupation with the many aspects of that subject. A contemporary British critic, Geoffrey Moore, has recently written:

If we cannot exactly agree with some American critics that the short story was an American invention we can at least say that, even before the Civil War, it was practiced in that country with an assiduousness and considered with a seriousness for which it had to wait half a century in England.

This is all we need to insist upon—the importance of the American short story not only in our own literary history but in the total history of the short story form. For the life it portrays is more than the American scene that it treats. It represents a microscopic examination of the most meaningful sensations of all modern life, through the American experience, which has in itself become a symbolic fact.

Atmosphere and Theme
in Faulkner's
"A Rose for Emily"

THE FIRST CLUES to meaning in a short story usually arise from a detection of the principal contrasts which an author sets up. The most common, perhaps, are contrasts of character, but when characters are contrasted there is usually also a resultant contrast in terms of action. Since action reflects a moral or ethical state, contrasting action points to a contrast in ideological perspectives and hence toward the theme.

The principle contrast in William Faulkner's short story "A Rose for Emily" is between past time and present time: the past is represented in Emily herself, in Colonel Sartoris, in the old Negro servant, and in the Board of Aldermen who accepted the Colonel's attitude toward Emily and rescinded her taxes; the present is depicted through the unnamed narrator and is represented in the *new* Board of Aldermen, in Homer Barron (the representative of Yankee attitudes toward the Griersons and through them toward the entire South), and in what is called "the next generation with its more modern ideas."

Atmosphere is defined in the *Dictionary of World Literature* as "The particular world in which the events of a story or a play occur: time, place, conditions, and the attendant mood." When, as in "A Rose for Emily," the world depicted is a confusion between the past and the present, the atmosphere is one of distortion—of unreality. This unreal world results from the suspension of a natural time order. Normality consists in a decorous progression of the human being from birth, through youth, to age and finally death. Precosity in children is as monstrous as idiocy in the adult, because both are unnatural. Monstrosity, however, is a sentimental subject for fiction unless it is the result of human action—the result of a willful attempt to circumvent time. When such circumvention produces acts of violence, as in "A Rose for Emily," the atmosphere becomes one of horror.

Horror, however, represents only the extreme form of maladjusted nature. It is not produced in "A Rose for Emily" until the final act of violence has been disclosed. All that has gone before has prepared us by producing a general tone of mystery, foreboding, decay, etc., so that we may say the entire series of events that have gone before are "in key"—that is, they are depicted in a mood in which the final violence does not appear too shocking or horrible. We are inclined to say, "In such an atmosphere, anything may happen." Foreshadowing is often accomplished through atmosphere, and in this case the atmosphere prepares us for Emily's unnatural act at the end of the story. Actually, such preparation begins in the very first sentence:

When Miss Emily Grierson died, our whole town went to her funeral: the men through a sort of respectful affection for a fallen monument, the women mostly out of curiosity to see the inside of her house, which no one save an old manservant—a combined gardener and cook—had seen in at least ten years.

Atmosphere and Theme in Faulkner's "A Rose for Emily"

Emily is portrayed as "a fallen monument," a *monument* for reasons which we shall examine later, *fallen* because she has shown herself susceptible to death (and decay) after all. In the mention of death, we are conditioned (as the psychologist says) for the more specific concern with it later on. The second paragraph depicts the essential ugliness of the contrast: the description of Miss Emily's house "lifting its stubborn and coquettish decay above the cotton wagons and the gasoline pumps—an eyesore among eyesores." (A juxtaposition of past and present.) We recognize this scene as an emblematic presentation of Miss Emily herself, suggested as it is through the words "stubborn and coquettish." The tone—and the contrast —is preserved in a description of the note which Miss Emily sent to the mayor, "a note on paper of an archaic shape, in a thin, flowing calligraphy in faded ink," and in the description of the interior of the house when the deputation from the Board of Aldermen visit her: "They were admitted by the old Negro into a dim hall from which a stairway mounted into still more shadow. It smelled of dust and disuse—a close, dank smell." In the next paragraph a description of Emily discloses her similarity to the house: "She looked bloated, like a body long submerged in motionless water, and of that pallid hue."

Emily had not always looked like this. When she was young and part of the world with which she was contemporary, she was, we are told, "a slender figure in white," as contrasted with her father, who is described as "a spraddled silhouette." In the picture of Emily and her father together, framed by the door, she would have become susceptible to the town's pity— therefore, human. Emily's world, however, continues to be the Past (in its extreme form it is death), and when she is threatened with desertion and disgrace, she not only takes refuge in that world, but she also takes Homer with her, in the only manner possible.

It is important, too, to realize that during the period of Emily's courtship, the town became Emily's allies in a contest between Emily and her Grierson cousins, "because the two female cousins were even more Grierson than Miss Emily had ever been." The cousins were protecting the general proprieties against which the town (and the times) was in gradual rebellion. Just as each succeeding generation rebels against its elders, so the town took sides with Emily against her relations. Had Homer Barron been the proper kind of man, it is implied, Miss Emily might have escaped both horns of the dilemma (her cousins' traditionalism and Homer's immorality) and become an accepted and respected member of the community. The town's attitude toward the Grierson cousins represents the usual ambiguous attitude of man toward the past: a mixture of veneration and rebelliousness. The unfaithfulness of Homer represents the final act in the drama of Emily's struggle to escape from the past. From the moment that she realizes that he will desert her, tradition becomes magnified out of all proportion to life and death, and she conducts herself as though Homer really had been faithful—as though this view represented reality.

Miss Emily's position in regard to the specific problem of time is suggested in the scene where the old soldiers appear at her funeral. There are, we are told, two views of time: (1) the world of the present, viewing time as a mechanical progression in which the past is a diminishing road, never to be encountered again; (2) the world of tradition, viewing the past as a huge meadow which no winter ever quite touches, divided from (us) now by the narrow bottleneck of the most recent decade of years. The first is the view of Homer Barron and the modern generation in Jefferson. The second is the view of the older members of the Board of Aldermen and of the confederate soldiers. Emily holds the second view, except that for her there is no bottleneck dividing her from the meadow of the past.

Emily's small room above stairs has become that timeless meadow. In it, the living Emily and the dead Homer have remained together as though not even death could separate them. It is the monstrousness of this view which creates the final atmosphere of horror, and the scene is intensified by the portrayal of the unchanged objects which have surrounded Homer in life. Here he lay in the roseate atmosphere of Emily's death-in-life: "What was left of him, rotted beneath what was left of the nightshirt, had become inextricable from the bed in which he lay; and upon him and upon the pillow beside him lay that even coating of the patient and biding dust." The symbols of Homer's life of action have become mute and silent. Contrariwise, Emily's world, though it had been inviolate while she was alive, has been invaded after her death—the whole gruesome and unlovely tale unfolded.

In its simplest sense, the story says that death conquers all. But what is death? Upon one level, death is the past, tradition, whatever is opposite to the present. In the specific setting of this story, it is the past of the South in which the retrospective survivors of the war deny changing customs and the passage of time. Homer Barron, the Yankee, lived in the present, ready to take his pleasure and depart, apparently unwilling to consider the possibility of defeat, either by tradition (the Griersons) or by time (death) itself. In a sense, Emily conquered time, but only briefly and by retreating into her rose-tinted world of the past, a world in which death was denied at the same time that it is shown to have existed. Such retreat, the story implies, is hopeless, since everyone (even Emily) is finally subjected to death and the invasion of his world by the clamorous and curious inhabitants of the world of the present.

In these terms, it might seem that the story is a comment upon tradition and upon those people who live in a dream world of the past. But is it not also a comment upon the present? There is some justification for Emily's actions. She is a tragic—and heroic—figure. In the first place, she has been frustrated by her father, prevented from participating in the life of her contemporaries. When she attempts to achieve freedom, she is betrayed by a man who represents the new morality, threatened by disclosure and humiliation. The grounds of the tragedy is depicted in the scene already referred to between Emily and the deputation from the Board of Aldermen: for the new generation, the word of Colonel Sartoris meant nothing. This was a new age, a different time; the present was not bound by the promises of the past. For Emily, however, the word of the Colonel was everything. The tax notice was but a scrap of paper.

Atmosphere, we might say, is nothing but the fictional reflection of man's attitude toward the state of the universe. The atmosphere of classic tragedy inveighed against the ethical dislocation of the Grecian world merely by portraying such dislocation and depicting man's tragic efforts to conform both to the will of the gods and to the demands of his own contemporary society. Such dislocation in the modern world is likely to be seen mirrored in the natural universe, with problems of death and time representing that flaw in the golden bowl of eighteenth and nineteenth-century natural philosophy which is the inheritance of our times. Perhaps our specific dilemma is the conflict of the pragmatic present against the set mores of the past. Homer Barron was an unheroic figure who put too much dependence upon his self-centered and rootless philosophy, a belief which suggested that he could take whatever he wanted without considering any obligation to the past (tradition) or to the future (death). Emily's resistance is heroic. Her tragic flaw is the conventional pride: she undertook to regulate the natural time-universe. She acted as though death did not exist, as though she could retain her unfaithful lover by poisoning him and holding his physical self prisoner in a world which had all of the appearances of reality except that most necessary of all things—life.

The extraction of a statement of theme from so complex a subject matter is dangerous and never wholly satisfactory. The subject, as we have seen, is concerned not alone with man's relationship to death, but with this relationship as it refers to all the facets of social intercourse. The theme is not once directed at presenting an attitude of Southerner to Yankee, or Yankee to Southerner, as has been hinted at in so many discussions of William Faulkner. The Southern Problem is one of the objective facts with which the theme is concerned, but the theme itself transcends it. Wallace Stevens is certainly right when he says that a theme may be emotive as well as intellectual and logical, and it is this recognition which explains why the extraction of a logical statement of theme is so delicate and dangerous an operation: the story *is* its theme as the life of the body *is* the body.

Nevertheless, in so far as a theme represents the *meaning* of a story, it can be observed in logical terms; indeed, these are the only terms in which it can be observed for those who, at a first or even a repeated reading, fail to recognize the implications of the total story. The logical statement, in other words, may be a clue to the total, emotive content. In these terms, "A Rose for Emily" would seem to be saying that man must come to terms both with the past and the present; for to ignore the first is to be guilty of a foolish innocence, to ignore the second is to become monstrous and inhuman, above all to betray an excessive pride (such as Emily Grierson's) before the humbling fact of death. The total story says what has been said in so much successful literature, that man's plight is tragic, but that there is heroism in an attempt to rise above it.

Katherine Anne Porter and "Historic Memory"

IN DESCRIBING MIRANDA, the little girl in the short story entitled "The Grave," Katherine Anne Porter wrote: "Miranda, with her powerful social sense, which was like a fine set of antennae radiating from every pore of her skin." Miranda appears as a character in "Old Mortality," "Pale Horse, Pale Rider," and in the short stories which open *The Leaning Tower*. In general, Miranda is the mask for the author when the short story is fashioned from autobiographical material and told from the author's point of view. Insofar as the short stories are concerned—as short stories—this fact is of no importance. Insofar, however, as we are concerned with Katherine Anne Porter as a Southern author, the fact is necessary information. Miss Porter's talent consists of just such a sensibility as she attributes to Miranda. She herself has said that her method of composition is to write from memory. When a remembered incident strikes her as having meaning, she makes a note; then, as details accumulate, she adds other notes. At some point in the process, all the individual details seem suddenly to merge into a pattern. With her notes about her, she sits down and writes the short story. Many of her notes begin simply: "Remember."

How such moments occur we can deduce from another passage concerning Miranda in "The Grave," where Miss Porter says: "One day she was picking her path among the puddles and crushed refuse of a market street in a strange city of a strange country, when without warning, plain and clear in its true colors as if she looked through a frame upon a scene that had not stirred nor changed since the moment it happened, the episode of that far-off day leaped from its burial place before her mind's eye." What "leaped," of course, was not merely the episode, but the full composition of the picture— the events with their pattern of meaning. "The Grave" is the story of how Miranda and her brother Paul discovered a gold ring and a small silver dove, which had once served as a screw-head for a coffin, in the emptied grave where her grandfather had lain before his final transfer from a home burial plot to the big new public cemetery; it is also about how Paul killed a rabbit which was just about to give birth to young, and how the knowledge of the young unborn bodies lying within the womb of the dead animal was first a secret between them, then finally forgotten, until it was suddenly remembered years later "in a strange city of a strange country." "It was a very hot day and the smell in the market, with its piles of raw flesh and wilting flowers, was like the mingled sweetness and corruption she had smelled that other day in the empty cemetery at home: the day she had remembered always until now vaguely as the time she and her brother had found treasure in the opened graves."

This "memory," as it became a short story in "The Grave," is much more than the remembered incident. It is a story about birth and death, about the beginning of life and the corruption of life. The words "innocent" and "evil" do not appear in the story, except symbolically and by implication, but the story is one of the initiation of the innocent by knowledge. The gold ring which Miranda received from her brother in exchange for the small silver dove symbolizes knowledge and suggests qualities which that knowledge possesses. It is about the time "she and her brother found treasure in the opened graves," and by the end of the story, when this passage occurs, we recognize the double intention of the words: the innocent "treasure" of childhood and the sweet, mysterious, guilty "treasure" of maturity.

How did the incident come to take on this burden of meaning? No complete answer can be given, of course. We must begin vaguely by saying that Katherine Anne Porter's creative sensitivity, like Miranda's, is a "powerful social sense," which detects special and subtle meanings in experience and translates them into fiction. By this, we mean that her senses, "like a fine set of antennae," detect meanings in experience which are then transformed into aesthetic experiences, where the meanings are made available through their embodiment in recognizable images, characters, and events. What we are to be most concerned with in this account is the nature of the experience upon which that sensibility operates.

Katherine Anne Porter was born in Texas in 1894, of a family which traced its ancestry to Daniel Boone, the Kentucky pioneer. If we take the account of Miranda's background in the stories from *The Leaning Tower* as being roughly autobiographical, we can say that the family had moved, within the lifetime of Miss Porter's grandmother, from Kentucky into Louisiana, and from there to Texas. As with most Southern families, it had retained a strong sense of family unity as well as an awareness of its place in the framework of Southern history and Southern society. The grandfather, although he had died before the family left Kentucky and even though the move itself was mainly necessitated by his imprudence, moved with the family each time they were uprooted, for his grave "had been twice disturbed in his long repose by the constancy and possessiveness of his widow. She removed his bones first to Louisiana and then to Texas as if she had set out to find her own burial place, knowing well she would never return to the places she had left."

Miss Porter's experience, then, is not only of the fixed, almost absolute values of Southern society, but also of our relationship to them in the face of a history of movement and change. In addition, the family was Scot and Presbyterian, inheriting a rugged stubbornness as its national inheritance, a determined set of moral values from its religion. When the grandmother talked about "all the important appearances of life, and especially about the rearing of the young," she "relied with perfect acquiescence on the dogma that children were conceived in sin and brought forth in iniquity. Childhood was a long state of instruction and probation for adult life, which was in turn a long, severe, undeviating devotion to duty, the largest part of which consisted in bringing up children."

I realize the dangers of talking about events from a literary work as though they were autobiographical facts. I think the danger in the case of Katherine Anne Porter is lessened, however, by the fact that so much of her subject matter lies within the areas of her own experience: her Southern background, her travels in Mexico and Europe, her Roman Catholic conversion, and her interest in liberal social causes. Also, in describing once how she had come to write the short story "Old Mortality," her tongue slipped, so that instead of saying, "Miranda's father said . . . ," she made the remark, *"My father said . . ."* In talking with her once about her stories, I asked her about the character Laura in "Flowering Judas." I had been puzzled by this character, because so many of the background facts concerning Laura were similar to those in Katherine Anne Porter's own experience: the strict religious upbringing, the interest in modern social causes, and the fact that Miss Porter had taught in Mexico and that when she returned she had brought with her an exhibition of paintings by Mexican school children. Why, then, wasn't this character called Miranda? Was Laura also an autobiographical figure? I asked. No. Laura was modeled upon a friend with whom Miss Porter had taught school in Mexico—but of course she was not merely a portrait of that girl; she was, Miss Porter supposed, a combination of a good many people, just as was the character

Braggioni, in the same story. At the same time, the events of "Pale Horse, Pale Rider"—which is a Miranda story—were many of them actual events which happened when Miss Porter was working as a reporter on the *Rocky Mountain News* in Denver during the first war.

The danger arises, of course, when a character possesses traits similar to those belonging to Miranda. But the important thing to notice is that in all cases, Katherine Anne Porter's characters possess qualities which have some point of similarity with her own experience. If they are Irish or Mexican, they are also Roman Catholic—or they are political liberals. They are usually Southerners. I don't mean to suggest this as a serious limitation, but it may help to account for the relatively small amount that Miss Porter has written. At the same time, it may also account for the consistently high level which her work represents, a level probably unsurpassed by any writer of her time. When necessary, she exhibits a range of perception of ordinary manners and mannerisms which is almost uncanny; but usually such qualities, as in the character of Mr. Thompson in "Noon Wine," are attached to a person well within the limits of her own experience. The whole atmosphere of the Thompson place, which is a Western Texas farm in the years between 1896 and 1905, seems to suggest that such an event must actually have occurred, even if not precisely as it is related in the story, and that the author knew very well the kind of people Mr. and Mrs. Thompson were, even if she did not know exactly these same persons. Mr. Helton, in the same story, who is a Swede and who came from North Dakota, is an interesting and successful character, but he does not occupy so prominent a position in the story and so does not bear so heavy a burden of probability. The events of "Noon Wine" center upon Mr. Thompson's guilt—the psychological effects of an unpremeditated killing; and we can imagine that the story began from a memory either of the event or of the character of Mr. Thompson, or both, in the mind of the author, who was probably about seven or eight years of age at the time of the murder and suicide. It could have begun from the events alone, and the character could have been supplied from other memories; but however it happened, the character at the center of the story was of a type that Miss Porter must have known well, while the less familiar Mr. Helton got into the story because he was necessary to the events.

The important point is that such memory as we are talking about in discussing Miss Porter's talent is not "mere memory," not only memory of something that occurred, but something that occurred within the long history of personal, family, and regional events—finally, within the history of mankind. In referring to the friendship between Sophia Jane, Miranda's grandmother, and her Negro maid in "The Old Order," Miss Porter writes: "The friendship between the two old women had begun in early childhood, and was based on what seemed even to them almost mythical events." Miss Porter treats her memories also as "mythical events."

Myth is, of course, a form of tribal memory, preserving events of the past as a means of justifying and explaining its views of the present. Every society adapts "myth" to its own purposes, either myths which it has transported from elsewhere and uses as a means of organizing its memories, or myths which it has created from events of its own past. Colonial America, as Constance Rourke has pointed out in her book on American humor, created its concept of the typical Yankee, which is as true of the frontier peddler as it is of the modern G. I.—and as untrue. The society of the South was particularly inclined toward the creation of myths—partly, I suppose, because of the amount of Latin influence in its history, partly because of the amount of Anglo-Catholicism, partly because of its Negroes, but mainly because of its closeness to nature and because of the rural nature of its plantation society. The Latin background gave it a regard for manners and romance; the Anglican, a respect for ceremony; while the Negroes fused the two with primitive magic. In addition, the aristocratic and paternalistic structure of the plantation represented a means not only of creating regional and family myth but also of preserving it in a more or less unbroken chain from earliest times down to at least the period of the Civil War.

There have been bitter quarrels with the nature of the Southern myth, but few deny its reality or its importance to the society which it reflected. We may say that the South spent the first years creating its myths, a few important years defending them (even in battle), and its most recent years utilizing them as the subject matter for literature. Perhaps their most complete use is represented in the novels and short stories of William Faulkner, where the timeless world of eternal values of the Southern past is posted against the fluid and pragmatic present. In one way or another these contrasts have gotten into most Southern writing, whether the poetry of Allen Tate, John Crowe Ransom, John Peale Bishop, Robert Penn Warren, and Donald Davidson, or into the prose fiction of Ellen Glasgow, Caroline Gordon, Stark Young, Eudora Welty, Peter Taylor, Carson McCullers, Tate, Warren, and Katherine Anne Porter. With a special emphasis, it is to be found in the writings of Truman Capote, Elizabeth Hardwick, William Goyen, Tennessee Williams, and Leroy Leatherman. With an inverted emphasis, it is utilized by Erskine Caldwell, Lillian Hellman, and most of the Negro writers of our time.

Yet each author poses a separate problem—not the least of them Katherine Anne Porter. She is less the self-conscious "professional" Southerner than either Donald Davidson or Truman Capote; she shares somewhat in the tendency toward inversion—the liberalism—of Erskine Caldwell. The question of how much an author owes to his region has been discussed endlessly and is now seen as a futile preoccupation, at least insofar as an evaluation of his work is concerned. Even as it concerns the author himself, it has only a limited and often questionable value. But it is tantalizingly present as a puzzle in personality. Just what kind of writer might Katherine Anne Porter have been if she had been born and raised in a Fundamentalist, Protestant New England family in, say, Rutland, Vermont? The question is hypothetical and nonsensical, but it does emphasize the importance of Miss Porter's Southern, and religious background. How much her sensibility was affected either by her place or her religion must remain a puzzle, but her sensibility is her *self*—including her memory, which she would have had in any case, and she herself *did* grow up in the South of a family with a long history of living in the South; she became Roman Catholic; and she did, as the result of an unusually perceptive mind, recognize the importance of that background, not only as subject matter for her works, but also as representing a point of view toward all experience.

Herman Melville has spoken of "historic memory," implying that it is at least one quality of the artist's general "prescience." I can think of no better phrase to describe Miss Porter's special sensibility than to call it "historic memory." Such memory, though it does, as Melville stated, go "far backward through long defiles of doom," begins with the specific present: the young girl finding a carved dove in an abandoned grave and trading it for a gold ring, another remembering the image of a dead aunt preserved in a family photograph and the family memory and contrasting them with the living present, the memory of illness and death during the influenza epidemic at the time of the First World War, the memories of Mexican revolutionaries, of moving-picture companies on location, of Mexican women and West Texas farmers stirred to violence by passion. Partly these memories are controlled by a Catholic sensibility, which seeks out the ceremony and order in the events, partly by a Southern habit of thought that metamorphoses reality into "romance"—not the romance of inferior Southern authors, who see the events as picturesque and quaint manifestations of a peculiar social order, but something nearer the "romance" that Hawthorne sought in his *The House of the Seven Gables,* a romance that links man of the present with the long, legendary concepts of man in a continued and continuing past.

The creation and utilization of myth is, then, in Katherine Anne Porter's work, both subject matter and method. Neither as a Southerner nor as a Catholic is she orthodox—that is, she does not mistake the myth for the reality; for her it is merely another kind of reality. Hawthorne called it "the truths of the human heart." Today, I suppose we should prefer a term such as "psychological truth." The important thing in a short story like "Flowering Judas" is not that Laura fails to escape the conflict between a conservative upbringing and the desire to assist in liberal political causes, but that such a conflict is at the bottom of the whole idea of man's Christian redemption; that there is something Christlike about such a dilemma. The important thing in "Pale Horse, Pale Rider" is not that a young Southern girl found the war horrible or that she suffered from influenza and lost her lover to it, but that the sequence of events mirrored the relationship of man to good and evil. The important thing about "The Jilting of Granny Weatherall" is not merely that a proud and stubborn old lady dies, unable to forget the jilting of a long-lost lover, but that the story reflects a particular, but common, attitude toward death.

Perhaps the most complete instance of a short story which utilizes a specifically Southern background and memory for the creation of this larger, more generalized "truth" is "Old Mortality," where Miss Porter's subject matter is Southern attitudes as expressed through family history, and where the theme is concerned with the nature of reality—particularly with self-definition. The story is told from the point of view of Miranda between the ages of eight and eighteen, and its details agree with all of the other Miranda stories insofar as they detail events in a family which had moved from Kentucky to Louisiana and from there to Texas. At the center of the story are the memories of a girl, Amy, about whose long courtship and brief marriage to "Uncle Gabriel" the aura of "romance" has accumulated. We meet her first in a photograph in the family parlor, "a spirited-looking young woman, with dark curly hair cropped and parted on the side, a short oval face with straight eyebrows, and a large curved mouth." The family legend represents her as a vivacious, daring, and extremely beautiful young girl, against whom the beauty and grace of later members of the family are forever being judged. It tells of her using her cruel beauty to tantalize Uncle Gabriel until he despaired of ever winning her, of her precipitating events at a ball which caused a family scandal and disgrace. It tells of her sad suffering from an incurable illness, of her sudden and romantic marriage to Gabriel, and of her early death.

But the legend, which is more than just a romantic memory of Aunt Amy, is also a reflection of the family's attitude toward all events of the past—memories which Miranda cannot share and an attitude which she cannot adopt because of discrepancies which she senses between such stories, as related by the family, and the actual facts which she perceives in the people and events which surround her in the everyday life of the present. In the photograph of Amy, for instance, "The clothes were not even romantic looking, but merely most terribly out of fashion"; in the talk about the slimness of the women in the family, Miranda is reminded of their Great-Aunt Eliza, "who quite squeezed herself through doors," and of her Great-Aunt Keziah, in Kentucky, whose husband, Great-Uncle John Jacob, "had refused to allow her to ride his good horses after she had achieved two hundred and twenty pounds"; in watching her grandmother crying over her accumulation of ornaments of the past, Miranda saw only "dowdy little wreaths and necklaces, some of them made of pearly shells; such moth-eaten bunches of pink ostrich feathers for the hair; such clumsy big breast pins and bracelets of gold and colored enamel; such silly-looking combs, standing up on tall teeth capped with seed pearls and French paste." Yet despite these disappointing incongruities, the child Miranda struggled to believe that there was "a life beyond a life in this world, as well as in the next"; such episodes as members of her family remembered confirmed "the nobility of human feeling, the divinity of man's vision of the unseen, the importance of life and death, the depths of the human heart, the romantic value of tragedy."

Another view is suggested in the second section of the story, when Miranda and her sister have become schoolgirls in a New Orleans convent. During vacation on their grandmother's farm, they had read books detailing accounts of how "beautiful but unlucky maidens, who for mysterious reasons had been trapped by nuns and priests in dire collusion, 'were placed' in convents, where they were forced to take the veil—an appalling rite during which the victims shrieked dreadfully—and condemned forever after to most uncomfortable and disorderly existences. They seemed to divide their time between lying chained in dark cells and assisting other nuns to bury throttled infants under stones in moldering rat-infested dungeons." In Miranda's actual experience at the convent, no one even hinted that she should become a nun. "On the contrary Miranda felt the discouraging attitude of Sister Claude and Sister Austin and Sister Ursula towards her expressed ambition to be a nun barely veiled a deeply critical knowledge of her spiritual deficiencies."

The most disheartening disillusion came, however, during this period, when Miranda came actually to meet the legendary Uncle Gabriel for the first time. His race horse was running in New Orleans and her father had taken her to bet a dollar on it, despite the fact that odds against it were a hundred to one. "Can that be our Uncle Gabriel?" Miranda asked herself. "Is that Aunt Amy's handsome romantic beau? Is that the man who wrote the poem about our Aunt Amy?" Uncle Gabriel, as she met him, "was a shabby fat man with bloodshot blue eyes, sad beaten eyes, and a big melancholy laugh like a groan. His language was coarse, and he was a drunkard. Even though his horse won the race and brought Miranda a hundred unexpected dollars—an event which had the making of a legend in itself, Miranda saw that victory had been purchased, not as a result of beauty, but at the price of agony; for the mare when seen close up "was bleeding at the nose," and, "Her eyes were wild and her knees were trembling."

In legend, the past was beautiful or tragic. In art, it might be horrible and dangerous. In the present of Miranda's experience, it was ugly or merely commonplace. In the first two sections of "Old Mortality," we get first the view of the past as seen through the eyes of the elders with their memories of the past, not as it actually was, but as they wanted it to be. In section two, we get the view of it through the eyes of Miranda herself, who judges it merely as it is reflected in her present. By section three, Miranda is eighteen. She has eloped and married, but she is still struggling to understand her own relationship to the past. To her, her elopement seemed in the romantic tradition of Aunt Amy and Uncle Gabriel, although we soon learn that it is, in actual fact, a failure. We meet her on the train, returning home for the funeral of Uncle Gabriel. His body has been returned to lie beside Amy's, as though in a final attempt to justify the dream, even though he has married again, and (it is hinted) there are better and more real reasons for him to be buried beside his second wife, who had shared the bulk of his wandering, homeless, and meaningless existence. On the train, Miranda runs into Cousin Eva, also returning for the funeral, whose own life had been burdened by a constant comparison with the legend of Amy. While Amy was beautiful, thoughtless, impulsive, and daring, Cousin Eva had been homely, studious, and dedicated to high purposes. Amy had died and had been preserved in the romantic legend; Eva had lived to develop a character and a reputation as a fighter for women's rights. In a sense, Cousin Eva's good works, too, were part of her legend of homeliness and dedication. At bottom, Miranda finds her a bitter, prematurely aged woman; but it is Cousin Eva who provides her with a third view of the legend of Aunt Amy. She hints that it was nothing but sublimated sex that caused the young girls of Amy's day to behave as they did. " 'Those parties and dances were their market, a girl couldn't afford to miss out, there were always rivals waiting to cut the ground from under her. . . . It was just sex,' she said in despair; 'their minds dwelt on nothing else. They didn't call it that, it was all smothered under pretty names, but that's all it was, sex.' "

The old, then, had two ways of looking at the past: the

romantic way of Miranda's father and of other members of the family, and the "enlightened" way of Cousin Eva. Each way was different, and each was wrong. But the old did have something in common; they had their memories. Thus, when the train arrived at the station, it was Cousin Eva and Miranda's father who sat together in the back seat of the automobile and talked about old times; it was Miranda who was excluded from these memories and who sat beside the driver in the front. Yet Miranda feels that she has a memory now and the beginning of her own legend—the legend of her elopement. Strangely enough, neither Cousin Eva nor her father will accept it. When reminded by Miranda of it, Cousin Eva says: "Shameful, shameful. . . . If you had been my child I should have brought you home and spanked you." Her father resented it. When he met her at the train, he showed it in his coldness. "He had not forgiven her, she knew that. When would he? She could not guess, but she felt it would come of itself, without words and without acknowledgment on either side, for by the time it arrived neither of them would need to remember what had caused their division, nor why it had seemed so important. Surely old people cannot hold their grudges forever because the young want to live, too, she thought in her arrogance, her pride. I will make my own mistakes, not yours; I cannot depend upon you beyond a certain point, why depend at all? There was something more beyond, but this was a first step to take, and she took it, walking in silence beside her elders who were no longer Cousin Eva and Father, since they had forgotten her presence, but had become Eva and Harry, who knew each other well, who were comfortable with each other, being contemporaries on equal terms, who occupied by right their place in this world, at the time of life to which they had arrived by paths familiar to them both. They need not play their roles of daughter, of son, to aged persons who did not understand them; nor of father and elderly female cousin to young persons whom they did not understand. They were precisely themselves; their eyes cleared, their voices relaxed into perfect naturalness, they need not weigh their words or calculate the effect of their manner 'It is I who have no place,' thought Miranda. 'Where are my people and my own time?' "

Miranda is not merely a Southern child, in Southern history, reflected through the sensibility of a Southern author—even though she is—partly, at least—all these things. She is any child, anywhere, seeking to come to terms with her past and her present—seeking definition. Katherine Anne Porter's Southern history, whether legendary or actual, provided the concrete experience through which her "historic memory" could function. Thus when she wrote the concluding sentence of "Old Mortality," she was expressing, not the dilemma of Miranda alone, but the dilemma of all of us who seek understanding. " 'At least I can know the truth about what happens to me,' " Miranda thinks, "making a promise to herself, in her hopefulness, her ignorance."

It is out of hopefulness and ignorance combined that myths are constructed and self-definition achieved, from a sense of social need and a vision of a society which expresses both the hopefulness and the need. Southern society represented the proper conditions for the perceptive talent of an artist such as Katherine Anne Porter, who responded both critically and with a warmth of admiration to her memories, thus transforming them, finally, into something more than mere memory.

Katherine Anne Porter: Symbol and Theme in "Flowering Judas"

K ATHERINE ANNE PORTER, in writing of Katherine Mans-
field's fictional method in 1937, said that she "states no
belief, gives no motive, airs no theories, but simply presents
to the reader a situation, a place and a character, and there
it is; and the emotional content is present as implicitly as the
germ in the grain of wheat." Of her own method she has written: "Now and again thousands of memories converge, har-
monize, arrange themselves around a central idea in a
coherent form, and I write a story."

Enlightening though these statements are concerning Miss
Porter's concept of a short story, true as they appear to be of
her own fiction and of the creative process, they still leave the
reader with his own problem of "understanding" when he is
confronted with the individual story. If we disregard the fact
that the first statement was made about a fellow artist (it is
still descriptive of Miss Porter's own stories), we must yet discover the "germ" which produced the emotion and which

flowers into the final form of the story. Though we might say that the converging, the harmonizing, and the arranging constitute a logical, though partly subconscious, activity which serves to bring the objects of memory into some kind of order, still it is the nature of this synthesis—particularly the predominantly social themes from "Flowering Judas" (1930) to *The Leaning Tower* (1944)—which puzzles most readers.

That Miss Porter herself was aware of the nature of her sensibility is clear from her comments concerning Miranda in a late story, who had, she says, "a powerful social sense, which was like a fine set of antennae radiating from every pore of her skin." Miss Porter's own social sense is most obvious (perhaps too obvious) in her latest long story, "The Leaning Tower," but it is not with the most obvious examples that the reader wishes to concern himself; rather, with the seemingly obscure; and since we have nowhere seen published or heard expounded an examination of "Flowering Judas," and since it is perhaps Miss Porter's best known story (to our mind, her most successful single work of fiction), let us examine that with the aim of understanding just what the author means by social sensibility—how it operates within the story itself.

The surface detail in "Flowering Judas" is relatively simple. An American girl who has been educated in a Southern convent is in Mexico teaching school and aiding a group of revolutionaries under Braggioni, a sensual hulk of a man, formerly a starving poet, but who is now in a position to indulge even his appetite for the most expensive of small luxuries. The girl (Laura) teaches her children in the daytime and at night runs errands for Braggioni, acting as go-between for him and the foreign revolutionaries, delivering messages and narcotics to members of the party who are in jail. At the point where the story opens, Braggioni has come to Laura's apartment to discover, if possible, whether it would be worth the effort to attempt an assault upon her "notorious virginity," which he, like the others, cannot understand. Laura is physically attractive, and this is not the first time that she has been courted by the Mexicans. Her first suitor was a young captain whom she evaded by spurring her horse when he attempted to take her into his arms, pretending that the horse had shied. The second was a young organizer of the typographers' union who had serenaded her and written her bad poetry which he tacked to her door. She had unwittingly encouraged him by tossing a flower from her balcony as he sang to her from the patio. A third person, Eugenio, is unknown to the reader until near the end of the story, when it turns out that he is expected to die of a self-imposed overdose of the narcotics which Laura had delivered to him at the prison. He is, however, the principal figure in a dream which ends the story, a dream in which Laura imagines him to have accused her of murdering him and in which he forces her to eat of the blossoms of the Judas tree which grows in the courtyard below her window.

All of the immediate action takes place in Laura's apartment after she has returned and found Braggioni awaiting her. He sings to her in a voice "passionately off key," talks about their curious relationship, about the revolution, and finally leaves after having Laura clean his pistol for use in a May-day disturbance between the revolutionaries and the Catholics of a nearby town. Braggioni returns to his wife, whom he has deserted for a month to pay attention to Laura, and who, despite the fact that she has been weeping over his absence, accepts his return gratefully and washes his feet. Laura goes to bed and has her dream of Eugenio.

It will be seen, even from this brief summary, that there are a great many details unexplained by the course of the action. There is the concern with revolutionary activities running throughout; there are the comments concerning Laura's religious training: the nun-like clothing, her slipping away into a small church to pray, the May-day demonstration. Obviously, a great many details have symbolic references, not the least of which is the title itself.

If we turn to any standard encyclopedia, we discover that the Flowering Judas is a tree commonly known as the Judas tree or Redbud. We learn further that a popular legend relates that it is from this tree that Judas Iscariot hanged himself. A second fact is that the exact title appears in a line from T. S. Eliot's poem "Gerontion":

> In the juvescence of the year
> Came Christ the tiger
>
> In depraved May, dogwood and chestnut, flowering judas,
> To be eaten, to be divided, to be drunk
> Among whispers.

This is scarcely a coincidence, since Eliot's passage so clearly suggests Laura's activity at the end of the story. Our first question is: what use is made of this symbol? The dividing, the eating and drinking among whispers suggests the Christian sacrament, but it is a particular kind of sacrament. "Christ the tiger" refers to the pagan ritual in which the blood of a slain tiger is drunk in order to engender in the participants the courage of the tiger heart. In a sense this is only a more primitive form of sacrament, one which presupposes a *direct* rather than symbolic transfer of virtues from the animal to man. In the Christian ritual, the symbolic blood of Christ is drunk in remembrance of atonement; that is, symbolically to engender the virtues of Christ in the participant.

If the Judas tree, then, is a symbol for the betrayer of Christ (the legend says that its buds are red because it actually became the body of Judas, who is said to have had red hair), then the sacrament in which Laura participated—the eating of the buds of the Flowering Judas—is a sacrament, not of remembrance, but of betrayal.

This leads us to other uses of the Saviour-symbol in the story. The first is Braggioni, who, at one point, is even called a "world-saviour." It is said that "his skin has been punctured in honorable warfare"; "He has a great nobility, a love of humanity raised above mere personal affection"; finally, he is depicted, like Christ, undergoing the final purification, the foot-washing. But there are important reservations in the use of this symbol: (1) the note of irony with which Braggioni is depicted and which suggests the attitude the reader should take toward him; (2) each time the Christ-like epithet is used, it is accompanied by other, non-Christian characteristics: "His skin has been *punctured* in honorable warfare, but *he is a skilled revolutionary*"; he is a *professional* lover of humanity, a *hungry* world-saviour. It is the use of the religious symbols alongside the secular which makes Braggioni the complex and interesting character that he is.

The second use of the Christ-symbol is present in the character of Eugenio, who is seen first as one of the revolutionary workers languishing in jail, but who figures most prominently as the person in Laura's dream. His name contains the clue to his symbolic meaning—well-born. As Christ is the Son of God, he is well-born. He is, likewise, a symbol of all mankind—Man. We say he is the "Son of Man." In this respect, Eugenio is also Christ-like, for he is well-born without the reservations noted in the character of Braggioni—in the highest sense. And as Judas was the direct cause of Christ's crucifixion, so Laura becomes the murderer of Eugenio (of Man) by carrying narcotics to his prison cell, the narcotics through which he (Christ-like) surrendered himself up to death.

We can say, then, that the use of religious symbolism by Miss Porter might suggest that her story be taken as a kind of religious allegory. But there are other, complicating symbols. There is, for instance, Laura's fear of machines such as the *automobile;* there is her dislike for things made on machines; and finally there is the statement that *the machine is sacred* to the workers. In the last instance, we may see how the word "machine" is coupled with the religious word "sacred," thus bringing the two kinds of symbols into juxtaposition, just as the same thing is implied in the descriptions we have had of Braggioni. For instance, "His skin has been punctured in honorable warfare" suggests the act of crucifixion, but "puncture" is not a word which we would ordinarily use in describing either the nailing of Christ to the cross or the piercing of his flesh by the spear of the Roman soldier. The most common use of "puncture" now is its reference to automobile tires (of which Laura is afraid). Likewise, the word "professional" used to modify "a lover of humanity" brings the modern idea of business efficiency into conjunction with the image of Christ, as though one were to say, explicitly: "Braggioni is an impersonal, cold-blooded Christ."

A third type of symbols is composed of love-symbols (erotic, secular, and divine). The story shows Laura unable to participate in love upon any of the levels suggested: (1) as a divine lover in the Christian sense, for it is clear that she is incapable of divine passion when she occasionally sneaks into a small church to pray; (2) as a professional lover in the sense that Braggioni is one, for she cannot participate in the revolutionary fervor of the workers, which might be stated as an activity expressive of secular love for their fellowmen; she cannot even feel the proper emotion for the children who scribble on their blackboards, "We lov ar ticher"; (3) as an erotic lover, for she responds to none of her three suitors, though she thoughtlessly throws one of them a rose (the symbol of erotic love), an act of profanation, since the boy wears it in his hat until it withers and dies.

Having located these symbols, it is now our problem to examine the use that is made of them. More specifically, we can say that the religious symbols represent the Christian ideology, while the secular are symbols most readily identified with the attitudes of Marxism. As philosophy, they would seem to represent the two most extreme positions possible; yet both claim as their aim the betterment of mankind. If we consider them as areas within which man may act, we might represent them as two circles.

The third field (love) is not so much an area within which man performs as it is an attitude toward his actions. The fact that we refer to "divine love" and "secular love" will illustrate this distinction. On the other hand, if we speak of a "code of love," then love comes to resemble a kind of philosophy and is similar to Christianity and Marxism. As there is evidence in the relationship of Laura to the young Captain and to her suitor from the typographers' union that Miss Porter had this relationship in mind as well as the other, we might represent our third symbolic field as a circle overlapping the other two, but also existing as a separate area.

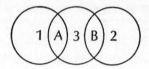

At this point, we must remember the relationship between "Flowering Judas" and Eliot's "Gerontion." The poem is concerned with a wasteland image; that is, with a view of life as a wasteland, sterile and barren as old-age, because of the absence of any fructifying element. Eliot's old man in the poem says:

> I have lost my passion: why should I need to keep it
> Since what is kept must be adulterated?
> I have lost my sight, smell, hearing, taste, and touch:
> How should I use them for your closer contact?

In "Flowering Judas" Laura has lost the use of her senses: when the children scribble their message of love, she can feel nothing for them. They are only "wise, innocent, clay-colored faces," just as the revolutionists have become "clay masks with the power of human speech." She is like the prisoners, shut off from human contact, who, when they complain to her, " 'Dear little Laura, time doesn't pass in this infernal hole, and I won't know when it is time to sleep unless I have a reminder,' she brings them their favorite narcotics, and says in a tone that does not wound them with pity, 'Tonight will be really night for you.' " Seeing the colored flowers the children have painted, she remembers the young captain who has made love to her and thinks, "I must send him a box of colored crayons." She confuses the children with the prisoners, "the poor prisoners who come every day bringing flowers to their jailor." "It is monstrous," she thinks with sudden insight, "to confuse love with revolution, night with day, life with death." Laura, like the figure in Eliot's poem, has lost her passion, she has lost her sight, smell, hearing, taste, and touch. She cannot use them for closer contact.

Now, if we return to our circles, perhaps this can be made clear. The philosophical systems represented by each circle (1. religion, 2. revolution, 3. love) represent a means of dealing with the wasteland. That is, faith in any one of the systems will provide a kind of signpost, which is the first step in transforming the wilderness of modern social living. By observing the signposts, we at least know where we are going or what we are doing there. Yet—it is still the wasteland. However, when we superimpose circle 3 upon either of the other two, the sterility disappears. In other words, either orthodox religion or socialism is a wasteland until transformed by the fructifying power of love; obversely, love is impossible without the object provided by either. In terms of our diagram, all is sterility outside the circles or at any point within the circles where 3 does not overlap either 1 or 2—that is, within the areas A or B.

Laura may be said to be outside any of the circles. Because of her early training, she is pulled away from a belief in the revolutionary cause of Braggioni. Because of her desire to accept the principles of revolution, she is unable to accept the principles of her religious education. Without either Christianity or Marxism, it is impossible for her to respond to her suitors or to the children. She cannot even feel pity for the prisoners; she can only supply them with narcotics, which likens their condition to hers, for her life seems to be a senseless kind of existence similar to the drugged sleep of the prisoners.

Braggioni's condition is likened to Laura's ("We are more

alike than you realize in some things," he tells her), but there are two important differences: (1) he has the revolutionary ideal as a guide; (2) he is capable of redemption, as the final, footwashing scene with his wife ("whose sense of reality is beyond criticism") shows. We can say, then, that Braggioni is not, as Laura is, outside the circles. He is within one of them, but it is not until he is touched with pity that he is brought wholly within the area of redemption (either A or B). Laura is not redeemed, even though she desires it, as the eating of the buds of the Judas tree suggests. Her sacrament is a devouring gesture and Eugenio calls her a cannibal, because she is devouring him (Man). She is, like Judas, the betrayer; and her betrayal, like his, consisted in an inability to believe. Without faith she is incapable of passion, thence of love, finally of life itself. Reduced to the inadequacy of statement, we might say that the theme, lacking all of the story's subtle comment, might be rendered as: Man cannot live divided by materialistic and spiritual values, nor can he live in the modern world by either without faith and love.

As the Nazi landlady in "The Leaning Tower" is made to say when overcharging the American student who wishes to cancel his lease: "Indecision is a very expensive luxury."

Laura's world, then, is as barren and sterile as the world of Eliot's "Gerontion"; it is a living death. Said another way, the living world exists only in our sensory perception of it, and any deadening of the senses (through a denial of traditional human values) constitutes a relinquishing of moral responsibility—the betrayal of mankind into the hands of the Braggionis or, as in "The Leaning Tower," into the hands of the Nazis.

This is, I suspect, what one reviewer discovered as early as 1938, when, in a review of the volume *Flowering Judas,* he wrote: "Miss Porter, I feel, is one of the most 'socially conscious' of our writers." But one might also fear that this reviewer was thinking in terms of the predominant Marxist movements of the thirties, into none of which Miss Porter could, obviously, be made to fit. "I do not mean," he continued, "simply that she is conscious of the physical suffering of her impoverished people; I mean rather that she understands the impoverishment of mind and spirit which accompanies the physical fact, and she sees too that some native goodness in these minds and spirits still lives."

But if "some native goodness" were all Miss Porter's characters had to recommend themselves to us as resolutions of our social dilemma, then every author who does not allegorize good and evil is still "socially conscious," and the reviewer's remarks represent a somewhat dubious compliment. The fact is, however, that he was right perceptually. Behind Miss Porter's elaborate structure of symbol and myth lies the psychological motivation which produces the theme. The germ which lies implicit in the grain of wheat is the central idea about which her memories cluster. An idea does not constitute her "meaning" in the usual sense of the word, but it represents a concept which makes the surface detail available to meaning. To put it another way, the very rightness of the *ideological* fact (the myth or symbol) charges the *particular* fact (the object as it exists in nature) with a meaning that is presented as an experiential whole, but which is available in all its complex relationships only when we have become aware of the entire field of reference.

Three Methods of
Modern Fiction

Ernest Hemingway, Thomas Mann,
Eudora Welty

MODERN CRITICISM has concerned itself more with poetry than with fiction for several reasons. First, fiction does not lend itself so readily as verse to the close analytical approach. Second, there is no body of critical theory upon the subject of fiction comparable to the poetic theory available to the critic of poetry. Third, the tremendous output of short fiction and novels tends to obscure the total picture and to make the initial problem of selection and evaluation extremely difficult. The result is that fiction, when it has been examined, has been subjected to the same criteria as those applied to verse; sometimes, as in the case of such authors as James, Joyce, or Kafka, with excellent results; at other times, with authors such as Tolstoi, Mann, or Hemingway, the results have either been bad or criticism has limited itself to discussions of the authors' lives, their social background, or their historical importance.

There are good reasons why contemporary criticism has been concerned primarily with elucidation. Understanding, as one critic has pointed out recently, demands a knowledge of the artist's technique. His technique is his work, for what is a novel or a short story but experience reflected, or distilled, or refined by the writer's sensibility? The metaphor is as near as we can come to generalizing the act upon its primary level— that of creation itself. It is only in specific instances that we can identify the fictional method as this or that and never without a primary consideration for the *heart* of the work— its theme. Consider the three following examples.

I. THEME THROUGH ACTION

Gertrude Stein called Ernest Hemingway the spokesman for the "lost generation," and critics have consistently pointed to his early novels as documents of despair and insisted that his early themes stressed the absence of all moral values except the isolated and subjective codes of the individual. "Morals are what you feel good after" is a famous statement from *Death in the Afternoon.* In *A Farewell to Arms,* Frederic Henry sees human life as comparable to ants on the log of a burning campfire. In an early essay, Hemingway wrote:

The first thing you found out about the dead was that, hit badly enough, they died like animals. Some quickly from a little wound you would not think would kill a rabbit. . . . Others would die like cats; a skull broken in and iron in the brain, they lie alive two days like cats that crawl into the coal bin with a bullet in the brain and will not die until you cut their heads off. Maybe cats do not die then. They say they have nine lives. I do not know, but most men die like animals, not men.

Now a concern with how men die is a concern with human morality. In the image of the ants and in the statement above, it would seem that Ernest Hemingway denies any *human* value to the act of dying. All men die like animals. There is nothing glorious about death in war. Yet the themes of two of the best known short stories, one early ("The Undefeated") and one late ("The Short Happy Life of Francis Macomber"), express almost the exact opposite. If we examine the latter, we discover that the death of Francis Macomber becomes the symbol of a final victory of Man over Death—a symbolic portrayal of the difference between the death of a man and the death of an animal, and that this concept is clothed in terms of the action through which the characters move.

The action is both simple and complex. It is complex in the sense that it does not begin at the actual beginning of the action but breaks into the middle, then flashes back to the earlier scenes, then picks up and continues to the end. It is simple in that the full course of events can be restated briefly, as follows: Francis Macomber, an American sportsman hunting with his wife in Africa, has earned the contempt of his wife through a display of cowardice on a lion hunt. The situation, however, brings the wife pleasure, because she is no longer in love with her husband, and his violation of the code of the hunter serves to justify her desire to violate their marriage contract; that is, it gives her a "moral" advantage over him by releasing her from the conventional obligation of marital fidelity. It also releases the guide, who becomes a party to her infidelity, from his obligation to his own code. When, however, Francis Macomber redeems himself by standing up to a charging water buffalo, the situation is reversed. Macomber regains his advantage over his wife; and she, in her frustration at losing and under the pretense of shooting at the animal, sends a bullet into his brain. Francis Macomber dies at the moment of his victory.

Retold thus, the story retains no remnant of its original power. It is the bare skeleton stripped of raiment. But it is with the skeleton that we are here primarily concerned. As in all successful stories, the framework (the action) is of the proper size and shape and density to fit the raiment (the tone, the style, and the characterization) which adorns it. Unsuccessful stories might be said to give the impression of bodies dressed in unsuitable garments—the sleeves and skirts too long or too short, of the wrong color or combination of colors, or patched with remnants of non-matching materials to cover holes or to extend to proper lengths.

The details of "The Short and Happy Life" fit like the parts of a pattern to form the whole. The action is, to use the term of Eliot, an "objective correlative." To state it another way, the theme is adequately embodied in the action, and it is properly intensified by the other elements. The dominant tone is ironic, and this includes, of course, the famous Hemingway style, by means of which the characters are given depth. The supreme irony appears in the facts of Macomber's death. It comes at the moment of his victory over his wife, as we have said, but this is depicted (expressed through the act itself)—not stated. We are not told that it represents a victory, but we know it as a result of the scene in which the man and the animal are seen lying together in death. For the buffalo, the combat was a mere gesture of self-preservation. For the man, it was an attempt to prove his manhood, a conscious and deliberate subjecting of himself to danger, a rational disciplining of his urge to flee. As for Margot Macomber, her final act—the shooting of her husband—is an intuitive recognition of defeat. As a matter of fact, we are not told that she intended to shoot him when she raised the rifle or even that she did do it intentionally. The fine line between intuition and reason is drawn carefully. Our clue to the full meaning of the act is given by the guide, who, in a sense, shares her guilt because of his participation in her act of infidelity, but who, we can be sure, would have acknowledged his error if Francis had survived the hunt: " 'That was a pretty thing to do,' he said in a toneless voice. 'He would have left you too.' "

We can restate the action, then, in the following manner: The situation consists of a state of tension between two characters—husband and wife. At the moment when we are first introduced, the wife is shown in a position of dominance over her husband, and this condition is explained through a depiction of the unsuccessful lion hunt and the incident portraying the unfaithfulness of the wife. During the ensuing scenes the situation is reversed by the successful enactment of the buffalo hunt and the final act of murder. On the level of pure action, we might say that Margot Macomber is the victor: she is alive, her husband dead by her hand. The ironic method of the author has, however, made us increasingly aware of a separate and distinct set of values which are presented in ironic counterpoint to the level of actual combat. We are shown the emergence of a value which transcends that of simply existing on the animal level. The final clue is obtained from the title: "The Short Happy Life." Why "short" and why "happy"? The implication is clear—Francis Macomber never really lived until that final moment when he had overcome his own fear of death. Margot Macomber and the buffalo both acted instinctively, that is, like animals. Francis Macomber died the death of a Man.

II. THEME THROUGH THEORY

Thomas Mann has been called the author of "psychological fiction." The term "psychological" has value only as it is applied to a particular kind of story. Generally speaking, there is no successful story that is not "psychological," since fiction must be concerned with the motivation of characters, and modern fiction in particular has become increasingly concerned with examining the mental processes which lead to action. In this respect *Macbeth* is no less psychological than Joyce's *Ulysses*, however. They differ not because Joyce had a greater interest in the inner motivation of his characters than Shakespeare but rather because of the different cultural (or mythical) attitudes which prevailed in their different ages. We might go further than this and say that, while there was a more or less generally accepted attitude toward Macbeth's guilt in the Elizabethan age, our own times have seen a dislocation of this traditional sense through the portentous, though often tentative, conclusions of modern science. In the field of modern psychology it is of course Freudian psychoanalysis (with its later modifications by Jung, Adler, *et al.*)

which comes the nearest to representing a general field of reference for the examination of a fictional character's acts and motives; but we cannot go so far as to say that Freudianism has become as completely a part of the modern consciousness as the Christian concept of sin and guilt was a part of the consciousness of the late sixteenth and early seventeenth centuries. It is entirely conceivable, for instance, that a modern reader may be simply puzzled (as indeed he often is) by a story, the motivation of which is based upon certain psychoanalytic concepts; or, if he is not exactly puzzled, certainly it is true that he does not possess a full understanding of the story until he learns to see the relationship between the ideology upon which the story is based and the action of the characters within that framework.

Indeed, it may be true that the author himself may come to have a clearer view of his own intentions and of the ideological climate of his time once he is aware of the particular source of his own, often unconsciously developed, concepts. For as Thomas Mann stated in a lecture which he delivered in 1936:

Indeed it would be too much to say that I came to psychoanalysis. It came to me. Through the friendly interest of some younger workers in the field for what I had written, from *Little Herr Friedemann* to *Death in Venice, The Magic Mountain,* and the *Joseph* novels, it gave me to understand that in my way I "belonged"; it made me aware, as probably behooved it, of my own latent, preconscious sympathies; and when I began to occupy myself with the literature of psychoanalysis I recognized, arrayed in the ideas and the language of scientific exactitude, much that had long been familiar to me through my youthful mental experiences.

Here clearly is an expression of the value which the term "psychological story" may have for us if it is properly defined. However, there is an additional distinction between the traditional story and the psychological story, which Mann makes clear when he quotes with approval from Jung's *Book of the*

Dead: "It is so much more direct, striking, impressive, and thus convincing to see how it happens to me than to see how I did it."

Mann might very well have been saying that it is more important for him to understand *how things happen to* the characters of his fiction than it is to see how they themselves act, which is, of course, a denial of the traditional concept of free will. The characters in the psychological story do not will their acts; *they are willed upon,* and an understanding of this distinction might well have been what Thomas Mann had in mind when he spoke of discovering with "scientific exactitude" the intentions of his own fiction.

Let us examine "Little Herr Friedemann" upon these grounds, particularly since it is an early story, presumably written before its author had become aware of the particular nature of its psychoanalytical background. It is the story of a man who was accidentally injured shortly after birth, so that he was forced to go through life a partial outcast, at least prohibited from participating in many of the normal activities of his friends and neighbors. The author focuses our attention particularly upon the sex relationship. When Herr Friedemann was sixteen, he realized for the first time that he was destined not to participate in the pleasures of physical love; for, as the author tells us, he realized that "to others it brings joy and happiness, but for me it can only mean sadness and pain." He turned to books and to the pleasures of his violin. Much later, however, through the interference of a woman who is depicted as possessing a strange physical attraction, Herr Friedemann's reserve is broken. In three important scenes between Little Herr Friedemann and Frau von Rinnlingen, Herr Friedemann is made to feel that here perhaps is one capable of understanding him and of releasing him from the pressure of his self-denial. In the end, however, he is cruelly rejected, so that, having lost the concept of himself as one triumphing over his physical deformity, he is completely degraded and ends his life in suicide.

It is important to note here that Herr Friedemann's death is depicted, not as the willed deed which might have given it some kind of dignity, but rather as the result of a kind of animal need:

> On his belly he dragged his body a little further, lifted its upper part, and let it fall into the water. He did not raise his head nor move his legs, which still lay on the bank.

He may think (assuming that he is a man still capable of thought) that he is imposing his own will upon himself. Had the story been told in the terms of Victorian literature, it might have depicted the triumph of so-called spiritual values, as represented in Herr Friedemann's ability to play the violin, to judge dramatic performances, and to enjoy good literature, over the grosser, physical side of his nature. Mann suggests, however, that the repression of physical desire is not so much a triumph as it is a necessary condition of Little Herr Friedemann's physical deformity (it happens *to him*); thus, the use of the Greek word *hubris* by the author as a description of his vanity in thinking that he can escape those conditions indicates an ironic contrast to the classic view of tragedy. The Greek heroes *willed* themselves to destruction somewhat in the same manner that Francis Macomber subjected himself to death; destruction comes to Little Herr Friedemann as a natural result of the condition under which he has lived.

If we rely upon the psychoanalytic explanation, we see that the drama has been transferred from outside the character (as in "The Short and Happy Life") to a conflict between the Id and the Ego and that the exterior events can be explained properly only in terms of this interior struggle. This relationship between the Id and the Ego, in Mann's own terms, is described as follows:

> It is the Ego's task to represent the world to the Id—for its own good! For without regard for the superior power of the outer world the Id, in its blind striving towards the satisfaction of its instincts,

would not escape destruction. The Ego takes cognizance of the outer world, it is mindful, it honourably tries to distinguish the objectively real from whatever is an accretion from its inward sources of stimulation.

In psychoanalytic terms, then, we can say that in "Little Herr Friedemann" the Id, which is the seat of Herr Friedemann's instinctive urges (the libido), has forced its request beyond the level of the unconscious, beyond the watchful care of the Ego, which would suppress it for its own good. When the Ego understands that it has been tricked, it retreats and transfers Herr Friedemann's emotion from love into hate; but even this act is unable finally to overcome the overwhelming feeling of disgust. The great mistake was that the Ego mistook the wished-for world for reality; the "real" world was the world of Herr Friedemann's deformity, and he could be protected from it only by escaping into fantasy. Once he has uttered his impassioned speech to Frau von Rinnlingen, retreat is no longer possible except in complete extinction.

Such are the terms of tragedy in the psychological story, and it is only in the acceptance of these terms that we can escape the judgment that the ending of "Little Herr Friedemann" is melodramatic—that the suicide of Herr Friedemann is inevitable and, therefore, unsentimental.

III. THEME THROUGH SYMBOL

In Eudora Welty's story "Powerhouse" we have, perhaps, the opposite pole to Ernest Hemingway—at least the Hemingway of "The Short and Happy Life"—for here is represented the slightest possible development in terms of action. The scene is a dance hall. The characters are Negro musicians. There is a minor shift of scene when, during the intermission, the musicians move to a small cafe for refreshments, and this change introduces briefly a secondary set of characters who participate for a moment and then disappear. The principal action level concerns only the playing of the musicians, there removal to the cafe, and the return to the dance hall. Another thread of action is maintained through the principal character, Powerhouse the band leader, who has received a wire saying that his wife is dead (or so he says). About this telegram he weaves a sequence of events, suggesting the details of the death; suggesting too the complication of a character named Uranus Knockwood, to whom Powerhouse attributes all his misfortunes:

"That no-good pussy-footed crooning creeper, the creeper that follow around after me, coming up like weeds behind me, following around after me everything I do and messing around on the trail I leave. Bets my numbers, sings my songs, gets close to my agent like a Betsy-bug; when I going out he just coming in."

Uranus Knockwood, according to Powerhouse's legend, has been following Powerhouse's wife, Gypsy, around. Somehow he is the cause of her death. He is the man who takes all their wives while they are gone.

This secondary thread is purposely vague. Does Powerhouse actually have a wife? Does she die? Has she been unfaithful to him? Is Uranus Knockwood responsible? Is there actually such a person as Uranus Knockwood? None of these questions is answered with any certainty. All we can say for the moment is that it is extremely unlike the usual "plot" of a story; it is even less real than the more concrete details—the playing of the orchestra, the movement of the dancers, the visit to the cafe, the meeting with the waitress and the local hero, the return to the dance hall. There is no certainty at all that anything has happened to Powerhouse's wife or even that the events concerning her are "true" in the usual sense that they actually happened.

The fact is that this story which deals with musicians is constructed in much the same manner as a musical composition. Its development is thematic. In a more limited way, the same might be true of Katherine Anne Porter's "Flowering Judas"; but in Miss Porter's story there is a greater importance given to external action even though that action is developed piecemeal and not as a continuous thread. Miss Welty also has her theme, but she is expressing it in an even more obscure manner than Miss Porter, for she has more completely adopted the technique of the musician.

Let us say that one of the chief features of a musical composition is its use of musical themes (not to be equated with the "theme" of fiction) which are developed in some kind of ordered progression. In extreme cases, such as Wagner where the music is combined with acting, singing, and staging, the musical form seems actually struggling to become something else. Wagner's musical drama, however, must make use of spoken words, for the instruments are only articulate as they become symbols—or as their playing of a particular musical theme becomes symbolic. The story "Powerhouse" reverses this process; it attempts, by using the characters and events as symbols (motifs) to usurp the function of a musical piece, even to approximating the obscurity (inarticulateness) of the instruments.

If we examine the individual characters, we find that the only musicians who really count are the small group who surround Powerhouse in the band. The others are anonymous like the bulk of the instruments in the orchestra. Just as Wagner selected the instruments which seemed best able to express the themes to accompany his principal characters in the musical drama, so Miss Welty gives us characters appropriate to the particular musical "theme" they are to represent. Thus we have Valentine, "A bass fiddler from Vicksburg, black as pitch . . . who plays with his eyes shut and talking to himself, very young," whose preference is for "Honeysuckle Rose." There is a clarinet player named Little Brother, who "looks like an East Indian Queen, implacable, divine, and full of Snakes," whom Powerhouse likes to listen to and approve. There is a drummer named Scoot, an unpopular boy, a disbelieving maniac. There is, finally, Powerhouse, the moving spirit in the entire organization, the dynamo. The appropriateness of the names is obvious. Valentine, Little Brother, and Scoot have their own individual functions, but in a sense Powerhouse combines them all. He provides the spark which sets them in operation, the power to keep them functioning as a unit, as well as the symbolic function appropriate to his instrument, the piano, which, in a limited way, is a combination of all the instruments. The other characters are limited, as are the functions of the instruments which they play. Scoot the drummer, for instance, supplies the rhythm, the metrical standard according to which all the other instruments play—even, at times, Powerhouse, who occasionally gets lost by the mystic sweep of a piece, yells up

like somebody in a whirlpool—not guiding them—hailing them only. But he knows really. He cries out, but he must know exactly. "Mercy! . . . What I say! . . . Yeah!" And then drifting, listening— "Where that skin beater?"—wanting drums, and starting up and pouring it out in the greatest delight and brutality.

It is appropriate that Scoot, the drummer, should be the realist, the cynic, just as it is appropriate that Powerhouse should occasionally play his piano as if it were a drum. Little Brother is Scoot's opposite, the mystic, least of all bound by the limitations of the rhythm. Of his playing, Powerhouse says, "Beautiful!" or, "He went clear downstairs to get that one." Valentine is the romantic who prefers "Honeysuckle Rose" (though they all like best of all "Pagan Love Song"), and he occupies the middle ground between the liberty of playing variations of the basic rhythm and assisting with the rhythmic base. He plays the bass fiddle, but he, like a lover, is hesitant and must be urged on by Powerhouse.

The actual *story* here, then, is not the suicide of Gypsy because she was being persecuted by Uranus Knockwood but the relationship between Powerhouse and his musicians (musically depicted attitudes ranging from mysticism to cynicism) to the story, just as their instruments depict similar relationships to Powerhouse's piano. Gypsy herself is a depiction of Powerhouse's love as well as a symbol of his suspicion (which is part of the quality of his love). Uranus Knockwood is the embodiment of his psychological defense against his suspicions—a kind of primitive superstition. Uranus, we are told in the story, is a star, perhaps the star upon which Powerhouse wishes; knocking upon wood is his conventional means of warding off danger.

When the story begins, Powerhouse says, "You know what happened to me?" Valentine, who is dreaming (romantically) at the bass, hums a response. "I got a telegram my wife is dead," says Powerhouse. His mouth gathers and forms a barbarous (pagan) O while his fingers walk up straight, unwillingly, three octaves. "Telegram say—here are the words: Your wife is dead." The drummer (cynically) replies: "Not but four words?" Powerhouse attempts to disregard him, but when Scoot asks in a moment: "What name has it got signed, if you got a telegram?" Little Brother (the mystic, the believer) glares at him. After the initial statement, the story is developed by Powerhouse in the cafe and in much the same manner as he plays the piano. He tells it looking into a ketchup bottle (like a fortune-teller) and slowly spreads his performer's hands over the damp, wrinkling cloth with the red squares.

"Listen how it is. My wife gets missing me. Gypsy. She goes to the window. She looks out and sees you know what. Street. Sign saying Hotel. People walking. Somebody looks up. Old Man. She looks down, out of the window. Well? . . . *Sssst! Plooey!* What she do? Jump out and bust her brains all over the world."

He plays variations upon the initial theme (four words), repeating them in several paragraphs, always with the combination of romance and realism (clarinet and drums). Little Brother agrees to everything, accepts the fiction, repeats phrases after Powerhouse. Valentine is slightly, hesitantly skeptical but accepts when reassured by Powerhouse. Scoot is openly doubtful. He asks Powerhouse why he doesn't go to a telephone and call up "just to see if she's there at home." All the others think: "That is one crazy drummer that's going to get his neck broken some day."

We see that the author is presenting her own myth through the story. Her story is setting up a myth, just as Powerhouse creates his *within* the story. Is it a comment upon the Negro race: their combination of imagination and reality, belief and skepticism, primitivism and creativeness? These are certainly her contrasts. In her final "meaning," however, she is going beyond the Negro and making it apply to all cases where the man of genius combines within himself the extremes. This, she seems to say, is what genius consists of, the ability to operate within the widest possible limits. The artist combines the primitive imagination with his sense of reality ("Where that skin beater?"). He calls for the drums at the proper moment.

A subtheme is introduced in the cafe, where Powerhouse is asked to meet the local mythmaker, Sugar-stick Robinson, who, though he could not swim, has dived down into the river and pulled up fourteen white people from a wrecked boat. He is the leitmotiv to Powerhouse's major theme. Sugar-stick, however, unlike Powerhouse, is inarticulate. He has become a mythmaker by accident (without knowing what he was doing; without being able to swim), yet he is, in his own way, more complete than either Little Brother or Scoot, and he has gained his local following. Powerhouse's genius is different in that it is often deliberate and always articulate. It is similar in that his actions are as natural as Sugar-stick's diving into the river: "Of course, you know how it is with *them*—Negroes— bandleaders they would play the same way, giving all they've got, for an audience of one. . . . When somebody, no matter who, gives everything, it makes people feel ashamed for him."

Here is the attitude of the indifferent audience toward the artist. Why does he do it, even when no one is listening? The man of genius creates because he *must*. When his audience is not in rapport with him, there is embarrassment—his acts seem barbaric and distorted; they are distorted except when motivated by the proper emotion, and they will always seem distortions unless they are participated in with the proper emotional attitudes. The only number Powerhouse will con- sent to play by request is "Pagan Love Song," and it is the playing of this number which suggests the fiction of Gypsy's death. It is, the author says, a sad song, and she implies that the story of the artist is a sad story—a pagan love song.

The subject matter of "Powerhouse" is the relationship between fiction and fact, and the story delineates through the intricate weaving of the symbolic themes their highest relationship as symbolized in the man of primitive genius, Powerhouse, his relationship to members of his orchestra, to members of his race, and to all mankind. At the end of the story Powerhouse played "a bass deep and coarse as a sea net—then produced something glimmering and fragile." The author suggests his similarity to Sugar-stick after all, for

who could ever remember any of the things he says? They are just inspired remarks that roll out of his mouth like smoke. . . . Now and then he calls and shouts, "Somebody love me! Somebody loves me, I wonder who!" His mouth gets to be nothing but a volcano. "I wonder who!"

"Maybe. . . ." He uses his right hand on a trill.

"Maybe. . . ." He pulls back his spread fingers, and looks out upon the place where he is. A vast, impersonal and yet furious grimace transfigures his wet face.

"Maybe it's you!"

The product of the artist is a vast, impersonal distortion, rooted in the public misery of the artist's private misfortune. Powerhouse is addressing his song to the dancers out of a sense of private need, just as he improvised his story of Gypsy's death out of a need to formulate his doubts and his suspicions. The artist in general, of whom Powerhouse in this story is the all-encompassing symbol, gives form to the doubts and fears of the race. This is Miss Welty's theme, presented in a form in which words share equally, both as meaning and as motif, with the musical motif as expressed in a music-like prose. If the theme-as-meaning is less pronounced here than in most stories, it is at any rate more "communicable" than the theme of a purely musical composition.

Of the three stories here examined, Ernest Hemingway's is,

on the whole, the most conventional in method. Yet to a teacher of fiction it is amazing how many students, when first confronted by it, find it simply incomprehensible. Its action is, for them—just action. A surprising number of them, when queried, explain that it is a conflict between a man and wife in which the wife comes out the victor by resorting to force. Irony, one of the principal products of artistic technique, is lost upon them. Perhaps as a result of Hollywood and the reading of stories in the popular magazines, they are not prepared for anything beyond the level of action, so that "Little Herr Friedemann" and "Powerhouse" leave them simply depressed and confused.

Yet there is good reason for this confusion. The chance is that the productions of Hollywood and the popular magazines, mass produced as they are, are nearer the level of popular culture than such artists as Mr. Hemingway and Miss Welty. We are living in an age which is suspicious of technique, as it is suspicious of anything which pretends to supply moral guidance, unless such technical training leads to an obviously practical end. Where aesthetic enjoyment (which is indissolubly bound to ethical instruction) is the only end, the modern reader becomes skeptical. Why worry about the subtle relationships between Margot and Francis Macomber, between Little Herr Friedemann and Frau von Rinnlingen, between Powerhouse and his wife Gypsy, if the only reward of such effort is a statement which might have come from any manual of religious instruction? More important is a knowledge of how much money an author made during a given year. If his technical ability was responsible, then the technique is justified.

This is undoubtedly a simplification, but it illustrates a common misunderstanding of the nature of technique. If we say that a moving picture or a radio program is bad but that it exhibited a remarkable technical competence, we are simply indulging in a *non sequitur*—we are disassociating the technique from the work itself. We are as wrong as if we were to say that the forms of religious worship are beautiful but that they have no effect upon the lives of the worshippers, or if we said that a certain doctor had great skill but that he had no interest in the patients whom he served. The doctor's interest in his patients *is* a great part of his skill, as it is the end of his art. In like manner, the technical ability of the writer *is* his work of art, objectified and embodied. Until this point is made, the reading of modern works of literature is sterile and unprofitable. Once understood, however, the reader is naturally alive to the most subtle nuances of theme. He is not interested merely in a story, a fabrication—he is interested in life.

The Modern Writer

JAMES JOYCE once said that he was not interested in the past, he was not interested in the present, he was interested only in the future. This is a puzzling remark when seen only in the light of his own work. Certainly Joyce was interested in the whole sweep of cultural history. His best-known work, *Ulysses,* is based upon a myth thousands of years old. Certainly he was interested in the past of his own country, for his work uses the Irish background as a basis for examining the action of his principal characters. If he was not interested in the present, why did he set his novel on a day in his own time, June 16, 1904, and why did he utilize places in Dublin so recognizable that they represent almost a guide-book description of his native city? What does he mean when he says he is interested only in the future?

The latter question can be answered only in terms of the large general intentions of art. A minor writer may be interested in imitating the achievements of the past and present. The major writer pushes on to what Hart Crane has called "new thresholds, new anatomies"—for the genuine artist sees not only the greatness of the past; he sees also its limitations.

What he writes today is based upon the vision he has of the present, but if he is successful his vision becomes society's vision tomorrow. It is this vision, incorporated in a work of art—a painting, a symphony, a poem, or a novel—which Joyce had in mind when he spoke of his interest in the future.

But, of course, to say this much is only to define the first stage in the process of creation. For it is not only the vision itself which is important. There are also the methods—the techniques—through which this vision is rendered or—as some critics say—discovered. A reader will ask: "Why does Joyce's novel look so little like any other novel I have read? Why is the punctuation different? Why does he not tell me who is speaking? Why do characters appear and disappear without any apparent reason?"

Such questions are almost impossible to answer. In the first place there are so many possible techniques, and in the second place an author never consciously uses a technique. The word "technique" is a critical term, devised as a means of explaining how an effect is obtained—after the fact. Except in the first stage of composition, before any writing is done, while the author is still schooling himself in his craft, and again after the principal labor of creation has been accomplished, when the author is applying the final correction and polish—at these times only is the author consciously concerned with technique. The full labor of creation is concentrated upon the vision itself (the painter calls it his "image"). Achievement depends first upon the quality of concentration, then upon the ability to render without spoiling either the concentration or the image. To be conscious of techniques, or of possible readers, or of anything extraneous to the concentrated vision would destroy or falsify the image.

To say this does not, I hope, make the process either mystical or magical. It is no more mysterious than the whole process of the unconscious, which is nevertheless mysterious enough. Sometimes, in an attempt to clarify this, I use the following diagram:

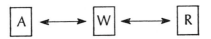

In the diagram the area *A* represents the author. Let us say that if he had perfect control of all his knowledge, conscious as well as unconscious, he might be said to have the intention of creating a certain work—the area *W*. If this intention were absolutely clear—and it is through what I have called "concentration" that it becomes clear—and if he were armed with a perfect control of technical means which he could utilize without spoiling that concentration, then he might conceivably re-create in the object *W*—the Work—that image or vision which he contained within himself. He might then, conceivably, have created the perfect work.

I hope it is unnecessary at this point to say that an author never succeeds to this extent. Nevertheless, such an example might well represent his aim, and in any case examples are clearer if we conceive of them as "pure" and then proceed to measure actual cases against this concept.

However, the process is not complete at this point. If the work is a novel, or a poem, or a short story, it exists on paper as a series of symbols which we call language. Thus far it has been imagined into being for the author; it must now be re-imagined by the reader from the printed symbols. Remember, we have had a perfect author, hence a perfect work. What we need now is the perfect reader. The author has projected his image onto the printed page. It exists there between the author and the reader—*R*. It is the job of the reader now to recapture the image through the medium of language. If he succeeds—and since he is a perfect reader he is bound to succeed—the image which he gains will be exactly the same image as that which the author conceived. Seen this way, the responsibility of the reader becomes only slightly less than that of the author himself.

"Very well," our reader may well reply, "but the authors I read seem intent only upon putting the greatest of difficulties before me. They seem to obscure, not elucidate, that image you speak of."

If this were true, all authors would certainly seem bent on self-destruction. However, there are difficulties which have to do with the limitations of the author, either his failure to imagine and to render or merely his limitations as a human being. No work completely succeeds—or can so succeed. On the other hand, if we grant this limitation to the author, we must also confess similar limitations in ourselves as readers. Isn't it, perhaps, possible that we do not always know enough to perform wholly that portion of the process which we alone can perform?

I am thinking now of our predisposition to see everything— to judge everything—from the point of view of the conventional and the familiar. We have seen that the kind of experience that art represents is a new experience—a new vision. One of the chief qualities of art is freshness, for art exists in time as well as in space. Only the very greatest artists defeat time, and then only in a relative degree. The genuine expression of art must be conceived afresh, and its impact must come with the immediacy of a never-before-known experience. If we do not leave ourselves open to fresh impressions, or recognize them only in the great works of the past, we are missing a whole area of aesthetic enjoyment.

But this does not answer the question of what it is the author does in order to make such enjoyment available. In general, as we have seen by our diagram, he does whatever he can do, and what he can do is done through language. His very style may suggest certain values, as Ernest Hemingway's suggests the importance of concrete objects, ordinary events, and simple actions, while the more ornate sentences of William Faulkner reflect a value in the more complicated forms and manners of society. Joyce's stream of consciousness affirms the value of those sensations which lie, as Harry Levin has pointed out, barely above the level of the unconscious: sensations which do not come in the usual, logical sequence but come as the result of their association with other sensations.

There is a point, however, beyond which no genuine artist can go. He cannot *imagine* the experience of the work for the reader. The difference between imaginative and unimaginative writing lies exactly here. The imaginative work calls always—even upon successive readings—for the fullest possible play of the reader's imagination. Great works, such as *War and Peace, The Brothers Karamasov, Moby Dick,* and *Huckleberry Finn,* continue to engage the reader time after time. Virginia Woolf, in a famous essay entitled "Mr. Bennett and Mrs. Brown," concluded that what was wrong with Arnold Bennett was that he wanted the reader to imagine his scenes for him. Caroline Gordon and Allen Tate, in their book *The House of Fiction,* have pointed to this distinction by examining closely examples of writing by Somerset Maugham and Stephen Crane. Mr. Maugham, they find, gives the reader too much—he allows too little room for the reader to share in the process of imagining the action or the scene. Stephen Crane forces the reader to participate, to recreate in his own mind this shared experience. As Henry James wrote in his Preface to *The Wings of the Dove:*

> The enjoyment of a work of art, the acceptance of an irresistible illusion, constituting, to my sense, our highest experience of "luxury," the luxury is not greatest, by my consequent measure, when the work asks for as little attention as possible. It is the greatest, it is delightfully, divinely great, when we feel the surface, like the thick ice of the skater's pond, bear without cracking the strongest pressure we throw on it.

One means by which the writer demands such attention is by using language in new, sometimes totally unconventional, combinations. Or he may gain startling effects by presenting us with unaccustomed shifts in the angle of vision from which we view the experience. He may throw us momentarily off balance by saying one thing when he means another, which is to utilize one of the many forms of irony. But such effects are not used merely to confuse the reader. They are not used even primarily to shock him. They must, in the long run, become also a part of the structure of the work—they must become a means of "rendering" a scene in such a manner that the complexity of the experience (despite the possible simplicity of the scene itself) may become *shared* by the reader.

The term "complexity of experience" might well be one to make a certain kind of reader pause. It is an expression which occurs often in modern criticism. "And what," he might ask, "if the reader does not see experience as complex?" What he would mean, no doubt, is that there are degrees of complexity. In English literary history we see the eighteenth and the nineteenth centuries as, each in its own way, seeking a relatively simple expression, taking a more straightforward view of life, than did the seventeenth century or does our modern age. This does not mean wholly that complex experience is reflected by complex forms, for to believe that would be to fall into what Yvor Winters calls the "fallacy of imitative form." But it may mean—to use simple examples—that a generation which sees simplicity or stability in experience will also put a high value upon simplicity or stability in its art forms. In one sense, then, the respect of the eighteenth century for fixed forms reflects an attitude of confidence in a stable society; the interest of the nineteenth century in the natural evolution of the common man is reflected in a descriptive and didactic literature addressed to a wide audience. The seventeenth century, its stability upset by Copernican science and an influx of rediscovered knowledge, reflected—as does our own age—its uncertainties and qualification in a literature of paradox and conceit.

To say as much is not to say that each age does not carry something over into the next. It is not to say either that a complex-minded age such as our own does not have its simplicities. Most Hollywood movies and much popular fiction reflect the tremendous desire many of us have to escape the "realities" of complexity, just as the Elizabethan bear pit must have represented an escape from the "realities" of Shakespeare's theater, as well as the "realities" of life.

But our problem is not with escape but with engagement, with the problem of making the literature of our own time available to as many readers as possible. It is my opinion that the chief difficulty is not so much one of recognizing the techniques by which the experience to be shared is created but an overcoming by the reader of his own prejudices. How many times have we not heard it said: "I have always intended to read *Moby Dick*, but I cannot get through the early chapters." The implication here is that Melville's novel would be worth reading if we could only put up with the perversities of its author. But even such an attitude is better than the one which says: "Why did Melville clutter his book up with all that difficult language?" For the implication here is that Melville failed. Such an attitude, when expressed without adequate knowledge, is arrogant, and it all but precludes understanding.

But by now Melville is a somewhat simple case. What about more recent novels? Even here the informed reader will be extremely cautious in making assumptions of failure. If the style or the structure of the work seems experimental and the reader brings to his reading a certain perception and a certain knowledge of how effects in literature are gained, and if the methods seem excessive in relation to this particular work, then he may suspect that the work is a failure—that it represents novelty, not true originality. This is, of course, a "loaded" statement. Just what do we mean by "a certain perception" and "a certain knowledge?" Let us consider the case of William Faulkner's *The Sound and the Fury*, a novel which utilizes apparently radical devices to tell its story.

The Sound and the Fury begins with a long opening section presenting events out of time order, with puzzling associational shifts from one time to another, and all limited to the sensory perceptions of a thirty-three-year-old idiot. It is unlikely that any reader, coming across it for the first time, would get anything more than a vague idea of the relationship of one event to another. The second section is not much clearer. It presents the stream-of-consciousness perception of a character bewildered by a confusion of values who is about to commit suicide. In Section III the time sequence of events becomes clear, but the tone shifts and the pace quickens. In Section IV all is resolved, but the inexperienced reader may well wonder why he has been conducted on so mad an excursion. He has a clue, of course, in the title, taken from one of Macbeth's best-known speeches: Life "is a tale told by an idiot, full of sound and fury, signifying nothing." Yet Faulkner's novel is not a mere illustration of Shakespeare's statement. It is also an ironic comment upon it. If the reader understands music, he will see that Faulkner's method is close to that of a musical composition, where themes are introduced in isolation or in simple combinations, then developed and worked into the total structure in a series of "movements" of varied length and tone. The reader will come to see that the isolated sense perceptions of the idiot boy in Section I are a better guide for conduct than the lengthy sophistries of his neurotic brother in Section II. He will see, too, that the author is utilizing a significant contrast between the life of the old and the new South and that much of what the novel has to say is related to these differences.

But I do not wish to make too much of technical innovation. Often what seems the most novel is, in actuality, merely the revival of something old. What this means can be seen best, perhaps, in the writing of modern poets. If we consider the writing done primarily between the end of World War I and the beginning of World War II, we can say—as, indeed, we have already implied—that our poets were greatly influenced by their rediscovery of the metaphysical poets of the seventeenth century and by their reading of the poets of the French *symboliste* movement.

We have already suggested what these attitudes mean in their relationship to the seventeenth century: that the Renaissance vision of life as complex, reduced better to paradox and conceit than to simple statement, seemed during the period between the wars, nearer our own view than did the more self-satisfied and straightforward views of the eighteenth and nineteenth centuries. They mean also that the associational and impressionistic methods of French symbolism appeared a truer reflection of the way man engages himself with the world than either the rhetorical regularity of the most skilful eighteenth-century verse or the lyrical simplicity of most nineteenth-century poets.

This explanation has been given so often that it is almost embarrassing to repeat it. Yet so long as there are readers puzzled by the attitudes and techniques of such modern poets as Pound, Eliot, Crane, Auden, Stevens, Cummings, or Tate, we can suppose repetition is necessary. To it may also be added the warning that, by the time the reader has mastered such poets as these, he may very well find that the next generation has turned elsewhere. I hope I have made clear, however, that such searching is not done frivolously. I do not wish, either, to imply that there is any one single key to a complete understanding. We live in an age which delights in "keys" and solutions and "how-to-do-it" formulas.

A reader should have his own likes and dislikes—his own personal preferences. These are a human necessity and lend color to his reading and thinking. What he should avoid, only, is prejudice—the holding of unconsidered opinions. To condemn William Carlos Williams or E. E. Cummings because their lines do not look familiar on the page or because they use words in an apparently new way is to display ignorance of the process by which poetry has always evolved. A poem may be *proved* obscure by careful reading, and there are more obscure poems written and printed every year than clear ones, but, once the poem is in print, the burden of proof is upon the reader. It may take several readings of Cummings' "A Man Who Had Fallen among Thieves" for the inexperienced reader to discover that the poet is merely telling an old story in a modern setting and with the intonations of contemporary speech. But surely this is little to expect.

Of course "The Man Who Had Fallen among Thieves" is a

short and relatively simple poem. What about the long works: *The Waste Land*, the *Cantos* of Ezra Pound, or *Paterson* by William Carlos Williams? *The Waste Land* is by now a fairly obvious case. When it first appeared, reviewers solemnly considered the possibility that it was a literary hoax. Today it is read intelligently by undergraduates in many of our colleges. The *Cantos* present a special problem, because they remain unfinished and because the relation of Ezra Pound's subject matter to his poem remains a controversial topic. Nevertheless, that it is a poem to be taken seriously, we must believe until convinced otherwise on grounds other than our feelings about the author's past actions or his present sanity or insanity. That real enjoyment may be gained from its individual parts is certain. Consider this single stanza from one of the late cantos:

> The ant's a centaur in his dragon world.
> Pull down thy vanity, it is not man
> Made courage, or made order, or made grace,
>   Pull down thy vanity, I say pull down.
> Learn of the green world what can be thy place
> In scaled invention or true artistry,
> Pull down thy vanity,
>   Paquin pull down!
> The green casque has outdone your elegance.

Tennyson observed a flower in a crannied wall, Ezra Pound an ant within the compound where he was kept prisoner; and if it were necessary to choose between the two images, Pound's would seem the more pertinent as well as the more beautiful.

Paterson by William Carlos Williams is a very new work. It has been in print in its entirety for only about two years. That it is being conscientiously read we know from the amount that has been written about it, and, whether or not it is a completely successful work, it provokes the curious mind by the degree of its originality. It may also puzzle even the experienced reader, so that he asks: "Why does Williams refuse to give us clues as to whether the main character or speaker of the moment is the city, the river, a man, or a woman?" My answer—a tentative one—would be that he does give clues but that there are times when the speaker is intentionally unidentified. I am not prepared to say that Williams always succeeds, and I suspect that he does not, but what he attempts is extremely interesting. Certain passages are clearly the expression of the poet, the city man, the physician, who is at once the man *and* the city. As a technique this might be seen as an expansion of the paradox of the metaphysical lyric, as when John Donne has man yearning after a woman who is the church—the bride of Christ—as well as a common prostitute. Williams seems to be attempting to merge the personal aspects of the lyric with the mythical qualities of a larger form, something very close to a modern epic.

Williams has written that art "is bred of the effort to take that momentous step into the imagination." We have asked the question: "Why do writers write?" We have also asked: "Is it to trick the public?" We might answer both questions by saying that a writer writes in order to trick the reader into seeing experience in a fresh light. He does not perpetuate a hoax, for a hoax is pointless, and too many years of discipline go into the writing of a novel, a poem, a story, to believe that a writer would dedicate his life to such labor in order to fool his contemporaries. Williams has also said: "If you write skilfully enough, sooner or later someone is going to find out and judge you for it." And we might add: "If you write badly, you will be found out too."

Let us consider a final example—one upon which I feel as a reader upon reasonably solid ground. Eliot's *Four Quartets* appeared in 1943. It is a work less well known than *The Waste Land*. It is my critical opinion that the *Four Quartets* will eventually come to be considered the better of these two long works. But there is a certain presumption in making such a claim. I would certainly not object to anyone making the contrary statement. *The Waste Land* was a revolutionary

work, which we have come to see as marking the serious beginnings of modern poetry. As such it has a special "historical"
significance. It was read first as a document of despair. We
read it today both as a foreshadowing of the direction Eliot's
verse was to take later in *Ash-Wednesday* and in the *Four
Quartets* and as an example of a new use of language. As Miss
Helen Gardner has stated it:

> Mr. Eliot approaches the problem of how the greatest thought
> can be expressed naturally, that is with the ring of the living
> voice, by concentrating on the problem of how we may "call a
> servant or bid a door be shut." If we can discover a poetic rhythm
> in the most commonplace speech, this rhythm may then be capable
> of refinement and elevation so that it may accommodate the greatest
> thoughts without losing naturalness.

The mood of *The Waste Land* emphasizes depravity and
loss. In the *Four Quartets* Eliot attempts to depict not only the
limits of man in nature and time but the extent of his hope
and his faith. It is both a personal poem, in which the author
examines his own background and the historical accident
which caused him to reverse the emigration of his ancestors
from England to America, and a public, religious, and philosophical poem. In it the dominant concerns of our age (man's
relation to nature and his relation to God) are given a remarkable degree of formulation.

"How do we know this?" the reader will ask. We know it by
reading the poem. "And how does one go about reading the
poem?" Yes, here's the rub. We are doomed to know less about
this particular poem than our grandchildren will know, and
the best advice I can think to give is to say, "Read it as though
you were born twenty, or thirty, or fifty years later than you
were." Read with the knowledge of the usable past, but think
of the contemporary work as though it were already a part of
that past—as indeed it now is, now that it is in print. Time
works rapidly, eliminating the inferior work and establishing
the successful. André Gide has written: "I write my books so

slowly that I often let the epoch catch up with me until I seem to be borne along by it, whereas I was originally reacting against it."

Perhaps we can make such a view clearer by saying that, when one of our first ancestors discovered the regularity of the sun and the moon, he had made an artistic discovery. When he went beyond this and attributed to the sun and the moon supernatural powers, made gods of them and worshiped them, he was expressing his complicated need for order in a world where natural forces overwhelmed him. He expressed his belief that order superseded disorder. He created an imaginative world which controlled psychologically the fear and uncertainty which he felt in his daily living.

Perhaps if no artist had appeared among subsequent generations, our race could have continued to exist upon the basis of such beliefs. The next artist to appear, however, probably began by feeling that so simple an explanation did not answer the complex questions which existence posed, even in so simple a society. The chances are that this second artist, who arose to challenge the complacency of his elders' views, was driven from society. The chances are, also, that the ideas which this artist (this "prophet") was crying were the very ideas adopted by succeeding generations. For he may have told them that the moon was no goddess, the sun no god, that both were merely the expression of a greater, unseen order which existed beyond the universe of Man. He may, even, have fashioned images of the original force, which came to represent for his people symbols of the order beyond sight which they believed the author of all order.

My point here is that the artist is both a myth-destroyer and a myth-maker. It is he in society who first recognizes the inadequacy of the old forms and who feels an irresistible impulse to strike nearer the heart of the truth. In our own day (and by "our own day" I mean the era of modern man) we have come to think two things about human experience. One is that mankind is capable of conceiving of some kind of almost-ideal order. Another is that man is incapable ever of achieving such order. Therefore, the artist is ever hopeful and ever defeated. If he were not hopeful, he would not create; if he were not defeated, there would be no need for creation after him. The artist is he who sees clearest the possibilities of existence, and it is he who is doomed to struggle most strenuously to achieve the impossible.

We should bear with him, but we won't. We shall continue to look back at the old familiar forms, and we shall leave it to our grandchildren to discover the new—in the old.